From Access to SQL Server

RUSSELL SINCLAIR

From Access to SQL Server

Copyright ©2000 by Russell Sinclair

ISBN (pbk): 1-893115-24-0

Printed and bound in the United States of America 12345678910

Technical Reviewer: Peter Vogel

Editor: Anne Marie Walker

Production Editor: Janet Vail

Page Compositior and Cat Herder: Susan Glinert

Indexer: Valerie Perry

Cover and Interior Design: Derek Yee Design

Distributed to the book trade in the United States by Springer-Verlag New York, Inc.,

175 Fifth Avenue, New York, New York, 10010

and outside the United States by Springer-Verlag GmbH & Co. KG, Tiergartenstr. 17,

69112 Heidelberg, Germany

In the United States, phone 1-800-SPRINGER; orders@springer-ny.com;

www.springer-ny.com

Outside the United States, contact orders@springer.de; www.springer.de; fax

+49 6221 345229

For information on translations, please contact Apress directly at 901 Grayson Street, Suite 204, Berkeley, California, 94710

Phone: 510-549-5930; Fax: 510-549-5939; info@apress.com; www.apress.com

Contents at a Glance

Contents

Introduction

There is considerably more TO MIGRATING AN ACCESS DATABASE TO SQL SERVER THAN Microsoft would have you believe. The fact that you are reading this introduction leads me to believe that you already know this, and that you are looking for more answers. This book provides those answers.

You may be wondering right now if this book is for you. Let me help you answer that question. This book is written primarily for Microsoft Access developers— those of you who create applications using Microsoft Access both as the database that stores the data, and as the development environment in which the user interface is created and maintained. The main purpose of this book is to aid Access developers in understanding how to modify their database and application, so that the data side of the application can be moved to SQL Server. All of the techniques described to access data and the information on how to plan the move assume you are migrating the back-end database only. Although this book does concentrate a great deal on Access as an interface development environment, Visual Basic developers and others may find this information helpful because many of the concepts can easily be applied to pure Visual Basic applications in which the database itself is being moved from Access to SQL Server.

In writing this book, I made a few assumptions about you, the reader, and your experience developing applications with Microsoft Access. I made the assumption that you have experience creating databases and user interfaces in Microsoft Access and know how to make the two cooperate. This means that you know how to design tables, queries, forms, and reports in the IDE. I assumed that you have at least tried to create an Access application that has separate database files for the back-end data and the front-end interface. It is not required but I would recommend that you understand at least how to do this. Finally, I made the assumption that you have done at least a little Visual Basic for Applications (VBA) programming. This is because the vast majority of Access development requires at least some rudimentary VBA programming. Although you can get by without needing any VBA code, Access really shines when you start to program it using VBA.

Where's the CD?

Okay, you caught me. This is probably one of the few application-specific books you have picked up in recent years that doesn't come with a CD (or a least a diskette). You may be wondering why.

When I originally started to write this book, I had every intention of creating a CD that you could use to follow the techniques described in each chapter.

However, as I progressed through the book, I realized that although I could go through the specifics of the sample database I created, it probably would not apply to your application. I didn't want to overload you with information on a sample database that did not teach you what you needed to know. Instead, I have concentrated on including the information that I have learned from *many* Access to SQL migrations. Any sample database that included all of the problems you should watch out for in your migration would seem like such a bad design to begin with that it would be doomed to fail no matter what.

However, there is a sample database that you can download from the Apress Web site at `http://www.apress.com` that includes all of the sample code listed in the book, along with one or two other useful functions. All of the code I have used in the book is complete in the text, there is nothing missing from the code that would prevent it from working on your database. I hope to keep this sample up-to-date for the next while, incorporating suggestions and questions from readers as they come in. It is always nicer when things improve over time.

Feedback and Information

The latest information about the book and a complete list of links that I think could help you in your migration can be found at the Apress Web site at `http://www.apress.com`. The downloads for the book will also be available from this site; just check out my section on the site.

Any questions, feedback, or other communications related to this book are welcome. You can reach me through email at `FromAccessToSQL@home.com` or `russellsinclair@home.com`. Either email account will go directly to me.

Acknowledgments

I would like to thank Peter Vogel, editor of *Smart Access* (a truly brilliant Microsoft Access developer magazine [http://www.pinpub.com/access]) and technical reviewer for this book, for giving me the initial opportunity to write back in 1997 and for being a great mentor and general sounding board over the past few years. I never realized how fun and frustrating writing could be.

Thanks to Karen Watterson for suggesting me to Gary Cornell when Apress was looking for an author. And to Gary Cornell and Dan Appleman for creating Apress, a publishing company with the radical concept of creating quality publications and making authors true partners in the publishing process.

Thanks to the great people at Apress who have cooperated to make this book a reality, among them Grace Wong and Sarah Jaquish, and freelancers Janet Vail, Anne Marie Walker, Susan Glinert, and Valerie Perry. I'm sure there are many others who work behind the frontlines whose names are not listed here. Your efforts are truly appreciated.

Thanks go very strongly to my parents Anthea, Colin, Jack, and Rosemary for encouraging me throughout the years and giving me the freedom to choose my own path. You see—it all worked out for the best in the end.

Thank you most of all to my companion Michele Vig, without whom this book could not have been written. Your understanding, help, and support throughout the creation of this book was immeasurable. Had it not been for your encouragement and understanding, this book may never have been written—certainly not anywhere close to schedule. I appreciate all that you have done. Dinner at Tundra—my treat.

CHAPTER 1

What Every Access Programmer Needs to Know about SQL Server

SINCE THE EARLY 1990S, Microsoft has been developing a relational database management system (RDBMS) called SQL Server. Microsoft first started working on SQL Server as part of a joint project with Sybase. After a few years, they decided to end their joint venture and continue development of the product on their own. Since then, Microsoft SQL Server has progressed to become one of the best selling RDBMSs on the market. It offers many features that make it an excellent database system for storing and managing data. Speed, ease of use, integration with other Microsoft products, and powerful management tools have all contributed to its success.

There are currently two versions of SQL Server that are commonly used. Version 6.5, the most commonly used version, has been in existence for a few years. The innovative features in version 6.5 include distributed computing support, Internet integration, and cross-platform replication. Version 7, released in early 1999, added a cohesive administration interface, better Internet integration, improvements in speed, and many new wizards designed to make the job of database administration and management, replication, and data transformation considerably easier. A separate, "lighter" version of SQL Server 7, called the Microsoft Data Engine (MSDE), is also available free of charge from Microsoft with the purchase of some of their development products including Access 2000, and it can be distributed to users royalty free.

Although SQL Server is often thought of as just being an RDBMS, it is really a suite of database components. One of these components is the RDBMS application itself, but there are many other components that are part of the suite. These components are used to manage, operate, and maintain the day-to-day workings of SQL Server.

SQL Server Architecture

SQL Server is a *Client/Server* (C/S) application. In order to understand SQL Server's architecture, let's take a step back to understand exactly what the term client/server means. The term client/server refers to a method of managing applications.

Most applications that are run on a PC are single-sided. All processing is managed by a single application running on a single computer. Client/server involves the cooperation of two or more processes, possibly running on two separate computers. These processes communicate with each other to provide an effective method of balancing the load of the processing between them. The advantage to this type of processing is that each application can specialize in a particular function. It allows them to be more efficient and to reduce the overall work that must be done. In many cases, the processes in communication are between separate computers. This improves the performance of the job in question by allowing different computers to cooperate to complete the task. The more computers involved, the greater the processing power that can be applied. In all of these cases, one application must initiate the process. This application is called the client. The other cooperating applications are called servers. Essentially, the client requests resources from a server or servers. The server(s) receives the request, handles any processing necessary, and then hands the end result back to the client. Because the server is dedicated to the task that it is called for, and because of its power, it is able to accomplish this task much faster than the client could. Servers often support multiple clients.

In the case of client/server database systems, the work is usually divided between an application, which runs as a client requesting data from an RDBMS, and a server, which is the RDBMS. When the client needs to obtain data from the server, it sends a request to the server telling it the details of the request. The server then processes the request, performs any needed manipulation of data, and sends only the results to the client. This procedure increases the speed at which data is processed and reduces network traffic in cases where the client and server reside on separate machines.

Because SQL Server is a client/server RDBMS, it allows client computers to request the use of resources available to the server. A computer on the network running a database application requests either data from SQL Server or that an action be performed on the data that SQL Server is managing. SQL Server processes the request and returns only the results to the client. This frees the client from having to do much of the processor intensive data access work.

This process can be contrasted with desktop database systems, such as Microsoft Access, which perform all processing of data locally. Even if the database resides on another computer, data is retrieved from the other computer and all manipulation, sorting, or modification of that data is done by the computer that initiated the request.

In cases where the client and the server are not located on the same machine, a network must be in place to allow communication between the applications. In order for applications to communicate with SQL Server, they must use special SQL Server packets called Tabular Data Streams (TDS). The data provider, which is the application library that handles the communication between the client and SQL Server, is used to build these packets from requests made by an application. OLE DB and ODBC (Open Database Connectivity) are common examples of these providers. TDS packets are sent from the provider to the SQL Server Net-Libraries, which convert the packets into network protocol packets for transmission to the server. The SQL Server Net-Libraries convert the packets back into TDS on the server, and then send them to a layer called the Open Data Services (ODS). ODS is an interface to the SQL Server DLLs and application framework. The ODS component examines each TDS request to determine what type of request it is and calls the appropriate function on SQL Server. The database engine on SQL Server then takes these commands, builds the execution plans for these requests, accesses any necessary data, and compiles the results for the client. The process is then reversed to return the results to the client.

The actual work of processing the requests and manipulating the data is done by the SQL Server Engine. This work involves the processing of requests and the manipulation of data or databases.

The SQL Server Engine can be divided into two main parts: the Relational Engine and the Storage Engine. In version 7, these components have actually been physically separated into different components. In previous versions, they were intertwined such that it was difficult to tell them apart.

The Relational Engine is the component that performs all of the parsing of SQL requests and creates execution plans that SQL Server uses to determine the best method to use to handle the data manipulation. The Relational Engine also executes these plans in conjunction with the Storage Engine. In fact, it is the thinking portion of the database engine.

The Storage Engine manages all of the physical handling of the data in SQL Server. It manages all input/output (I/O), database maintenance, concurrency issues, logging, and recovery. The Storage Engine performs all of the manual labor. The presence of the two engines allows SQL Server to divide two primary processes—planning to work with the data and actually working with the data—so that each process can perform its task faster and more efficiently.

SQL Server is designed to manage many databases in one RDBMS. The administration utilities included in SQL Server display all of the databases together. This allows you to administer several databases from a single interface without having to open different instances of the same application to administer each database.

Transact-SQL

The acronym SQL (pronounced "seekwal") stands for Structured Query Language. SQL is a language used for communication with relational database management systems to perform data definition and manipulation. This language, like many programming languages, has been standardized by the American National Standards Institute (ANSI). In order to be compliant with the ANSI standard, each database vendor must implement the language in its own system such that it includes the necessary syntax and behavior outlined in the standard. Although it is up to the particular vendor as to how the standard is to be implemented, the vendor must ensure that this implementation is seamless to the user. Consequently, you could use the same language to achieve the same results on two different RDBMSs if they both comply with the same standard.

As with other standards, the SQL standard is revised from time to time. There are currently two major revisions in use in the major RDBMSs: SQL 89 and SQL 92. These standards are named for the year in which they were finalized. The SQL 92 standard improves on SQL 89 in that it adds more features to the language. However, the standard does not necessarily provide access to all the capabilities of each RDBMS. Most vendors try to meet one of these two standards in their RDBMS products but will also add on their own extensions to the language. These extensions allow users to access the "extra" features implemented by the vendor. Microsoft has chosen to comply with SQL 92 for SQL Server 6.5 and 7. As a result, if you know ANSI-Standard SQL, you can easily port your knowledge to SQL Server.

However, like other vendors, Microsoft has added its own extensions to the SQL 92 standard in its implementation of SQL Server in order to implement features not supported by the standard. The extension of SQL 92 that is implemented in SQL Server is called Transact-SQL (T-SQL). This extension of the standard is one of the important reasons why SQL Server is so popular. T-SQL adds core functionality, such as stored procedures, distributed transactions, operating system functions, and other improvements. Transact-SQL is the native language of SQL Server.

You can think of T-SQL as a cross between Visual Basic for Applications (VBA) and SQL. T-SQL includes all the functionality necessary to retrieve, modify, delete, and add data to tables in a database. It can also be used to perform functions that are available in many programming languages. T-SQL has the ability to accept and return parameters, perform calculations, run built-in and custom functions, copy data between servers, and perform many other tasks. Combined, these capabilities make it an extremely powerful tool when working with SQL Server.

Main Database Components

In SQL Server, databases consist of two components: a transaction log and a database. They do not necessarily represent separate operating system files, but they are separate entities.

The transaction log is a file that is maintained by SQL Server, which is used to recover the database to the last known "good" state in case of system failure. It contains a list of all changes to the database. Every time a transaction starts in SQL Server, a Begin Transaction event is recorded in the log. The data modification that is to take place is then added to the log. If the transaction finishes successfully, a Commit Transaction event is logged. All of this information is used by SQL Server to recover in case of error or in case of system failure. If SQL Server shuts down unexpectedly, it uses this information to return to the last known good data state.

The database component houses the data for the system. It also contains all of the tables, stored procedures, user information, and other system objects.

Database Files

Databases in SQL Server are really one or more physical files that are managed by SQL Server. These files differ considerably between versions 6.5 and 7 in how they are used and organized.

SQL Server 6.5 databases consist of at least one file and possibly many files. Before a database can be created, the system administrator must create a *database device* on which to load the database. A database device is a file that houses the database and can also be used to house a transaction log. Usually, a database is created with two database devices, one that houses the database and one that houses the transaction log. This configuration ensures that corruption in the database file does not destroy the log device and vice versa. In cases where the database is extremely large, or in cases where administrators want to perform complex balancing of data, multiple devices can be used for the same database and the database will be spread through the selected devices. Devices usually have the file extension DAT.

In SQL Server 7, however, the database is comprised of at least two files: the *primary data file* and one or more *log files*. Databases can also have one or more *secondary data files*. The primary data file is used as the starting point for the database and includes some or all of the data and pointers to all of the secondary data files. Primary data files have an MDF extension. The secondary data files have an NDF file extension and contain any data for the database that does not fit on the primary data file. There can be any number of secondary data files if the database is large and the administrator configures the database in this manner. There is always at least one transaction file and sometimes more. These files contain the transaction logs for the database and have an LDF extension by default.

You should keep one detail in mind if you are planning to run SQL Server on a machine that is regularly backed up: Do not plan on restoring your database from the database or log files. In SQL Server 6.5, this is simply not possible. In SQL Server 7, there is no guarantee that this works. And, even if it does, your data may well be corrupt. Instead, you should back up your database using the SQL Server backup and restore utilities, and copy these SQL Server backup files to your backup drive.

Security Modes

SQL Server security can be configured to run in one of three modes: SQL Server/ Standard authentication, Windows NT authentication, or mixed authentication. The type selected for the server is usually chosen based on user needs or system requirements, but can also be chosen based on limiting factors of the environment.

SQL Server authentication, or *standard* authentication in SQL 6.5, is designed so that the database administrator creates the users who can log in to the system. The system is not dependent on Windows NT login information to allow access to different databases. Instead, all of the user names, passwords, and other authentication details are managed within SQL Server itself.

NT authentication, or *integrated* authentication, obtains user information from the Windows NT network or computer that SQL Server is running on. This allows users to directly access the database without having to specifically log in to SQL Server. Instead, the necessary Windows NT login information is passed to SQL Server when the user connects to the database. It requires that the user be logged into a Windows NT account that is set up with access to the appropriate databases. This login information is configured in SQL Server using the Windows NT login information available on the network. Integrated authentication can be very troublesome in version 6.5. In version 6.5, the Windows NT security information is not truly integrated, but instead is derived from information obtained from Windows NT, as it is in version 7. However, version 6.5 does not always maintain a connection to the Windows NT login information after the security is set. This means that changes to Windows NT security may not be propagated to SQL Server. Integrated authentication of security has been much improved in version 7. SQL Server now properly handles changes to Windows NT security. However, if your users do not log in to a Windows NT or Windows 2000 network, you cannot use integrated security. Integrated security is limited to Windows networks only.

Mixed security enables both integrated and standard authentication, allowing users to access the database with either type of information. A user can log in to the system by using the standard security or by entering a user name and password, or SQL Server can use login information derived from the Windows NT login server to allow users to access the database.

System Databases

The first time you start SQL Server, you will notice that there are already a few databases in the system. Four of these databases are system databases that SQL Server uses to administer the server and as temporary storage space. Specifically, these databases are called *master*, *tempdb*, *model*, and *msdb*.

The most important of these databases is the *master* database. It contains all of the system level information about SQL Server as well as all other databases managed by the installation of SQL Server. It stores all of the logical and physical layout information for SQL Server. The master database includes information about objects in other databases, files that other databases are stored in, all current database login information, and initialization information that is used to configure SQL Server when the server application is started. SQL Server prevents users from directly modifying the master database. All information in this database is modified through graphical utilities included with SQL Server or through system commands. This database is extremely important and regular backups of it must be maintained if the administrator wants to be able to restore any other database after a system failure occurs. If the master database is damaged, it is next to impossible to recover any other databases on the system if a backup is not available.

The *tempdb* database is used for storing temporary data. This storage can be requested by the system for transaction processing, or a user or user-driven code can explicitly request it. Tables and other objects created in tempdb are dropped either when a command such as an update query completes or when a connection to the database is terminated. Consequently, the tempdb database always starts out empty. In fact, this database is re-created each time SQL Server is started.

The *model* database is a template database that all new databases are created from. Event tempdb is created from the model database, so the model database must exist on all SQL Server systems. When a database is created, it is created by copying the model database to the new database file. Users can then create the objects in the new database as necessary. It is possible to make changes to the model database, so that all new databases that are created from that point on have those modifications in them. It may be tempting to add objects that you regularly use in each of your databases, however, I do not recommended this type of action. Keep in mind that the model is the template for all databases including tempdb. Any objects that you add to the model will automatically be added to tempdb each time the server is started. This could clutter tempdb with unused objects that will degrade the performance of the system.

The final system database that exists on all SQL Server systems is *msdb*. This database is used to manage SQL Server maintenance commands. Maintenance jobs are handled by SQL Server Agent in SQL 7 and SQL Executive in SQL 6.5. Whenever an administrator configures a maintenance command of the SQL Server system, the information about this maintenance task is stored in msdb. SQL Agent or SQL Executive then looks to this database for details on any maintenance commands that need to be run, such as database backups, operator notification in case of error, or database tuning commands.

Along with the system databases, each database also contains its own system tables. These tables contain information that is used to manage and keep track of the design of the database they reside in. They include information on all objects, relationships, fields, user defined datatypes, indexes, user permissions on each object, and other necessary information.

Do not attempt to make changes to the master database or any system tables in a database. Making changes to these objects incorrectly can corrupt SQL Server or the database in which they are modified. Because this corruption is not easy to recover from, it is best to leave these tables to SQL Server to manage. SQL Server provides tools for modifying all of this information in a controlled manner through system stored procedures and graphical interfaces.

Because tempdb is re-created each time SQL Server starts, there is little point in trying to make permanent changes to it. Your changes will not survive a restart of SQL Server. However, tempdb is a great place to create and destroy temporary tables that you may need to process specific data. In Access, developers often create temporary storage tables permanently to avoid having to re-create them each time a command is run. In SQL Server, it is better to create temporary tables in tempdb because it is designed for exactly this purpose and will save you from the added overhead of maintaining extra objects in your database.

Database Objects

Each SQL Server database contains a number of different object types. Each of these object types fulfills a particular function in the database.

Tables

Tables in SQL Server are similar to those in Microsoft Access. Database designers create tables in order to hold related information in a logical information structure. Each table consists of *fields* that define the type of data being stored in each column. Each *row* in a table represents an individual record.

Tables can also have indexes. Indexes access data, so that SQL Server can retrieve data in that index faster than nonindexed data. As in Access, indexes can be unique (the same data cannot appear twice in the same index), and they can be built on many fields forming what is called a *composite* key. However, SQL Server has one major difference in the way it handles indexing. In Access, the data in a table is stored sorted on the primary key. This allows for faster access to the data when the table is queried on the fields defined in an index. SQL Server does not require that data be sorted by the primary key. Instead, indexes have a property defining whether they are *clustered*. Any index in a SQL Server table may be clustered, but only one clustered index is allowed per table. The data in the table is sorted on disk using this key. Clustering can be very useful for tables that are accessed most often by a nonprimary key field because it allows you to cluster on the index that is most frequently used rather than be forced to cluster on the primary key. For example, a Customer table could have a primary key of a unique ID field called CustomerID. However, users search for data most often by the CompanyName field. By defining an index on the CompanyName field and setting its clustered property to true, data access is optimized for the CompanyName column. User queries against this column run faster because SQL Server does not have to look at an index that is unsorted or stored off the table. Nonclustered indexes require SQL Server to maintain separate information that contains pointers to the location of the data in the table. When you query an index that is not clustered, SQL Server must first find out where that data is by querying the index. This takes more time than querying a clustered index because the table is actually sorted on disk by the clustered index. When a query is run against a clustered index, SQL Server can retrieve the data as it searches the index without having to use secondary information.

Tables can also be in *relationships* with other tables that define how the data in one table is related to the data in another table. For example, an Order table that contains information about orders placed by customers could include the CustomerID. In order to link the CustomerID back to the Customer table, a relationship would be set up by the database designer. This link would define how the tables are related and is thus called a relationship. For those of you who are used to using relationships in Microsoft Access, you will probably notice that there is one feature that SQL Server is missing in relationships—cascading changes. Cascading allows you to define a relationship in an Access database, which specifies that when information in the primary key for a parent table is changed, the related data in child tables will automatically be updated. Cascading also allows you to specify that when records are deleted in a parent table, the child records in the related table are automatically deleted. This feature can be very useful in Microsoft Access. However, cascading is not supported in SQL Server for relationships. Instead, *triggers* (discussed in the section "Triggers" later in this chapter) should be used.

Relationships, primary key definitions, and unique indexes in SQL Server are implemented through SQL *constraints*. Constraints can most easily be described as a set of rules to which data entered into a table must conform. Constraints are used to define relationships and primary keys. Constraints can also be used to define the default value for a field, set whether a field can accept null values, limit the values that the column accepts as input, or define a rule for how data should be entered for each record in the table.

Views

Views in SQL Server are similar in some ways to SELECT queries in Access. Views represent SQL statements that return data from a table or from other views. Instead of an application using a complete SQL statement, such as a SELECT query to select certain columns from a table or multiple joined tables, a view can be called by an application to return the necessary data. Views can be used to maintain data security. By only allowing a user to access data through views, you can restrict the data a user can see and how that data can be retrieved from the database. For example, you can remove permission for a user to directly view an Employee table that contains salary information, but instead give the user access to a view that doesn't include the salary field, keeping the salary information secure from unauthorized users.

Stored Procedures

Stored procedures are sets of instructions for SQL Server that are compiled into a single plan. Stored procedures are written in Transact-SQL. In many ways, they are a cross between a VBA procedure and a Microsoft Access query. Stored procedures combine into one convenient package a set of instructions and queries that can return or modify data and/or perform some other function.

There are two types of stored procedures that you will probably use— *system stored procedures* and *user defined stored procedures*. System stored procedures are predefined SQL Server stored procedures. These procedures carry out common tasks for SQL Server users, look up information about the database, and return information about SQL Server, the operating system, or the network it is installed on. One such system stored procedure is called "sp_help." Calling sp_help in any SQL or T-SQL code provides information on SQL Server databases or the objects the databases contain. There are also system stored procedures for managing logins, creating or deleting objects, setting up replication, checking server statistics, and many, many other functions. The other type of stored procedure is a user defined stored procedure. These are created by users of SQL Server. User defined stored procedures can be very small, such as a simple statement to return data from a table, or very large, such as a complete transaction management function for transferring money between bank accounts.

Triggers

Triggers are actually stored procedures that are run whenever data in a table is modified. Triggers can be used to enforce referential integrity through user-defined cascade updating or deleting; they can be used to ensure that data in multiple tables is properly synchronized; or they can be used for any one of a myriad other functions.

Triggers are executed in response to data in a table being updated, deleted, or inserted. Triggers can be written in such a way that they run only if data in a particular field is updated, or they can be designed to run regardless of which field is affected. This allows you to respond to data changes only in those situations that call for some action to be taken. An example of where a trigger could be used is in a table designed to track the history of an employee's job position. Each time the Title field in the Employee table is updated, the EmployeeHistory table would be updated by a trigger on the Employee table with the employee's last position, title, and end date. Creating a trigger on the table would allow you to maintain a running history of changes to the data in the Employee table without having to write code to handle the transfer of the data or requiring a user to enter the historical data.

Rules

Rules are a component of SQL Server that have been partly kept for backward compatibility, but are also used in user defined types, which are discussed in the "User Defined Data Types" section later in this chapter. Rules are used to define the policies to which data in a table column must comply when entered. The concept is similar to the Validation Rule property of a field in Microsoft Access. However, rules are created as a separate entity and are then bound to a field. When defining validations that must be run against only one field in a table or a few fields on a few tables, you should use constraints instead of rules because constraints are more versatile. However, rules can be useful because you can define one rule and bind it to many tables. If your data must conform to a complex set of policies, it is often easier to create a single rule for a field that must conform to those same policies rather than having to rewrite a constraint for each affected field.

Defaults

Defaults are used to define an initial value for a field in a table. Like rules, defaults are supplied partly for backward compatibility with older versions of SQL Server. Defaults can best be equated to the Default setting for a field in an Access table. As with SQL Server rules, once a default is created it must be bound to a field. In most cases, you should use default constraints instead of defaults because default constraints are automatically deleted when a table is deleted. However, defaults can be useful if you are applying the same default to many fields on many tables.

User Defined Data Types

One of the great benefits of SQL Server over application databases, such as Access, is the ability to create user defined data types (UDDT). Each created data type must be based on an existing SQL Server data type. The advantage of a user defined data type is that it can define and enforce rules and defaults against the type itself, set its field size and *nullability* (whether or not it can contain null values), and use the new data type in any table in the database without the user having to set those properties each time a field of that type is needed. For example, many tables in a database include phone numbers. You can define a phone_number data type that is set to the exact number of characters with default values filled in for the area code and define rules that restrict the area codes that can be entered. When you need to create a field that is used to store a phone number, just select the data type you created. You don't have to worry about reimplementing its functionality because it is already built-in to your UDDT. One detail that should be noted about user defined data types is that you must use rules or defaults to define these properties. You cannot use constraints on a user defined type. This is the main reason rules and defaults still exist as individual entities.

11

Logins

In SQL Server, logins do not apply only to a single database. Instead, they are global items for the server. After a login is created by an administrator, rights must be assigned to that login to allow it to access different databases. However, each login does not need to be specifically assigned rights to a database. Instead, you can *alias* it to another login for a database; thereby giving it the same rights as the login alias it is using. You can also add any login to a group (or role in SQL 7), and then assign rights to that group, saving you from having to remember every detail of a user's rights. Instead of having to assign particular rights for each user, you can assign rights for a group, and rights for the users will be inferred from the groups to which their login belongs.

Groups (SQL 6.5)/Users

Groups, replaced in SQL 7 with roles (which is discussed in the next section), are a way of grouping people in an easy-to-administer package to allow users in the group to have access to various portions of the database. SQL 6.5 groups are similar in many ways to Access security groups in that you can define rights for the group and not have to worry about assigning rights for individual users within that group. Groups in Access can be used to allow selected users access to database objects without having to specify rights for each user. However, SQL Server's implementation of this feature is considerably better. It does not suffer from the issues that Access security does when individual users are assigned particular rights. When individual rights are assigned in Access, the user's rights replace any group rights, and the change cannot be reversed. In SQL Server, it is reasonably simple to reset the rights for a particular user, so that the group the user belongs to takes precedence over individual rights.

The *users* item, available in SQL 7 and 6.5, allows you to assign access rights to individual logins or alias logins to other IDs. Aliasing logins is a method of telling SQL Server that when a particular login is used in a database, it should act as another login for that database. This can make administration of the database easier in that you can create a single login for the database and assign security rights only to that login, rather than having to set them for each SQL Server login. By aliasing other users to that login, your database needs only to have the rights set for the alias that is used.

Roles (SQL 7)

Roles are a new concept introduced in SQL 7, so you cannot use them in 6.5. Roles allow you to create a single object to allow users permission to perform certain functions. Roles go one step beyond SQL 6.5 groups in that they can be nested, and they can easily be used in concert with Windows NT security information. Roles can also be used to define who has rights to perform system maintenance as well as which users have rights to access or update data. Groups in SQL 6.5 are created to be local to a database; roles can be local to a database or can be designed for the entire SQL Server.

Diagrams (SQL 7)

Diagrams, introduced in SQL 7, are similar to the Access relationship window. Diagrams allow you to define relationships between fields in various tables using a graphical interface. Unlike Access, SQL Server allows you to define many different diagrams for a database that can affect many of the same tables. By creating multiple diagrams, it becomes easier to administer different areas of the database and still have complex relationships defined. Multiple diagrams can be used to separate relationships in different areas of the database, so that you only need to view the particular sections of the relationships in which you are interested. Anyone who has worked with an Access database that contains a large number of related tables will appreciate this feature.

Using Enterprise Manager (SQL 6.5)

SQL Server 6.5 is managed through an application called SQL Enterprise Manager. This application is a graphical interface used in all areas of SQL management.

Before you can use Enterprise Manager to manage SQL Server 6.5, you must add the information necessary on your computer to define how Enterprise Manager should connect to SQL Server. This is done using the SQL Client Configuration Utility. This utility tells the various utilities used to connect to, work with, and administer SQL Server, where to find the server, and how to communicate with it. To add a server to your list of SQL Servers, start the SQL Client Configuration Utility in your SQL Server program group from the Start menu and select the Advanced tab when the application has started (see Figure 1-1). Enter the details necessary to connect to your server. This information should be available from your database administrator, or if you are the administrator, you should use the configuration you selected when SQL Server was installed. You do not need to type the name of the DLL in the *DLL Name* box. Instead, use the drop-down list to display the common names used to refer to the Net-Libraries. The selected network library is translated into a DLL name when you apply the configuration settings. The Net-Library you choose should be the one that your network uses. If you have a Windows NT network, choose TCP/IP Sockets; if you are on a Novell network, select NWLink IPX/SPX; or choose another protocol that your main network works on. You should also ensure that the server is configured to listen on this library. The Net-Library is determined when SQL Server is configured, and the person who installed SQL Server should be aware of these settings. If SQL Server is not configured correctly to handle your network protocol, consult the SQL Server documentation for information on how to change these settings.

Figure 1-1. SQL Client Utility

Note that when using TCP/IP Sockets as your network library, you must enter the IP address of the computer on which SQL Server is running (if it is the same as the one you are using to open the client utility, use "127.0.0.1", which is the network address for the local computer) followed by a comma, and then enter the number of the port that SQL Server is configured to listen on. This port is set when SQL Server is installed and is, by default, port 1433. If you are the person who installs SQL Server, keep in mind that it is best to accept port 1433 as the default because it is the standard used for all Microsoft SQL Servers. Changing the port could cause conflicts with other applications on the server that may need those ports to communicate.

Once the server is added to your network libraries configuration, you must then add it to SQL Enterprise Manager. To do this, start SQL Enterprise Manager from the SQL 6.5 program group on your Start menu. In order to register the server, you must add the server information to a group. Server groups are an arbitrary categorization that are used to separate multiple SQL Server systems. They allow you to group and administer multiple servers in an organized manner. If there aren't any groups defined or you don't want to use one of the groups that are defined, you can add a new group by selecting Server Groups from the Server menu in Enterprise Manager. Typically, server groups are set up by geographical area, business function, or some other logical grouping that applies to your own situation. Feel free to name the group, so that it is easier for you to remember which group to open in order to access the server you need.

To register the server for administration using SQL Enterprise Manager, select Register Server from the Server menu. The Register Server dialog appears. For the server name, use the name you added in the Client Network Utilities in the Server section. Then, enter into the login information the *sa* login or another login that has system administrator privileges (see Figure 1-2).

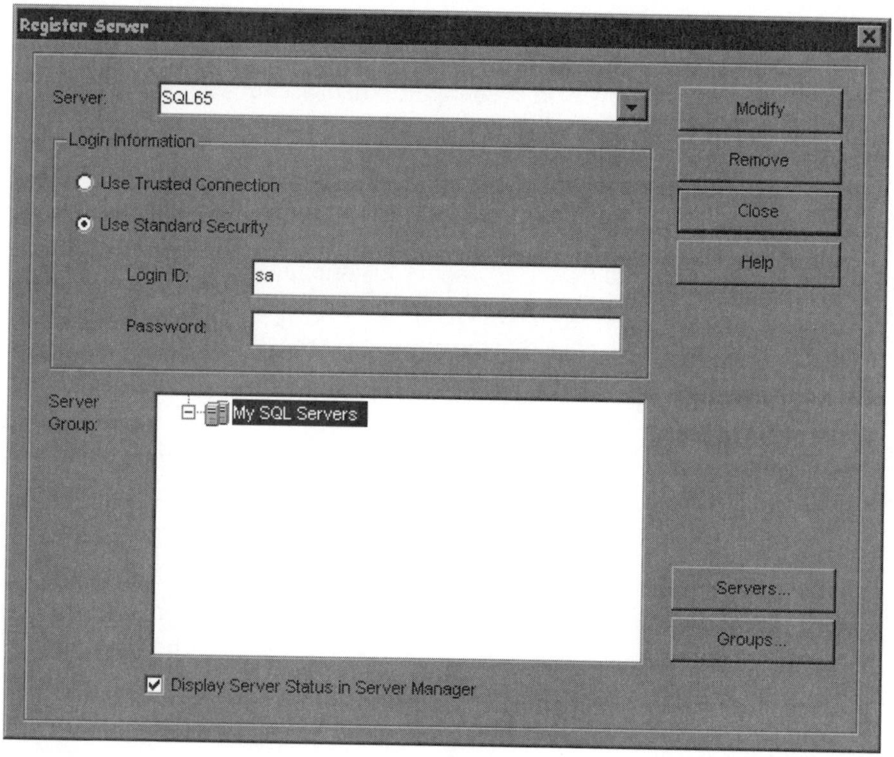

Figure 1-2. Register Server

Finally, select the group that the server is to be added to, click Register, and then close the window. Your server should show up in Enterprise Manager under the group you selected.

Explore the sections in your SQL Server by expanding the name of the server in the tree view in Enterprise Manager. You will see six items under your server name. These items are

- SQL Mail

- SQL Executive

- Database Devices

- Backup Devices

- Databases

- Logins

The *SQL Mail* entry allows you to configure a mail account for SQL Server to use with MS Mail or a selection of other mail systems. The *SQL Executive* item allows you to configure, manage, and run all of the maintenance jobs that have been or will be set up for the databases on the server. *Database Devices* allows you to set up and maintain all of the database devices that are used by each database and transaction log. *Backup Devices* is where you configure and maintain devices to which databases and transaction logs can be backed up. The *Databases* section gives you access to all of the objects and users in each database. And, the *Logins* section is used to set up and maintain SQL Server logins.

The most important item in the list is, of course, the Databases section. This is the area that you will use most because it allows you to create, configure, and update your databases. To view a database and its objects, expand the Databases section and select the database you want to view. By expanding a database item in the tree, you will be presented with all of the database object collections. Also, by right-clicking on the database name in the tree and choosing Properties from the context menu, you will be allowed to view or modify the main properties of the database.

Viewing Data

In order to view data in SQL Enterprise Manager, you must open an ISQL/w window and execute a SQL statement. This can be done in Enterprise Manager by selecting Tools ⇒ SQL Query Tool. This window can also be accessed through the ISQL/w program item in the SQL 6.5 program group on the Start menu. From the query window that opens, you can view data, execute stored procedures, execute action queries, or even run database maintenance and change database options. All of these functions can be performed in this tool using Transact-SQL. Database maintenance and administration, although possible using textual commands, is much easier using the graphical utilities provided in Enterprise Manager.

In order to run a command against a particular database, you must select the database you want to work with from the DB drop-down list in the SQL Query Tool. You can then run any valid Transact-SQL statements against the database. For example, selecting the pubs database and running the SQL statement

```
SELECT * FROM Employee
```

returns all of the rows from the Employee table in the Results pane (see Figure 1-3).

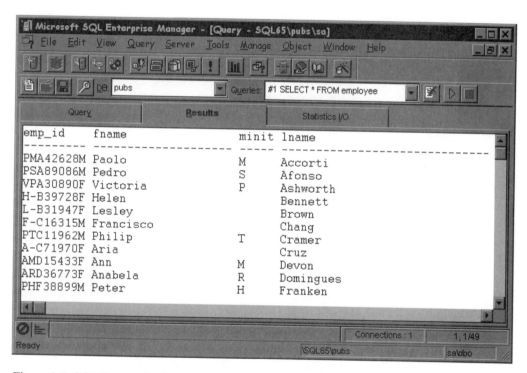

Figure 1-3. SQL Query Window—Results

ISQL/w is limited in that it is not designed for editing data in a grid, such as the one Access uses. All data that is returned to this window is static and cannot be modified. In order to modify data in ISQL/w, you must write the SQL statements that will make the modification for you. However, one of the advantages of ISQL/w is that you can run multiple statements from the same window without having to execute two separate queries. You can do this by entering both statements in the

Query pane, one after the other, and executing them using the run command (CTRL+E or click on the Execute Query toolbar button). You can also enter as many statements as you like and only execute a particular one by highlighting it in the Query tab, and then using the run command. Only the highlighted code is executed.

Executing the following SQL statements in the Query pane:

```
SELECT * FROM Employee
SELECT * FROM Authors
```

in the pubs database returns all of the rows from the Employee table followed by all of the rows in the Authors table. However, selecting only the first line, and then executing, only returns the data from the employee table. Being able to run multiple SQL statements in one function is one of the advantages of using SQL Server over Access.

Using Enterprise Manager (SQL 7.0)

SQL Server 7 is managed through an application called Microsoft Management Console (MMC). MMC is Microsoft's new standard administration tool for all Microsoft server products and for Windows 2000. A plug-in is used in this application to enable administration of SQL Server systems. Although it is possible to load the plug-in yourself, it is easier just to use the Enterprise Manager shortcut that is created when the SQL administration tools are installed.

If you are using Enterprise Manager on a computer other than the computer that has SQL Server installed, you first need to add to your computer the information necessary to connect to the server you will be using. In order for Enterprise Manager and most other applications to access SQL Server, you must add the connection information to the Client Network Utility in the SQL 7 program group on the Start menu. This is a newer version of the same utility used for SQL Server 6.5. This utility configures SQL network information, so that the SQL Server tools will know where your server is and how connections should be established. Open the Client Network Utility and if your server is not listed in the server alias information on the first table, you can add it by clicking on the Add button. The Add Network Library Configuration window, shown in Figure 1-4, appears, allowing you to specify the protocol to use when connecting to the server.

You must then provide an alias for the server. This is the name that is used by all applications to access the server from this computer. You can use any name that you want to refer to the computer, but it is usually easier to remember which server you are connecting to if you use its real network name. Select a protocol to connect to the server. This is the protocol that was selected when the server was installed. The Net-Library you choose should be the one that your network uses. If you have a Windows NT network, choose TCP/IP Sockets; if you are on a Novell

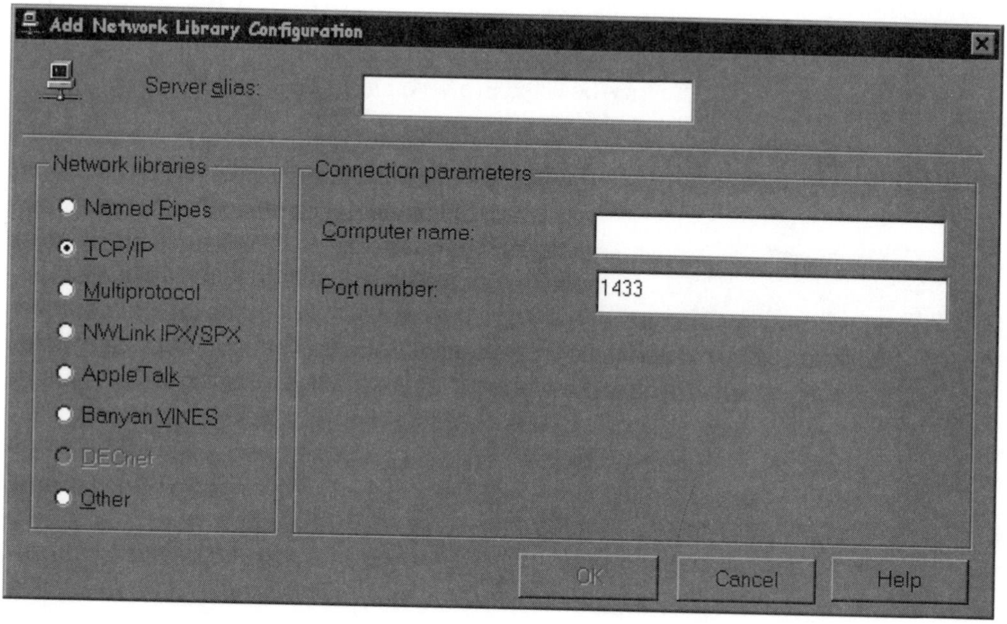

Figure 1-4. Add Network Library Configuration

network, select NWLink IPX/SPX; and so on. You should also ensure that the server is configured to listen on this library. The Net-Library is determined when SQL Server is configured, and the person who installed SQL Server should be aware of these settings. If SQL Server is not configured correctly to handle your network protocol, consult the SQL Server documentation for information on how to change these settings.

The computer name you enter must be the name or IP address of the server that SQL Server resides on. By default, port 1433 is the port that is used for Microsoft SQL Server. This port number differs only if it was modified during the installation. Click OK after selecting the name and port for your server; your server appears in the main Client Network window. Close the window to complete this task.

You then need to register the server, so that it can be managed in Enterprise Manager. To do this, start Enterprise Manager from the SQL 7 program group on the Windows Start menu. When Enterprise Manager opens, right-click on a group or the main Microsoft SQL Servers item in the tree view pane, and choose New SQL Server Registration. Select the server you just added to the Client Network Utility from the list and use the Add button to add it to the list of servers that can be managed by Enterprise Manager. Click Next, and select the security method that you will use to connect to the server. If your server is configured under Windows 95 or 98, note that Windows NT Authentication is not supported on those platforms. Click Next, and enter the user name and password you will use if you selected SQL

Server Authentication. Finally, select the server group you want to add your server registration to or create a new group.

Your server should then be listed in a server group. Explore the server by expanding it in the tree view in Enterprise Manager. See Figure 1-5 for the items that should be listed under the server name.

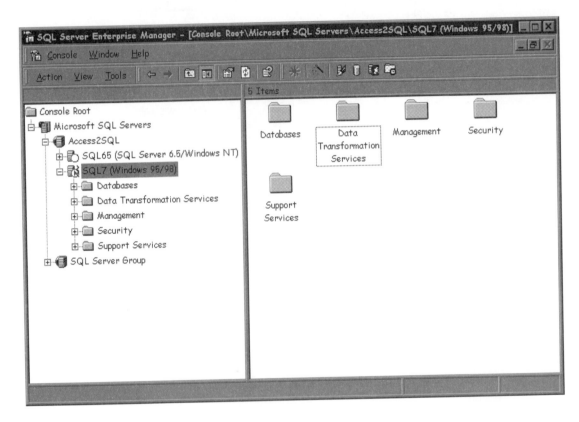

Figure 1-5. Enterprise Manager

There are five main folders shown in each registered server when you expand it. They are

- Databases

- Data Transformation Services

- Management

- Security

- Support Services

The *Databases* section provides access to the databases currently set up on the server and all of their objects. The *Data Transformation Services* provides functions for importing, exporting, and transforming data between SQL Server and any OLE DB or ODBC data source. The *Management* section provides access to SQL Server management and diagnostic tools. The *Security* section provides access to security management and maintenance functions. And, the *Support Services* section provides management access to services that SQL Server uses and supports, specifically mail and Distributed Transaction Coordinator.

In order to view a database and its objects, expand the Databases section, and select the database you want to view. If you select the name of the database by clicking on it, Enterprise Manager shows you some quick statistics for that database in the details window, shown on the left. It also gives you access to commonly used wizards. You can also right-click on the database, and choose Properties to view or modify properties of the database.

Viewing Data

One of the improvements in management in SQL 7, which did not exist in 6.5, is that you can view data in a table without having to write any SQL. Select a table in the database, and then, from the Action menu or by right-clicking the table, select Open Table, Return All Rows to view the entire contents of the table. You can also choose Return Top to return only a specified number of rows. Figure 1-6 shows the window that these selections display, where you can see all of the data and modify the SQL. The toolbar buttons on this screen provide access to different options for viewing and modifying the SQL string that returns this data.

There are four different panes that can be used to help design a SQL statement. These can be accessed through the toolbar or through the right-click context menu in this window.

Diagram Pane: This pane is used to graphically select the tables you want to use in a query and to select the fields that should be included in the results of the query. It is very similar to the table pane in query design view in Access. However, instead of having a separate field list, fields can be added to the query simply by placing a checkmark beside them.

Grid Pane: This pane is used to show the results of the fields that are selected in a grid and provides the capability to add criteria, such as sort by, group by, and alias fields. It is similar to the field pane in query design view in Access.

SQL Pane: This pane shows the actual SQL statement that is generated by the graphical selections. You can still modify the SQL directly if you want or need to do so. There are many situations where it is quicker to write the SQL than try to use the graphical tools.

Results Pane: This pane shows the results (if any) of executing the SQL statement after you run the query. It is possible to directly edit the data in this pane as you would in an Access query result set.

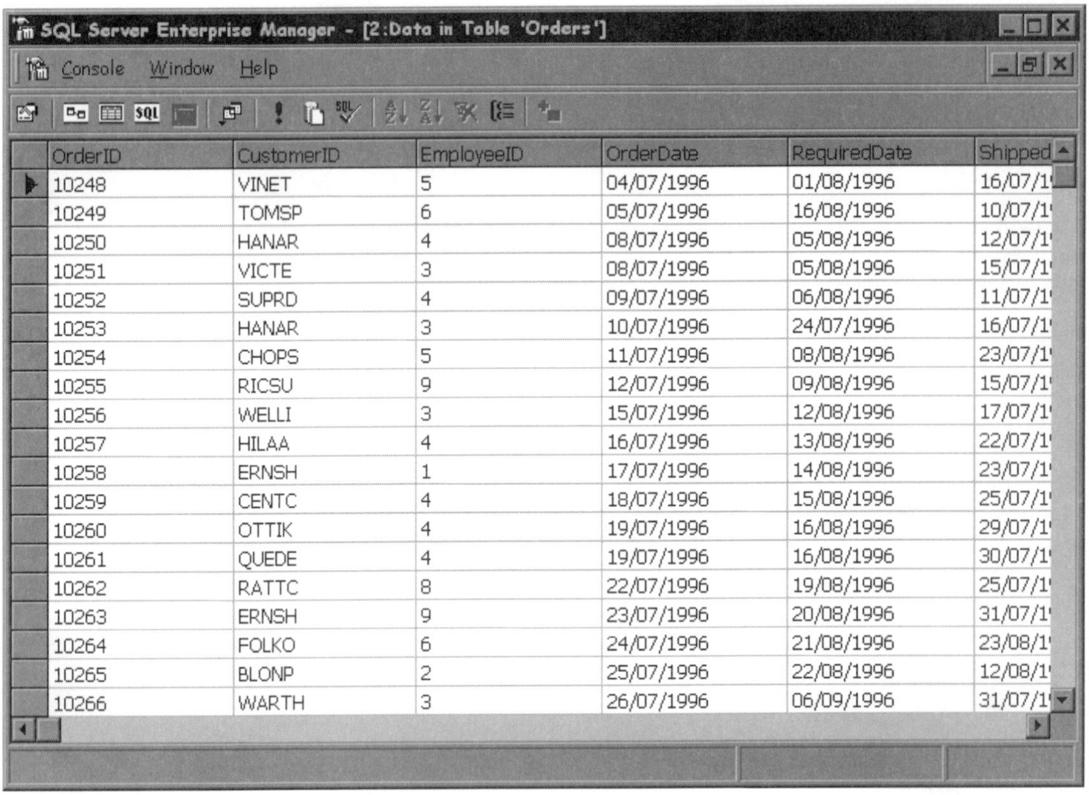

OrderID	CustomerID	EmployeeID	OrderDate	RequiredDate	Shipped
10248	VINET	5	04/07/1996	01/08/1996	16/07/1
10249	TOMSP	6	05/07/1996	16/08/1996	10/07/1
10250	HANAR	4	08/07/1996	05/08/1996	12/07/1
10251	VICTE	3	08/07/1996	05/08/1996	15/07/1
10252	SUPRD	4	09/07/1996	06/08/1996	11/07/1
10253	HANAR	3	10/07/1996	24/07/1996	16/07/1
10254	CHOPS	5	11/07/1996	08/08/1996	23/07/1
10255	RICSU	9	12/07/1996	09/08/1996	15/07/1
10256	WELLI	3	15/07/1996	12/08/1996	17/07/1
10257	HILAA	4	16/07/1996	13/08/1996	22/07/1
10258	ERNSH	1	17/07/1996	14/08/1996	23/07/1
10259	CENTC	4	18/07/1996	15/08/1996	25/07/1
10260	OTTIK	4	19/07/1996	16/08/1996	29/07/1
10261	QUEDE	4	19/07/1996	16/08/1996	30/07/1
10262	RATTC	8	22/07/1996	19/08/1996	25/07/1
10263	ERNSH	9	23/07/1996	20/08/1996	31/07/1
10264	FOLKO	6	24/07/1996	21/08/1996	23/08/1
10265	BLONP	2	25/07/1996	22/08/1996	12/08/1
10266	WARTH	3	26/07/1996	06/09/1996	31/07/1

Figure 1-6. Data View

If you right-click the Employee table in the pubs database, and choose Open Table, Return All Rows, you see all of the data contained in the Employee table. By showing the Diagram Pane, you can even drag another table from the database window onto this pane to have it included in the query. If a relationship has been defined between the tables, the relationship is shown in much the same way that Access shows you the relationships between tables when you create a query. You can then select fields to display or view other panes to modify other properties of the query.

Finding Information

This book does not purport to be a replacement for a good information source for SQL Server. It is a solution aimed at those who want to migrate from Access to SQL

Server. As a result, there are quite a few topics in SQL Server that won't be discussed in this book. So where can you go for answers?

The Books Online feature is an invaluable resource for any SQL Server administrator or programmer and can be found in your SQL Server program group on the Start menu. It contains complete information on the architecture, administration, programming, and operation of SQL Server. In SQL Server 6.5 Books Online, you can find an introduction to the database objects and how to work with them in the Database Developers Guide section. Similar information is presented in the Creating and Maintaining Databases section of the Books Online in SQL 7. Each of these resources provides detailed information on creating databases and the objects that comprise them. They are the first places you should look for answers to your SQL questions because many solutions are usually found in this documentation.

One of the indispensable resources that Microsoft gives developers and users alike is the Microsoft Knowledge Base. SQL Server and Access have large communities that use these programs. If you run into trouble, the Knowledge Base can often help to answer your question. In recent revisions, Microsoft has added the SQL online documentation to the Knowledge Base, making it easier to use one resource to find the information you need. If you haven't used it before, you must check it out. The Knowledge Base can be found at `http://support.microsoft.com`.

The Internet also has many public newsgroups that can help you in your search. Most news servers have access to the newsgroups `comp.databases.ms-access` and `comp.databases.ms-sqlserver`. Posting a message to one or both of these groups gives you access to a wide audience of people who have experience with these applications and may be able to offer you help. Microsoft also manages its own news server located at `msnews.microsoft.com`. These differ from the "public" Usenet groups in that they are all aimed at people who are using a particular Microsoft product and even specific uses for different products. There are many newsgroups pertaining to various aspects of SQL Server and Access, where people who also have experience with migrating from one application to another can help you. In addition, you can search the past postings on the Microsoft newsgroups and the public newsgroups at `http://www.deja.com`. Formerly known as DejaNews, this site contains a searchable index of all past and present postings to all of the Microsoft and general Internet newsgroups. If you think that someone else may have had the same issue you currently have, it is a very good place to start.

You should also check my section on the Apress Web site at `http://www.apress.com`. This site contains the downloads for this book and a list of sites that you can use to obtain information on the various topics I discuss. This site will be updated periodically to ensure that you are receiving a list of the most up-to-date resources available on the Web.

CHAPTER 2
Why Migrate?

MIGRATING AN APPLICATION from Access to SQL Server can be a daunting task. Preparation and careful planning is essential to make the transfer of data go smoothly. Before a migration can take place, a complete evaluation of the migration and the reasons behind it must occur. In this chapter, we'll review the different types of migration, the advantages of SQL Server, the reasons to migrate, and the reasons not to migrate. In order to evaluate a migration, you first need to understand exactly what migrating is.

What Is Migrating?

Migrating from Access to SQL Server involves evaluating, categorizing, and moving tables, data, objects, and functionality from an Access application to SQL Server. It also requires that you preserve—and possibly enhance—the functionality available to the user. Migrating is not a simple matter of transferring all of the Access tables to a SQL Server database and then linking the new tables into Access. You must perform a complete analysis of the items being migrated before the migration takes place. This analysis includes evaluating queries, macros, form and report data sources, ADO, DAO, and VBA code, and tables and their properties. You should also determine how your Access objects will scale and whether their implementation should be modified or remain the same in the new system. You should consider the timing of the migration in the lifecycle of the application because it affects how much work has to be done and how that work occurs. The decisions that the analysis helps you make will have a dramatic effect on the methodology you use to migrate your application. Before I get into the specifics of the migration itself, I will examine the different types of migrations that can occur.

Many applications are prototyped in Access because it is much faster to develop a database in Access than in SQL Server. An application is prototyped in Access with the knowledge that the application will be moved to SQL Server before it is rolled out to users. Once potential issues and development changes are finalized based on the prototype, the database is migrated to SQL Server. This type of migration is often one of the easiest to perform because the original design of the application takes into account the fact that the backend RDBMS will be SQL Server. It allows a developer to follow certain practices that can make the migration easier. Also, because the application has not been rolled out to the general user community, there is often little or no data that must be migrated to the server.

As you will see, this eliminates many of the potential issues that are encountered during a migration. In this chapter, I will take an in-depth look at the issues that you need to consider in order to migrate an application to SQL Server.

Migrations sometimes take place shortly after a system is rolled out into a production environment. Developers using Access for the first time or using it in a different way than they normally do, often find that Access does not give them the performance and functionality they need for the successful implementation of their system. Sometimes Access simply does not meet all of the requirements of the application. This can be the result of poor planning, but is just as commonly a result of greater use of the system than was originally anticipated. A migration immediately after implementation is usually one of the hardest migrations to deal with. Confidence in a system that is withdrawn after it is released to users can be very low. This can lead to difficulty dealing with users and management when justifying the migration and the extra development time involved. However, because the original developers are available to support the migration, the planning of the changes can take place very quickly. Less time is spent in "discovery" learning the functionality of the system because the knowledge of the system is still fresh in everyone's minds. The system is already well understood.

By far the most common time for an Access database to be migrated is after the system has been in a production environment for some time. This type of migration can occur for any number of reasons, but the most common reasons are performance and security concerns. This type of migration is usually the most difficult to plan and implement for a number of reasons. Often, the original developers are not available to help out in the planning. This means that a significant amount of time is spent in learning how the application works and determining all of the purposes it fulfills. Developers must evaluate the entire application to ensure that none of the components of the system are missed in the migration. This type of migration can also be the most risky. Applications that reach the point where they need to be migrated are often critical applications in a business. If a migration fails or does not meet the new or old requirements for the system, it can end up completely destroying an application unnecessarily.

Because of the problems involved in moving from Access to SQL Server, it is imperative that the person performing the migration has a solid understanding of the Access application that is being migrated as well as the reasons the application should be migrated. In order to understand the reasons behind migrating, you need to take a look at the major differences between Access and SQL Server that cause people to want to upgrade. This will help you to better understand the specific set of problems that can be solved by moving to SQL Server.

Access versus SQL Server

Access and SQL Server are very different systems. SQL Server is a client/server RDBMS, whereas Access is a file-based application. They have very different limitations and work very differently.

Size Constraints

One of the major differences between SQL Server and Access databases is the maximum size of a database. Despite what many people believe, Access databases can support a great deal of data. Access 97 and earlier versions have a documented size limit of 1 gigabyte. In Access 2000, this limit has been increased to 2GB. However, anyone who has experience with a shared Access database over 10MB is well aware of the fact that the larger a database gets, the worse the performance from the Jet Engine. This is especially true if the majority of the data is housed in only a few tables. Attempting to retrieve data from one very large table can take a long time. Attempting to retrieve data from multiple large joined tables can take even longer. Needless to say, this is not the desired behavior for an application.

SQL Server can support much larger databases. The maximum size of a single database in SQL Server 6.5 is 1 terabyte. In SQL 7, this has been increased to 1,048,516 terabytes. A terabyte is equal to 1,024GB. Consequently, the limit of a SQL Server database in version 7 is approximately 536 million times larger than the limit of an Access 2000 database.

Recently, some changes were made to SQL Server to optimize its support for what the industry has termed Very Large Databases (VLDBs). These are databases that house millions of records of information. VLDBs can be very difficult to manage without the appropriate RDBMS. If the RDBMS is not designed to handle these types of databases, the methods they use to work with data may cause large degradations in the performance of the application that accesses that database. The definition of this name is somewhat subjective, but it is doubtful that anyone would dispute that VLDBs include databases over 100GB. Microsoft SQL Server can handle these types of databases and even does it well. When a SQL Server VLDB is designed correctly, it can support lots of users without any problems and still respond quickly to requests from other applications.

Transferring Data

As discussed in the previous chapter, SQL Server and Access return data in very different ways. Access must retrieve all of the data in a table to the local computer in order to filter and manipulate the data. SQL Server has the capability to process a request for data, perform any data manipulation on the server, and only return the resulting records to the client application. How the data is handled by an application once it is requested can also differ a great deal between Access and SQL.

When you run a query against a Microsoft Access database, the Jet Engine goes out to the database, retrieves the entire contents of the table that the data is requested from, and copies that data locally for the client. The Jet Engine then handles this data in local memory to filter it according to the specifics of the request that was generated. When you run a similar query in SQL Server, the server takes the request for data and processes it on the server. The requested data is extracted from the table by the server, and then sent across the network to the client. The client then works locally with the data that was requested.

Due to these differences, more memory is required on the client when using Access than is required with SQL Server. If the Access database resides on a disk drive on a remote computer on the network, the network load is also much higher because more data must travel over the network to the client.

Another major difference between how Access and SQL Server deal with data is how they support cursors. Cursors define where and how data is updated. They can be server-side or client-side. With server-side cursors, a constant connection is held to the database. Any changes to data are immediately transmitted to the server. All indexing of data and changes to data take place on the server. As a result, server-side cursors use the network a great deal. As each change is sent back to the server, sorting of the data and data changes made by other users must be passed back and forth between the client and the server. With client-side cursors, all sorting, updating, and manipulation of data takes place on the client. Once the server has sent the data to the client, it becomes the client's responsibility to handle the data until it is resubmitted to the server in a batch update. The server only tracks the fact that the data is currently being used by another system.

SQL Server 6.5 and 7 fully support client-side and server-side cursors. You can request data from the server, and then completely disconnect from the database once the data has been sent to the client. The application then works with the data locally. You can also maintain your connection to the server and have each update sent to the server as it occurs. On the other hand, the Jet Engine does not truly support cursors through DAO. Although it is possible to implement cursor types in ADO, you cannot use the DAO interfaces to implement cursors. When using DAO, the server handles all updates to the data. Sorting changes and updates to the data are transmitted to the client as they occur. Access 2000 offers better support for cursors using ADO, but in Access 97, you cannot bind any objects to data that uses client-side cursors because ADO binding is not supported. Essentially, this means that an Access 97 application must maintain a constant connection to the server. This increases the load on the network as changes are constantly being sent back and forth between the backend database and the client application.

Multi-User Constraints

Anyone who has developed an Access application that is used by more than 10 people concurrently has probably run into the dreaded "record locked by another user" error that is common to multi-user Access databases. This error is a result of how Access locks records and how concurrency is managed.

When a user is updating a record, an RDBMS locks that record or the table the record resides in, so that other users cannot make modifications to it. This prevents multiple users from being able to update the same record at the same time. Access's record locking locks not only the record that is being edited, but also some of the other records physically stored close to it. As a result, two users may not be able to add records at the same time. Access locking information is stored in an LDB file that is kept in the same directory as the database that is being used. This file is created when a user connects to the database and is deleted once the last connected user leaves the database. The locking that is implemented by Access in this file tends to have a number of problems when many concurrent users are accessing the database. This can create a severe limitation to an application when the user base starts to increase. SQL Server handles locking considerably better than Access. SQL Server can handle thousands of concurrent users, all accessing the same data. Of course, they can't all be updating the same information at the same time, but the potential to have a large user community sharing data is there. Access can have a large community too—as long as users don't all show up at the same time.

Implementation of the security model is much different in Access than in SQL Server. In Access, all security information is kept in the system.mdw file. This file contains all of the user IDs, groups, and passwords for each defined user on the system. In order to connect to a database using customized login information, users must have access to a copy of the version of this file that was used to develop the application. If this file is lost or damaged and proper documentation on it is not kept, a database can become completely inaccessible. Also, in order to implement security on the database, either a new version of this file must be created or all permissions must be explicitly removed from all objects for the default user "Admin." The Admin user ID is common to all Microsoft Access systems and if the permissions for this user are not properly removed, anyone with a clean copy of Access can open the database and modify it. The security administrator must remove these implicit permissions, which can be a long and tedious process.

SQL Server security is implemented locally to the system. All user and group information is stored in the master database on the server, so there is no conflict with different versions of the security implementation. Security is also set to the highest possible level by default: Only the system administrators have access to all databases, for instance. User permissions must be assigned as needed and are not given explicitly. The default admin user, "sa", can have his or her password changed for the entire server, so that users cannot access the server where the change occurred using the "sa" login from their own server. . This prevents unauthorized access to the database at a level that Access cannot even come close to.

Maintenance and Administration

Administration in Access may seem rather simple. However, there are some maintenance tasks that must be done to a database in order to ensure the optimal performance of the system. When using Access, each database must be repaired and compacted on a regular basis. Repairing rebuilds the indexes in the database, and compacting clears out any empty space or deleted objects in the file. Repairing and compacting can prevent the database from becoming corrupted by high volume usage or improper application shutdown. Databases should also be backed up on a regular basis as a precaution against unexpected events, such as hard disk failures or accidental deletion. Each of these Access maintenance functions must be run separately for each database either manually or by using a third-party tool that comes at an extra cost. And, there is no facility in Access that records this activity. There is no central administration point for all Access databases on a computer, and there is no common way to schedule these tasks to occur at times when users are unlikely to be in the system. When fatal errors, such as a corrupted database, are encountered, the only way for administrators to know about the problem is when users contact them. This notification is inefficient and can become a problem if the support staff is not around to take the call.

SQL Server administration and maintenance is run through stored procedures included as system utilities or through SQL Server Agent/SQL Executive. Maintenance for all databases on a server is performed through one entry point and is therefore centralized. Rebuilding indexes, removing unused space from databases, checking database integrity, and backing up the database and transaction logs can be done for one or many databases using the tools supplied with SQL Server. Jobs can be scheduled at times when users are not on the system and can even be executed from remote servers. These tools maintain logs of all activities and, if configured to do so, notify users if any of the jobs failed or page someone if a fatal error has occurred on the server. You can even configure the server to email or page someone when an unexpected error occurs during the normal operation of the databases.

Replication

Access has the capability to create databases that replicate their data to other Access databases. This can be quite useful if users outside the normal network require access to information contained in a local database, if you're trying to reduce the number of users on a single MDB, if you're supporting a data warehouse, or for many other reasons. However, replication in Access is not without its problems. Replicated databases that become corrupted are no longer replicable and trying to determine what changes occurred in the database since the last time it was synchronized can be a difficult, if not impossible task. Access replication must also be managed through a separate utility called Replication Manager and can be difficult to administer. Replication Manager does not handle conflicts between the replicas very well and if a replica becomes damaged and needs to be repaired, it will lose its capability to be replicated. Also, you cannot create a database in Access that automatically replicates its data to another RDBMS.

SQL Server replication is much more robust. The replication that SQL Server uses is much more reliable and less prone to conflict errors or outright failure. It can replicate SQL Server data with another database on a separate SQL Server system, with an Access database, with an Oracle database, or with any other ODBC or OLE DB compliant data source. A SQL Server database can, therefore, share some or all of its data with completely different database systems. SQL Server Replication is configured through the same interface that is used to manage the rest of SQL Server's functionality. It can also be managed through system stored procedures or programmatically. In addition, replication can be scheduled through these interfaces and notification of job status can be configured.

Cost

The difference in cost between a purely Access-based application and one that uses SQL Server is considerable.

The costs of the software alone are quite different. A copy of Microsoft Office Developer Edition can be purchased for approximately $1,000. This allows royalty free distribution of the Access runtime engine with your Access application. SQL Server, on the other hand, must be purchased as a separate application and costs approximately $1500 with 5 client licenses. Extra licenses must be purchased depending on the number of users that will be accessing the server. These extra licenses cost approximately $100 per additional user and can become very expensive if the number of users who will be accessing the server is sizable. On top of this, there is still the additional cost of the Office Developer Edition (or all users must have a licensed copy of Access) if you want to create an Access database or project to manipulate the data in the SQL Server database.

The hardware requirements for SQL Server are more stringent than the hardware requirements for Access. Access applications rarely require purchasing new hardware because the computers and network that the applications run on usually exist before an application is designed. Users can run Access on the equipment they already use for their word processing and spreadsheet applications. SQL Server, however, is best run on a dedicated server, so that the maximum performance of SQL Server can be extracted. Because servers are not usually purchased and left unused, a new server will almost certainly have to be acquired for SQL

Server. For a mission-critical application, the minimum cost of an adequate server is about $3000.

The cost of development and maintenance of a SQL Server application is also higher than one that is purely designed in Microsoft Access. Often, a professional database administrator (DBA) must be hired. This person must have the knowledge and the experience to maintain the server in optimal condition and to ensure that developers are using best practices when designing the database. If any of the developers is unfamiliar with SQL Server and how it works, there can be extra costs in development trying to get these developers up to speed with a new development environment.

The difference in costs between a SQL Server application and one developed solely in Access can be anywhere from $500 to $50,000.

Reasons to Migrate

Now that we've reviewed the differences between Access and SQL server, let's discuss the reasons that people migrate their Access applications to SQL Server. Although there are almost as many reasons to migrate as there are Access databases, you should be prepared to justify your reasons for upgrading to yourself as well as others. Making the move with poorly defined reasons can cause you to address the wrong areas for improvement when you plan your upgrade.

Size

Probably the most common reason that people have for migrating an application from Access to SQL Server is the amount of data. Many users notice that the performance of a networked Access application tends to degrade once the database expands to between 10MB to 20MB. This is because Access must constantly deal with the passing of large amounts of data back and forth between the database and the client. When a database reaches 100MB, it can take a very long time to run complicated queries against the data. Despite the absolute 2GB physical limit of the size of a database, performance is usually degraded long before the limit is even approached. This is a very good reason to migrate an application to SQL Server.

Number of Users

Due to Access's problems with multi-user access, SQL Server is often a viable alternative to using Jet. Access tends to run into problems with more that 10 concurrent users. SQL Server can handle thousands of concurrent users and can help administer them much better than Access can. If you are building a large system where there are many different types of users, SQL Server can make it easier for administrators and users to add and remove logins with appropriate permissions.

Network Traffic

As previously mentioned, SQL Server reduces the amount of data traffic between the database and the client. If you are planning on running an application over a slow network, it is best to reduce, as much as possible, any traffic on the system. This frees resources for other users. Even if you have a fast network, if Jet-based applications are a significant portion of the network's number of requests or packets, then a migration might extend the life of the system.

Response Issues

SQL Server is much faster at working with and returning data across a network than Access is. This is because of the reduced amount of data that must be transferred across the network. If you have a table with hundreds of thousands of records in it, Access has to return the entire contents of the table. SQL Server only returns the requested data, and it will retrieve it faster than Access can. This is because SQL Server can take advantage of the processing capability of the computer on which it resides. The computer that requests the data must do all of the processing of an Access database. The server running SQL Server can also handle all of the indexing and updating of the data, freeing the client to implement the rules required by the business case.

Maintenance and Administration

The centralized administration interfaces provided by SQL Server can be used to justify a migration. They allow one entry point for all activities including the ability to schedule jobs, which can guarantee the state of the database and provide the added security of constant backups. SQL Server also supports rollbacks when the server fails. If SQL Server stops unexpectedly, once it is restarted, it attempts to restore all of its databases to the last known good state. This means that any transactions that were committed before the crash remain in the database. When this occurs in Access, a corrupted database will often have to be recovered from a physical backup if one exists. The data changes that took place since the previous backup are lost. Although this is also possible with SQL Server databases, it is much more likely that the server will be able to recover from the damage and only those changes that were not complete at the time of failure are lost.

Replication

Access does not have the native capability to replicate to other RDBMSs as SQL Server does. If an application needs to retrieve data from multiple systems with a minimum of user intervention or development effort, migrating to SQL Server may be able to solve this issue. For example, SQL Server can be configured to replicate its data to another data source that is used to do reporting on actions within multiple systems. You can also use SQL Server 7 with any OLE DB compliant data source to bring data together into one place. You can replicate external data into SQL Server or replicate SQL Server data to these data sources. The number of OLE DB drivers available is growing and includes such systems as AS/400, Oracle, Sybase, Btrieve, and Informix. Any of these systems can be replication partners with SQL Server using the built-in capabilities of SQL Server. If multi-system replication is a requirement for a system, SQL Server's capabilities can be used to justify a migration.

Reasons Not to Migrate

Just as there are reasons to migrate an application to SQL Server, there are also reasons not to migrate an application. Take a good look at your motivations in migrating the application and make sure they are sound. You should ensure that the migration is necessary (after all, it is a lot of extra work) and that migrating the application will not negatively affect users.

Size

Just as size is a reason to migrate, it is also a reason not to migrate. Access is very good at dealing with small databases. You may find that migrating a database that is less than 10MB is not worth the effort involved. Also, SQL Server has a certain amount of overhead that can degrade the performance of a small database. You will probably find that a small database in Access performs better than the same database on SQL Server because of the index processing that must take place.

Organization of Data

If you are using size to justify your migration, you may also want to take a look at how the database is designed. Running queries against an Access database that has 100 tables, each containing 1000 records can be very quick. This may seem like a large database, but Access returns the data in much the same way that it would if there was only one table containing 1000 records. If, however, your database has one table with 1,000,000 records, you can safely assume that this database should be migrated. SQL Server will deal with this database much better than Access will.

User Connectivity

One of the problems with using SQL Server as your database is that users must have constant access to the server. In some applications, this is not possible. If each copy of the application runs separately from each other and has its own data file, you probably should not move the application to SQL Server. Doing so would eliminate the users' ability to work with the application when they are not connected to the network. Although it may be possible to redesign the application so that all users access the same database, it may not be practical. Because the original database was running locally on a user's PC, the original design will probably run much faster because it does not need to engage network resources to work with data.

Cost

Cost is always a major factor in each migration from Access to SQL Server. It is often a very good reason not to migrate an application. There are multiple costs that are incurred in the process of migration and any one or all of them should be considered carefully before a migration takes place.

Migration Considerations

Any migration should be thoroughly analyzed before it takes place to ensure that it is justified and that it will give you the benefits that you expect. Part of this analysis must include your reasons for migrating. The reasons given in this chapter are by no means exhaustive. There are many more reasons that you or your company may need to consider before migrating an application. The reasons may not only need self justification, but may also need to be justified to colleagues and, more likely, a management team. If the migration is not justifiable, the developer should take a second look at the motivation for performing the upgrade. This is not to say that migrating for the sake of migrating is not justified. There is a lot to be gained in learning to migrate an application. And sometimes, the reason to migrate may be the learning itself.

CHAPTER 3

Planning the Upgrade

WHEN AN APPLICATION IS MIGRATED from Microsoft Access to Microsoft SQL Server, it is usually done using one of two methods. The first type of migration is a database migration. It involves migrating the backend Access database to SQL Server while maintaining the application interface in Access. The other type of migration involves migrating the interface to another development environment, such as Visual Basic, as well as migrating the backend database to SQL Server. The second type of migration is considerably more complex as it involves two migrations and extensive knowledge in each area. In this book, we will only be looking at the first type of migration, migrating the backend to SQL Server. However, the lessons learned in this type of work can easily be applied to a complete migration of the application and data. The steps involved are very similar, and the planning that is necessary in each type of migration is very important.

Before you begin your migration, you must create a plan. Your plan should address a couple of key issues. It should address how SQL Server data will be accessed from your application. Your plan should also address what objects will be migrated and how. All of this information should be thoroughly documented, so that you go into the migration with a good idea of what has to be done and how much work is involved. Without this analysis, the migration can easily fail and the credibility of the application could be jeopardized.

Planning How Data Will Be Accessed

Before any part of the migration can take place, you should decide how you plan to access data from SQL Server from your application. Although you can make modifications to the data-access methods as the migration progresses, deciding how data will be accessed has a pronounced effect on what development will be necessary and how you should plan the migration.

Data Access Methods

The method that you use to access data can change depending on where and how you are using it. This includes whether the data needs to be bound to objects in the Access application, such as forms and reports. The data access method you choose also depends on how you plan to use SQL Server data in code or macros.

Any analysis should take into account what object model will be used for programming and what the capabilities are of the version of Access you are using.

There are two main methods used to connect to a SQL Server database from Access: ODBC and OLE DB.

ODBC

Open Database Connectivity (ODBC) is a standard protocol for accessing relational database systems, such as Microsoft SQL Server, Oracle, or Sybase Adaptive Server. It is designed so that computers can connect to a SQL data source and work with the data from that system. In Access 97, when using data from another relational database, most data manipulation takes place through ODBC. In fact, if you want to bind non-Jet data to Access objects in Access 97, you must use ODBC. ODBC binding is still supported in Access 2000.

When you connect to ODBC data in Access, Jet retrieves the data using one of two methods. If the data has a unique index that Access is aware of and the data is updateable, Access retrieves the requested fields for the current record (with the exception of text and image fields, which are downloaded when they are accessed) and also retrieves the fields for 100 records surrounding the current record to make browsing the data faster (this can be configured through a Registry setting). It also generates bookmarks for the entire recordset based on the unique index in use.

> **NOTE** *The unique index that Access uses is not necessarily the primary key. Access selects the first unique index on a table in order of index name and uses the values in that index to generate the bookmark values. This knowledge can be very useful because you can force Access to select a particular unique index in a table by naming it, so that it will be sorted (alphabetically) before all others. This trick can be handy if you want to force Access to select a unique index built on a single field over another index that is built on more than one field.*

When your application is idle, or as you browse the records, Access queries the details of other records in the database. This method of retrieving data allows much faster access to immediately visible records and reduces the overhead to access any other records. If the data does not have a unique index that Access can use or is not designed to be updateable (through security or some other definition), Access retrieves all of the fields and rows requested. This ODBC data is returned as a snapshot-type recordset. This type of recordset cannot be updated. Storing and working with the entire recordset in Access does require more memory to be used locally, but the benefit is that Access does not maintain a constant connection to the server. Because the connection to the server does not need to be maintained in order to work with the recordset, network traffic is reduced. Only the initial transfer of the data takes place over the network. The traffic associated with a connected recordset, where the client is requesting data from the server regularly, is not generated.

Access provides a number of ways of using data through ODBC. You can link ODBC tables directly into your Access database much as you would a regular Access table. With this type of connection, you use the ODBC data through a Jet interface. The Access Jet engine maintains some of its own indexing on the connected data in order to allow the data to be navigated and updated. This means that you are really using two different interfaces to the data: the Jet engine connection to ODBC and the ODBC connection to the server. This type of connection can be used in linked tables or linked views, and the data in the linked ODBC table can be manipulated using Data Access Objects (DAO).

You can also manipulate ODBC data by directly connecting to the ODBC data source and bypassing the Jet engine. This type of ODBC data manipulation can be accomplished through the use of SQL pass-through queries or through the use of ODBCDirect workspaces. SQL pass-through queries are queries in which you can enter a statement that is passed directly to the ODBC driver without the Jet engine validating it or parsing it in any way. When working with linked ODBC data, Access parses a statement locally to translate it for the ODBC driver and determines how much of the statement can be sent to the server. Access also checks the syntax of the statement to ensure that it is valid. SQL pass-through queries bypass this feature of Access. However, there is a drawback to using pass-through queries. Although pass-through queries can return data, that data is always read-only to the Access application. Another method of connecting directly to the server and bypassing Jet's parsing functions is to directly modify data in code by using an ODBCDirect workspace. This is essentially a wrapper around the ODBC driver to allow you to use DAO-like code to modify ODBC data. It can be very useful if you want to perform quick data manipulation and have the server handle all of the work.

OLE DB (ADO)

OLE DB is a new Microsoft standard for accessing data in the enterprise. It goes beyond ODBC in that it is a standard for accessing relational and nonrelational data stores. This means that you can use OLE DB to access not only a SQL database, but also any data store for which an OLE DB driver can be or has been created. These data stores include relational databases, file directories, mainframe data, and email systems. A Microsoft Access programmer cannot directly access OLE DB. Instead, a wrapper called ActiveX Data Objects (ADO) is used to manipulate OLE DB data. This wrapper is basically a programming framework that makes all of the low-level functionality of OLE DB available to you without requiring you to possess the knowledge of what is going on at the system level.

ADO provides some functionality that ODBC does not. A useful capability of ADO data allows you to disconnect from the server once data has been retrieved from the client. This data can then be used locally as if you were still connected, but the network communication that is normally required becomes unnecessary. When processing of the data is complete, the data can then easily be reconnected to the data source and submitted to the server, so that the changes are submitted. ADO also provides the capability to run commands against the server asynchronously (without stopping code execution). When such a command is created, ADO can notify the application when processing is complete. This can be very useful for long running commands that would otherwise freeze the application. ADO also provides one function that ODBC and Jet have never been able to provide: the ability to create recordsets on the fly. Recordsets that are defined on the fly can be filled with data and then added to a data store or saved to disk with only a little added code. This additional capability to database programming of creating datasets on the fly will revolutionize the industry.

ADO and OLE DB can be used in an Access database in a number of ways. In Access 2000, you can use ADO code to modify data local to the database in which the code is running, and you can use ADO code to manipulate data in any other OLE DB data source. Access 97 does not have native support for OLE DB—all data connections use the Jet engine natively; therefore, code is the only place where you can use ADO. And, in order to use ADO with Access 97, you need to install the Microsoft Data Access Components (MDAC) and the Development Kit (DA SDK) available at `http://www.microsoft.com/data`. In Access 2000, the default programming model for database information is ADO, so you can use it without having to add any references to your application. Also, the connections that Access makes to SQL Server in a database project actually use the OLE DB driver for SQL Server to make the connection. This means that ADO and OLE DB are much more tightly integrated into the environment.

Analyzing Objects

Once you understand how Access can connect to other databases, you can proceed with analyzing the objects in your database for the migration. Take the time and analyze each object in the database. You can dramatically improve the performance of your application if you can migrate as much functionality as possible to SQL Server. Let's take a look at all of the objects as well as what you should be looking for when you plan the migration.

Tables

Any migration from Access to SQL Server must start with an analysis of the tables that make up the database. After all, they contain all of the information that you need in your application. There are a number of items you should consider when analyzing the tables: data organization, data types used, indexes, defaults, rules, and relationships. You should take as much time as possible to ensure that you do not miss any items because table migration is where the greatest performance gain can be achieved.

Data Organization

Each table should be analyzed to determine how the data is organized. All organization of data should be logical and resistant to problems as the database grows. Apply all rules for sound database design before the migration takes place. The topic of good database design is well beyond the scope of this book. Tomes have been published on this subject, and your best bet is to purchase one of these books if you are unfamiliar with the rules of good database design. There are many books available on this subject, but my personal preference is *Database Design for Mere Mortals* by Michael Hernandez (Addison-Wesley, January 1997). It is designed for anyone who is unfamiliar with the concepts of normalization, and it is not specific to any RDBMS. If you are looking for something a little more advanced without getting extremely technical, try *Handbook of Relational Database Design* by Fleming and von Halle (Addison-Wesley, August 1988).

It is important to make sure that your database is in at least third normal form. Problems that can be papered over in a Jet database will become major issues as your database expands. Large SQL Server databases are much less forgiving concerning database design than small Access databases. The level of normalization you choose is dependent on the purpose of your database. Operational databases must be in third normal form to ensure that the database will function properly. If your database is only used for data warehousing or reporting, then first normal form is all that needs to be satisfied.

Data Types

The wizards that are available to upsize a database from Access to SQL Server have their own translation algorithm for creating a SQL data type equivalent to an original Access data type. However, the translation the wizards choose is not always appropriate for your use of the data type. There are a number of items to watch for in your data type conversion when you move to SQL Server. In order to make informed decisions that will lead to a successful migration, you should know the various data types that SQL Server makes available to you and the sizes and limitations of those types.

Table A-1 in Appendix A contains a complete list of all the SQL Server data types. You can see from this table that there are many more data types in SQL Server than in Access. Most of these types are simply larger versions of data types that Access uses and are reasonably simple to understand. However, one data type requires special attention: the timestamp data type. A timestamp field is not a field that you edit, and contrary to its name, does not hold time or date data. Instead, it is a system field for which SQL Server generates values to uniquely identify each row in a database at a single state in the data composition.

Timestamp values are always unique within a table. When you update data in a row in SQL Server and a timestamp column is in the same row, SQL Server changes the timestamp to a new value. When a user updates the data in a table, the timestamps for the affected rows are also updated. This allows Access and SQL Server to easily determine if the data has been modified by the fact that the timestamp has changed. If a second user is updating one of the same records that the first user already updated, they will get an error telling them that the data is no longer valid because the record has changed.

The timestamp is automatically updated by SQL Server when a change is made to the record. If two users "take out" a record at the same time, the value of the timestamp field comes with it. When the data is returned to SQL Server and modifications have been made, the value in the submitted timestamp field is compared with the value still in the table. If they match, the update is allowed to go through. If the first user updates the record, the timestamp changes. When the second user submits changes, the timestamp in the submitted record does not match the timestamp in the table; therefore, a nasty error message occurs. When the second user attempts to commit the changes to the record, the update fails because the application tells SQL Server to update a record that contains a particular timestamp value. This value no longer exists because the first user has modified the record before the second user could commit his changes.

SQL Server prevents you from creating more than one timestamp column per table. Because the timestamp data type is designed more for the use of the data provider than for users to view, you will only need one timestamp column per table. It is recommended that you give this column the name "timestamp" (this is the only occasion when I will tell you to name a field the same as its data type). The reason for this is, if you open an ODBC linked table in design view, the data type of the field will appear as a binary field. Because you want to ensure that you don't attempt to work with this field as you would other fields, you should name it "timestamp," so that you will always know what the purpose of the field is. Access handles concurrency in tables without timestamps by comparing each field in the table to its original value. Adding a timestamp field to a SQL Server table forces applications, such as Access, to use this column to enforce concurrency without having to compare each field in the table. Only the unique index Access uses to identify records and the timestamp are compared against the table to enforce concurrency. Adding a timestamp field to frequently updated tables can dramatically improve the performance of your application when applying updates.

You should ensure that the data types you use in SQL Server are large enough to hold all possible values for the field in the future. Autonumber fields in Access (called Identity fields in SQL Server) are always of type Long Integer. This data type, equivalent to SQL Server's *int* data type, can hold whole number values between -2,147,486,648 and 2,147,483,647. Although this may sound like a very large range of numbers, you must keep in mind that not all numbers are used, especially in Access. Some numbers may not be used due to failed or canceled updates or if records are deleted. SQL Server also skips numbers for the same reasons. If an update fails or if a record is deleted, an identity number becomes unavailable for use. Identity columns in SQL Server can be of any Integer data type (except bit), so you are not limited to the int data type (equivalent to Long Integer in Access) when creating identity columns. You must set their seed value (starting ID) and the number that will be used to increment them. By selecting a data type that is appropriate for the data requirements of the table, you can either reduce the storage space necessary for the field in the parent and any related tables, or choose a larger Integer data type that will ensure that you do not run out of numbers any time in the near future.

Text data types should also be looked at to ensure that your data types are sufficient for the application they will be used in. In Access, any Text field over 255 characters must be a Memo field. Text and Memo fields in Access are variable length, meaning that the data only occupies as much space as is necessary. In SQL Server, varchar and text data types are both variable length data types. However, the char data type is always fixed-length and always occupies the same amount of disk space. If you do not enter enough characters to fill the char column, it will be padded with spaces when the data is stored in the table. When running comparisons on a text field, you should be aware of whether or not it is a char field because the extra padding may cause comparisons to fail. The advantage to using the char data type is that it is easier for SQL Server to work with than varchar is. Varchar requires extra processing from SQL Server to handle the fact that the length can vary. SQL Server performs better when using a char column. This performance gain only applies to small fields. In fields that are greater than approximately six characters, SQL Server handles variable length fields much better. If you require a small text field, use the char data type if possible. For larger fields, use varchar.

You can also make improvements on how precise your data is with SQL Server, or reduce the precision if high precision is not required. SQL Server decimal and numeric data types allow you to set the scale of a field (the number of digits right of decimal) with more flexibility than Access. If your application deals with statistical data and requires a specific degree of precision, you can use this characteristic to set exactly how precise your data will be. You can also choose larger data types, such as float (scale cannot be modified, set at 53 digits), to store your data if your numbers are larger or if you require more precision. Access, on the other hand, is limited to the Single and Double data types, which have variable precision but a fixed maximum and minimum size. If you want to ensure that your SQL Server data conforms to the data rules required by your application, setting the scale and precision of the numeric data you use can help to fulfill these rules.

Indexes

In Access, indexing is implemented using one of a few methods. You can set indexing directly by setting a field's Indexed property in the field properties in the table design to Yes (No Duplicates) or Yes (Duplicates OK). You can create indexes in the Indexes property sheet in table design view. And, you can have Jet create indexes by specifying a foreign or primary key. All indexes in a table should be analyzed to determine if they are needed. Indexes are not required on fields that are not often used as the basis for criteria in searching, on fields that are not related to fields in other tables, or on fields that are not used to sort the data in the table or in queries.

SQL Server indexes have a characteristic that is not revealed to a user in Access tables: clustering. A clustered index is the index that a table is sorted by on disk. Each table can have only one clustered index. When SQL Server needs to access data in an index, and that index is not clustered, SQL Server must look at an index that is stored off-table. Off-table indexes contain pointers to the location of their data in the parent table. This means that searching a nonclustered index is slower than accessing a clustered index because the server must look at the index and follow the pointers back to the original data. In Access, the primary key is always a clustered index. In SQL Server, you can choose which index is to be clustered, and it doesn't have to be a unique index. If your data is most commonly accessed by a nonprimary key, you should set the index on that field to clustered because it will improve the access time for that field.

You should also ensure that all of your indexes are necessary and logical. Adding an index to a table adds overhead for updates to the table. Each time a record is inserted, SQL Server must maintain all of the indexes. You should check all of the indexes on your table and ensure that they do not add unnecessary overhead to your application. You may require an index for any number of reasons: criteria are regularly used against the column to search for or update data; data needs to be sorted by this column often in forms or reports; or the column is a primary key. Indexes can benefit an application in any of these situations. However, you must balance the need for faster performance when querying the database against the need for faster performance when updating data. Searching data should receive greater consideration because it is usually more cumbersome and can span large numbers of records. In nonindexed columns, SQL Server must scan the entire table when you search on that column. This is in contrast to indexed columns, where SQL Server can quickly move to the first match in the index and just retrieve the matching data from that point on. But keep in mind that if you have too many indexes on a single table, you could make updates to the data extremely slow. In a reporting database, lots of indexes are good, but in an operational databases, fewer indexes are better because of the maintenance overhead.

Defaults and Rules

Defining default values in Access is quite simple. In fact, if created using the user interface, all of the numeric data types in Access automatically define a default value of zero when you create a numeric field (a feature that can be very annoying for those of us who don't want it to happen). In SQL Server, defaults are just as easy to set and can be configured in one of two ways: added to the field as a constraint or created as a Default object and linked to a field. The constraint method is the better choice if the default value is not complex and is not reused in many tables. In cases where the default is complex and must be applied to multiple fields or if you need to bind it to a user defined data type, use a Default object.

A problem arises when you use defaults for fields in SQL Server and bind the fields to an Access form. Access, when working with Jet data, shows the default value in a form even before the record is added to a table, saving the user from mistakenly thinking that the value will be Null. When using SQL Server, the default values for the fields are not shown on an Access form until the record is saved. This may cause the user to think that they must enter data in the field at all times. If a field is not used in the data entry form, you should set the default on SQL Server if you want to prevent the field from being set to Null when a record is inserted.

Rules in Access can be defined against a field or against a table. Rules are defined by setting the Validation Rule property for the fields against which they are to be applied. Each field can have only one validation rule as can each table. Validation rules can be very complex if the application requires them to be, but they are usually fairly simple. Validation rules in Access are limited to 2048 characters in length.

In SQL Server, you can add multiple rules or CHECK constraints to a field or to a table and make them as complex as necessary. Again, you should ensure that the items you add are necessary because they add overhead to your tables. Each time a record is modified SQL Server must run the rules against changed fields. If you put the data validation in the application itself, the amount of time that is required to update the record is reduced once it is sent to SQL Server, and the user receives immediate notification of the violation. When a rule is violated on SQL Server, the validation does not run until the whole record is submitted. You must balance the importance of having a single point of control in SQL Server against user considerations.

Relationships

Relationships in any database can become quite complex. Access is very good with how it manages relationships in that you can create enforced relationships with cascading updates and/or deletes. In SQL Server, this is not possible. You can either create relationships that prevent the insertion of unrelated records or deletion of parent records while child records exist, or you can maintain the integrity of data in related tables through the use of triggers. As described in Chapter 1, triggers are Transact-SQL code that runs in response to data being modified in a table. They can be used to validate changes to a record, cascade updates and deletes, or even maintain data in derived fields or in other tables. Triggers can be defined to run in any or all of three possible situations: record deletion, addition, or modification.

The type of enforcement you use in your relationships depends on the design of your tables. If you use identity columns as the primary keys on your tables, you often do not need cascading features. Cascading an update would be useless because you cannot update the identity column. However, you may want to add cascading deletes to your table, in which case, you cannot define a relationship and you must create a cascading trigger. In SQL Server, relationships always take precedence over triggers and therefore a delete on an enforced relationship will fail because the relationship will prevent the delete and, as a result, the trigger will never fire. In this case, you should remove the relationship and enable the cascading delete by creating a DELETE trigger. This trigger will be fired each time a record is deleted from the table.

Similarly, updating a column that has an enforced relationship will fail if there are related records for that row in another table. If you want updates to cascade to other tables, you must create an UPDATE trigger to make the modifications for you. One of the benefits of SQL Server triggers is that you have the ability to determine whether particular columns were modified in an insert or update. This means that you can shorten the processing SQL Server needs to do by forcing the trigger to only execute commands when certain columns are updated. SQL Server simply executes the trigger to the point where the cascading fields are singled out. If the field being updated is not in this list, the processing of the trigger does not go any further. This allows you to guarantee referential integrity without taking unnecessary performance hits.

When defining relationships you may also want to determine if your primary key in the parent table can be improved upon. Integer data types are by far the best fields to use for primary keys because the data that is stored in them is more readily handled by the computer processor, and they are always the same size and length, regardless of their value. This is in contrast to textual data that can change length or precision numeric data types that can also vary depending on the data they contain.

You can also use Integer data types to increase the speed of those relationships where multiple fields are related in different tables. Multiple field relationships require a great deal of extra processing to handle joins. Linking the tables involved in the relationship requires the RDBMS to search an index that contains a large amount of data. To avoid this problem, add an identity field to your table, and then use that as the primary key. You can still create a unique index, and even cluster it if you like, on the multiple fields, maintaining your requirements. With the new primary key, queries that join the table to other tables based on this key will perform much faster, and you will be storing less data in the related table, reducing the size of your database.

Queries

Migrating access queries to SQL Server can make dramatic improvements in an application. Determining the correct way to migrate a query depends on the purpose of the query and the purpose, in turn, affects how it should be evaluated for migration.

If your query is used as the source for a form and the data the query returns needs to be updateable, the best way to migrate the query is to move it to a SQL Server view. Views in SQL Server allow you to define a SQL statement that returns records and can be linked into an Access project as a view (Access 2000). It can also be linked into a standard database as if it were a table when using ODBC. Views can include multiple tables in their definition, but only one of those tables can be updated at a time. Attempting to update data for more than one base table in a single record in a view will raise an error from SQL Server. However, views can be very useful for retrieving and organizing data. If your application does not require all of the fields in a table, you can use a view to retrieve only the fields you need. This reduces the amount of data that must be transferred across the network. It also allows Access to work with the data more efficiently because it does not have to track fields that will not be modified.

If your query is used as a source for reports or drop-down lists, you may be better off using stored procedures and/or SQL pass-through queries to get the data, rather than using a view. Stored procedures can be very powerful. One major advantage to using stored procedures is that you can run multiple data manipulation functions in one procedure. For example, suppose you had a sales database that required some data for a report. The data for this report must come from multiple unrelated tables to merge the data for the different sales types. In Access, you would have to create multiple queries to retrieve the data into a temporary table. Each of these queries would have to be called independently through code. In SQL Server, you can run a single stored procedure that creates a table in the tempdb database, appends the necessary data from each source table to the new temporary table, and then returns the data in the temporary table to the client. The temporary table only lasts as long as the data is in use. Once the report is closed, the table is deleted. The main advantage to using a stored procedure under these circumstances is that you only need to call one stored procedure. This greatly simplifies the coding on the client-side and reduces the number of permanent objects required in the database. Using SQL pass-through queries, Access can call the stored procedure and the pass-through query itself can be bound by the report.

When planning the migration of queries to SQL Server, you should watch for queries that use Access or user defined functions in their definition. Visual Basic functions that are used in queries cannot be directly migrated to SQL Server. Instead, you should try to find equivalent functions in SQL Server, create stored procedures, or use SQL statements that implement the same functionality. For example, Access domain functions, such as DMax and DMin, do not have equivalents in SQL Server. Results similar to the results provided by these functions have to be derived from SQL statements in a view or with stored procedures that create the same functionality. Some aggregate functions do have equivalents in SQL Server. The Access Jet functions Max and Min can be replaced with SQL Server MAX and MIN functions where necessary, however, you should check the SQL Server documentation to ensure that their implementation achieves the results you need.

User defined VBA functions cannot be directly migrated to SQL Server. In many cases, the functionality they implement cannot be directly duplicated. In such cases, it may be better to retrieve the necessary information from SQL Server, and then use the VBA functions against the data once it has been passed back to Access. Caution should be exercised with such functions, however, as working with data in this manner can be quite cumbersome and can lead to bottlenecks in the application. If you call the function directly in a query based on a linked table and you use the function itself to filter the resulting data, the Jet engine will assume that none of the processing of the query can be run by SQL Server, and it will retrieve the entire contents of the table before running your function to filter the data. This means that the entire table is returned to the client. Network load is increased, and the performance of your application suffers.

In some cases, you can create equivalent functionality in Transact-SQL stored procedures. Running stored procedures on the server instead of using VBA functions can help you increase the response time of the application because any processing that takes place on the server before the application receives the data increases the speed at which the data you require is summarized. SQL Server is much faster at handling data requests than Access is, and if you can make the server do the work, you reduce the time it takes for the data to be presented to the user.

One function of Access SQL that is not supported in SQL Server's version of SQL is cross-tab queries. A cross-tab query derives its columns not from the columns in the tables it takes its data from, but creates a column for every unique value in one of the table's columns. The SQL statements that you use in Access to create these queries are not valid for SQL Server. Creating a cross-tab query in Access from SQL Server data generally means that you must reduce the records returned by SQL Server to the absolute minimum before sending them to Access, and then create a local cross-tab query to create and summarize the data in the desired format.

Forms

When evaluating a form for migration, the record source should be analyzed. If you base all of your forms on queries, you may have already completed some of the analysis for this migration in your query analysis. If your forms are based on SQL statements or tables, you should evaluate what data is being retrieved and how that data is retrieved.

In Access 2000, you have much more versatility with form data sources than you do in Access 97. Using a database project or ADO code in Access 2000, you can base a form's data on a table, a view, a stored procedure, or a SQL statement. In Access 97, your best choice on bound forms is to use views or tables linked in through ODBC when working with remote data servers. Forms bound to stored procedures are read-only because a SQL pass-through query must be used to run the stored procedure (and pass-thru queries are always read-only). Choosing the appropriate object to supply the data to your form can be very complex. When you make a choice as to which object type you will use, you should keep a few concepts in mind.

If a form is always opened with supplied criteria in Access 2000, you will probably want to use a stored procedure because stored procedures can accept arguments, whereas views cannot. For example, if you normally open a Customer Details form with only one customer shown at a time, you can use a stored procedure that takes a Customer ID and returns only the supplied customer. Consider the following stored procedure:

```
Create Procedure spGetCustomer (@intID int)
/* retrieves only one customer id */
As
    BEGIN
        SELECT * FROM tblCustomer WHERE CustomerID = @intID
        RETURN @@error
    END
```

For now, it is not really necessary to understand how to write a store procedure or how this particular stored procedure works. You only need to know how it is called. To run this stored procedure in SQL and have it retrieve information for a customer with CustomerID 12, you would use the command *Exec spGetCustomer 12*. There is a benefit to using a stored procedure that is written this way. Supplying the procedure with a Null value as the parameter returns an empty recordset to which data can be added. Therefore, setting a form's record source to *Exec spGetCustomer NULL* returns a new blank record that a form can use as a base to add more data. Because the amount of data retrieved is small, network traffic is reduced.

If your form is used only to display data and does not directly modify it, it is best to use a stored procedure. However, if you filter the data in the form regularly and different columns are used to filter the data each time that the stored procedure is called, you may have to create multiple stored procedures to handle the different situations.

If you are using Access 97 with ODBC, your choices are reduced. The only updateable connections to SQL Server are linked tables or views. Because of this limitation, any form that updates data must be linked to one of these objects. However, it is almost always better to use a view, especially if your form does not show all of the fields in a table. Using a view to retrieve only the necessary fields can reduce the amount of network traffic and reduce the memory requirements on the client because less data is handled.

Controls on forms that display data in lists (such as list boxes or combo boxes) provide opportunities to make performance improvements. The list of items in these objects does not often change. When the list is static and small, it is best to use a nonupdateable stored procedure (called through a pass-through query if using ODBC) to return the required data. Creating a stored procedure to retrieve the values in the list allows you to transfer some of the processing of data to the server, and using a nonupdateable recordset allows Access to avoid some of the overhead that updateable recordsets require. If a list is long, you may want to return only some of the top values from the database unless the user requests more. For example, you could have a drop-down list of customers that, by default, lists only the top 10 values and a value called "More…". When a user selects the "More…" item, you could run code that requeries the stored procedure and tells it not to limit the list. The following stored procedure would accomplish just this in the Northwind sample database included with SQL Server 7:

```
CREATE PROCEDURE spGetCustomers (@bitLimit bit)
AS
BEGIN
    IF @bitLimit = 0
        SELECT CustomerID, CompanyName FROM Customers
        ORDER BY CustomerID
    ELSE
        SELECT TOP 10 CustomerID, CompanyName FROM Customers
        UNION SELECT 'ZZZZZ', 'More...'
        ORDER BY CustomerID
END
```

Calling this stored procedure with 1 as the parameter value tells the stored procedure to return the top 10 with a "More…" item added to the end of the list with a SQL UNION statement. Calling the same stored procedure with 0 as the parameter value returns all values in the list. The only detail you must ensure is that the "More…" is displayed last in the list. This can be done by creating a false sort in the stored procedure on the server (as was done in the previous code) or in code by dynamically adding an entry after the data has been returned to the client. When the user selects the "More…" item from the list, you can force the list to change to a full list of customers, as in the following code on a combo box:

```
Private Sub cboCustomers_Change()
    If Me!cboCustomers = "More..." Then
        'Change the RowSource to another pass-through
        'that lists all customers
        Me!cboCustomers.RowSource = "qptCustomersAll"
        Me!cboCustomers.Requery
        Me!cboCustomers.Dropdown
    End If
End Sub
```

Normally, the RowSource property for this combo box is a pass-through query that calls spGetCustomers with the bit parameter set to 1. When the user selects the item "More…" from the list in the combo box, the Change event fires, and the source of the data in the list changes. The combo box is then requeried, so that the new data is shown, and the list is dropped-down, so that the user knows that they can now select a different item.

Code behind Forms

Event-driven code behind forms should be thoroughly analyzed when planning a migration. Much of the functionality that needs to be programmed into forms to ensure data integrity can be moved to SQL Server. The most common migration technique is to move functionality in the Before Update and After Update events to SQL Server triggers. For example, if you have a need to update the quantity of a product on hand in the Inventory table whenever an item is ordered and quantities are entered into the OrderDetails table, in Access, you would accomplish this through code or macros in form Update events. A form will call the necessary code to update the quantity on hand and ensure that the totals in the Inventory are correct. This kind of update has one major failing, which is when a user updates the data directly in a table, the code in the form will not be executed. Because the update to the Inventory information is only fired when the data is changed in the form, entering data directly into the table would break the consistency of the data and could cause problems in reporting or in the ability to deliver the product to a client because the quantity of product on hand would not be correct. In SQL Server, adding a trigger to the OrderDetails table that fired an update to the Inventory table whenever the quantity of a product order changed would force any update to the data to trigger the update on the quantity on hand in the Inventory table. In this case, it does not matter where the OrderDetails table is updated, in a form, in code, or directly in the table, the trigger will always run. You can also use triggers to prevent updates that do not satisfy your own criteria, thereby enforcing business rules for the application. Look for code in your forms that performs these kinds of actions and plan to move the functionality to SQL Server.

In planning the migration of your forms, you should also look for any code that directly accesses the database or uses DAO or ADO to update data. The functionality that these procedures implement can often be successfully migrated to SQL Server. For example, you may have a master/detail form where the items in the subform cannot exist without the master form data. In this case, you want all the subrecords deleted if the parent record is deleted. Although you can accomplish this functionality in Access through cascading deletes, it is often run through form events instead of through cascades. This is because enabling automatic cascading deletes is risky. You want to ensure that this type of cascade only occurs from the form in question. However, when you do this from your Access forms for SQL Server data, you should encapsulate the detail data deletion into a stored procedure that takes the master primary key information as a parameter. This reduces the amount of network traffic because all of the records are deleted with a single command. This allows SQL Server to manage most of the deletion and enforces any rules against the data that are necessary without having to implement the same functionality in two places. It also makes the system more secure by forcing deletions to occur in a controlled manner.

Reports

Reports are probably the easiest item in a database to analyze for migration because there is very little that needs to be done. The main portion of a report that needs to be analyzed is the report record source. It is almost always easiest to migrate the record source definition to a stored procedure that returns records. There is only a small amount of analysis that is really necessary. The main feature to watch for is if your reports are often opened using a specific criteria. For example, if you want to print a customer record, the main filter you need to apply against the data is a customer ID. Creating a stored procedure that takes the CustomerID as its sole parameter can speed the previewing and printing of a report because SQL Server will precompile the stored procedure such that it retrieves the data in the fastest possible manner. It also allows you to use complex SQL functions, such as nested queries or multiple SQL statements. The record source should be analyzed in much the same way as queries are and the same caveats should be kept in mind.

Macros

It is common for Access applications to use macros that update data. Because of this, you need to analyze all of your macros and determine what they do. Look for any actions that interface with data, especially those that modify data. The most important actions executed in a macro to watch for are ApplyFilter, FindRecord, OpenQuery, OpenTable, and RunSQL because they are all used against data. Any of these actions in a macro work with or modify data in such a way that their functionality may degrade the performance of an Access or a SQL Server application, so each action that takes place should be carefully analyzed. The most important one, RunSQL, directly executes a SQL statement against a database and should be analyzed using the same criteria as a query. Moving macros to stored procedures can often accomplish the same task with less work, especially when the macro contains multiple steps to accomplish a complex task. Stored procedures can include as many commands as necessary, and they will benefit from the increased performance of SQL Server. You will also be reducing the network traffic because you will only make one call to the stored procedure as opposed to running multiple functions on the data through macros.

Modules

Much of the processing that takes place in database modules is designed to perform detailed functions against data from a database. The most critical code to look for is code that performs any data processing using DAO or ADO, especially those routines that use multiple tables and/or recordsets to achieve a business goal. The type of SQL Server object you will use to replace this code depends on what the purpose of the routine is, how many database objects it accesses, and whether or not it needs to modify data.

Developers often create VBA modules that retrieve data from the database, and then navigate that data to update other tables or perform some other complex function against the data. This record processing code often takes the form of the following pseudocode:

```
Set rst = cnn.Execute("Select ….")
While not rst.EOF
    If rst("f1") = "some value" Then
        rst("f2") = "some other value"
    End If
    rst.MoveNext
Loop
```

Because this type of procedure is mostly data oriented, it should be moved to SQL Server by creating stored procedures that achieve the same functionality. You may not have access to some functions that VBA provides, but there is almost always a way to achieve similar functionality in Transact-SQL. To this end, you should familiarize yourself with the various Transact-SQL functions that are available by looking at the Books Online. As part of creating the stored procedure, you should consider eliminating this record-by-record processing. Even though you can navigate individual records by defining special Transact-SQL variables called cursors, it is not the best solution. Typically, you get better performance from bulk update commands than you do from cursors. You also get less code, which can reduce the number of bugs as well as your maintenance costs. You should attempt, as best you can, to use pure SQL in your functions. Many of the functions developed in VBA that navigate individual records can be rewritten to use pure SQL with a bit of time and effort.

You should look at the code and determine whether it will be able to stay as it is in the migration or if changes will be necessary. Some of the most common places where changes are required are in the connection information to the database and the type of recordsets that are used. You should be conscious of whether the recordsets you use are being updated or if they are just read-only data used for other purposes. If you do not need to update the data, tell the server that this is the case by using a read-only recordset. The server will understand that it does not need to track any changes to the data that you make, and that you will not be returning the data at any time. This reduces network traffic and server load. This technique should be used wherever possible. Also, you cannot open table type recordsets on ODBC or OLE DB data sources because these are only supported for Jet tables.

SQL strings that appear in code are a very important aspect of the migration. You should avoid SQL strings used in code as much as possible. Instead, use views or stored procedures to retrieve your data. Although this increases the number of objects in your database, it is a much better method of retrieving data for a few reasons. Saving stored procedures on the server, rather than passing SQL statements allows the server to precompile the T-SQL code before you call it. SQL Server compiles the stored procedure with an execution plan that it thinks is the most efficient plan to perform the necessary functions against the data when the object is saved. This allows SQL Server to execute the procedure without having to compile each SQL string as it is passed. As a result, the stored procedure returns the data faster than a SQL string could. The same is true of SQL Server Views. An added benefit is that saving the SQL as a stored procedure or view on the server makes the SQL more maintainable. If someone changes the name of a field or some other information on the server, it is much easier to determine what code and queries are affected by that change if the code and queries are stored on the server. The SQL Server administration utilities include a tool to automatically determine the dependencies of an object. If your SQL string is stored in an Access database and not on the server in a stored procedure or view, SQL Server has no way of notifying you of the possible repercussions of a change in the database design. In addition, rewriting code to move functionality to the server sends the more complex functions to the server and saves your application from having to call on the memory and processing power of the local client.

When analyzing your code, you should also keep in mind that SQL Server stored procedures can encompass many operations. Unlike Access queries, you can define multiple statements for a single stored procedure. Much of the code that is written for Access applications is designed to work around the fact that Access cannot handle multiple statement queries. When migrating to SQL Server, you may be able to completely eliminate some VBA procedures from your database and rewrite them as stored procedures. T-SQL has much of the procedural functionality that you need to accomplish the same tasks as your VBA code, so you should take advantage of this functionality.

General Considerations

When you analyze the objects in your database, there are a number of general considerations you should take into account. First, the more objects you can move off the client, the better the performance of the application will most likely be. Mixing objects between the server and the client can cause a lot of unnecessary overhead in the application. Mixing causes greater network traffic as data must be exchanged between these objects more often. Also, you are forcing two systems to share the work on the data when in truth, one of them is much better at it. Second, you should check the importance of the objects in the new application. Do you really need all of the objects in the new application? Do they add value to the application? Are they designed to accomplish a task in the most efficient manner? Is there a better way to implement them? Sometimes, these questions can only be answered by testing the application under different situations. Third, you should take into account that if concurrent user problems are forcing you to upsize, you may find that your current design is aggravating the problem and, as a result, moving to SQL Server by itself won't solve the problem. You should consider how a large number of users will affect your application and if the design can be improved upon, so that these users can be handled. Finally, if you are upsizing an application that ran on the client's computer, you should take into account that your application will now need constant access to a network. Failures in the network mean that your application cannot function, and your users will become very unhappy. Having good network support can mean the difference between an application that is productive and one that is wasting space on a user's hard drive.

Documentation

In any migration plan, there can never be too much documentation. Documenting your database design and migration procedures not only allows you to keep a record of the migration, it also helps you think through the various aspects of the analysis. You should begin your documentation with a general description of the migration including why you are planning to move the database to SQL Server.

This allows you to explain to others and to yourself why the migration is happening. You should include information, such as what problems currently exist, how SQL Server will solve those problems, costs involved in the old and new application, maintenance considerations, and any other information that you think is pertinent. You should then document the physical name and location of the database before and after the migration, how large the database is, how large it will be initially in SQL Server, and what application or scripts will be used to migrate the data from one database to the other. Finally, you should include thorough documentation on the migration plan for each object in the database and the purpose of each object. This will be the object documentation that you will return to as you redevelop portions of the application to take advantage of the new environment and avoid future problems. This documentation should include all of the following information and any other information you deem necessary.

Tables

- Table name and purpose

- Field names

- Field source and destination data types

- Defaults and rules

- Triggers that will be needed

- Relationships and how they will be enforced

- Indexes and their characteristics

Queries

- Query name and purpose

- Destination object type and name

- Considerations for VBA code calls

- Relationship to other objects

Forms

- Form name and purpose

- Record source for the form and its destination

- List box and combo box source data and destination object and name

- Code behind form purpose and destination if any

- Triggers that can be created from code

Reports

- Report name and purpose

- Record source for the report and its destination

Macros

- Macro name and purpose

- Migration potential and destination object

Modules

- Module name and purpose

- Description of each procedure in module

- Migration destination of procedures if any

- Areas where code needs to change for access to another system

This documentation should be used to understand how the migration work will be done and what improvements will result.

Once the documentation is complete, you should be ready to begin the migration to SQL Server.

CHAPTER 4

The Microsoft Wizard

SINCE THE FIRST VERSION of Microsoft Access was released in 1992, developers have been using it as a rapid development platform for database applications. However, almost as long as this has been going on, some of these developers have found that their applications often hit the limits of what Access can efficiently manage. Too many users attempting to use the same database at once, too much data stored in the database, and other problems are common to Access applications. As a result, many applications have needed to be migrated to more robust, client/server database systems. In the early days of Access development, this meant having to manually re-create the database on an RDBMS, such as SQL Server, and then revamping the user interface to handle the new backend. Creating a duplicate of the original Access database from scratch on another system was a very difficult task that was prone to error. Tables could be missed, field translations could be done incorrectly, stored procedures and views could have errors, and generally the application might not function properly. There was also no easy way to migrate the data that was contained in these databases. Often, the databases being migrated contained a large amount of data that users wanted to retain in order to have an historical record.

In view of these facts, the task of migrating essential data had to become an easier task that produced more accurate results faster. Wizards were developed to do just that. They are designed to provide developers with tools for doing some of the more tedious tasks involved in migrations. They are not comprehensive devices, and, as you will see, there are advantages and disadvantages to using wizards.

Introducing the Upsizing Wizard

In October of 1994, Microsoft, in response to the need to make this process easier and less prone to error, released the first version of the Upsizing Wizard designed for Access 2.0 and SQL Server 6.0. Because Microsoft already had their own RDBMS—SQL Server—on the market, Microsoft designed the Wizard to work best with their product. In order to make the product as easy to use as possible for developers, they designed the Wizard to allow a user to migrate the table structure and data in an Access database to SQL Server while maintaining the interface that was already available in Access.

One of Microsoft's main goals in developing the Upsizing Wizard was to allow a user to migrate an application to SQL Server without having to do any work other than specifying the settings in the Wizard. The Wizard then modifies the Access application, making the changes to the data seamless. The introduction of the

Upsizing Wizard was a major step in the drive toward making Access a valid development platform for client/server database applications. The Wizard has always been available from Microsoft free of charge, avoiding any extra investment in order to smooth the migration.

Obtaining the Wizard

If you are using Microsoft Access 2000, you don't need to worry about obtaining a copy of the Wizard. The Wizard in Access 2000 is now fully integrated into Access—it is not a separate add-in like it was in earlier versions of Access. However, you should ensure that your copy of Access is up-to-date by checking the Office Update Web site at `http://officeupdate.microsoft.com` and downloading any patches or service packs. If you are using Microsoft Access 97, you must obtain the Wizard from Microsoft. (It is best to do this even if you already have the Wizard because it was updated for SQL Server 7 and will likely be updated for SQL Server 2000). The Access 97 Wizard can be downloaded from `http://www.microsoft.com/AccessDev/ProdInfo/AUT97dat.htm`. The file you download is an executable that you should run once the download completes. The executable installs both the Upsizing Wizard and an interface called the SQL Server Browser that allows you to design a SQL Server database using an Access-like interface.

Preparing to Use the Wizard

Before you use the Wizard, there are a few tasks that you should carry out to ensure that the Wizard can complete its job without errors. The first of these is to ensure that SQL Server is configured with enough user locks to allow the upgrade to complete successfully. Locks are objects that SQL Server uses to ensure that no two users or processes act on the same data at the same time. When actions are run against data, a lock is created for each page of data that will be modified. What this means in SQL Server is that when you run large queries against SQL Server data, a large number of locks are required to ensure that no conflicts occur. Once changes are committed, all locks involved in the transaction are released. Because the Upsizing Wizard often works with large tables, the number of locks it requires to migrate the data that the tables contain can be quite large. The number of locks available to the server at any one time is limited in SQL Server 6.5, but this limit can be modified. You should modify the available locks before running the Wizard to ensure that the Upsizing Wizard can do its job without failure. If insufficient locks are encountered, the Wizard displays an error message before the upsizing takes place, which allows you to cancel the operation or continue the upsize.

SQL 6.5 Locks

Before you configure the locks in SQL Server, you should determine how many locks will be needed. To determine the number of locks required, use the following formula: Locks = Number of Records / ((SQL Server Page Size - SQL Server Page Overhead) \ Max Record Size).

> **NOTE** *If you have never seen the \ operator before, it is simply a division that returns only the integer portion of the result, ignoring any remainder or decimals.*

This process may sound a bit confusing but it is actually quite simple to figure out. SQL Server Page Size in SQL 6.5 is 2048 bytes and the overhead is 32 bytes. (This means that the formula really works out to: Number or Records / (2016 \ Max Records Size). You can determine the maximum record size by adding the storage size of each data type used in the table being converted. The easiest way to do this is by checking the *size* property of each field in the table using VBA code. You can use the following code to check the number of locks needed for a table:

```
Public Function LocksNeeded(ByVal strTableName As String) As Long
On Error GoTo Err_LocksNeeded
    Dim db As Database, tdf As TableDef, fld As Field
    Dim lngMaxSize As Long
    Const lngcSQLPageSize As Long = 2048
    Const lngcSQLPageOver As Long = 32
    lngMaxSize = 0
    Set db = CurrentDb
    Set tdf = db.TableDefs(strTableName)
    For Each fld In tdf.Fields
        lngMaxSize = lngMaxSize + fld.Size
    Next
    LocksNeeded = tdf.RecordCount / _
    ((lngcSQLPageSize - lngcSQLPageOver) \ lngMaxSize)
Exit_LocksNeeded:
    Exit Function
Err_LocksNeeded:
    MsgBox "Error " & Err.Number & " " & Err.Description
    Resume Exit_LocksNeeded
End Function
```

Check each table using this function in your database and ensure that you use the maximum returned value to determine what you should set the locks to in SQL Server. You may want to add 1,000 to this number to give the Wizard a little bit of leeway just in case your situation requires a few more locks than the formula prescribes. It is easier to perform this task now than to have to run the Wizard twice to recover from a locking error. In order to configure the locks in SQL Server 6.5, open Enterprise Manager and select the server to which you are migrating your database. Right-click the server name and select Configure from the drop-down menu. Select the Configuration tab and scroll down to the locks Configuration value, as shown in Figure 4-1. Change the number in the Current column to the number of locks required. Click Apply Now, and then click OK to exit the configuration screen.

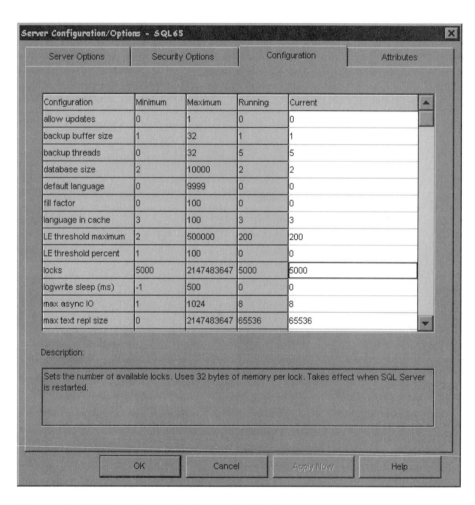

Figure 4-1. SQL Server Locks Configuration/Options

Once you have set the locks option, you must stop and restart SQL Server in order for the change to take effect. You can do this by right-clicking the server name in Enterprise Manager, choosing Stop from the menu, and then choosing Start after a few seconds. The ability to start and stop SQL Server is not available from Windows 9x, so it must be done from a Windows NT or 2000 computer. Once SQL Server has restarted, return to the Configuration utility and ensure that the numbers in the Running and Current columns match the number that you just entered.

SQL 7 Locks

If you are migrating your database to SQL Server 7, you probably do not have to make any changes to the server. In version 7, locks are, by default, set to zero, meaning that they are allocated as necessary. Consequently, there is no graphical utility that allows you to view the locks available on the system, but you can use a system stored procedure. You can run this stored procedure with Query Analyzer from the SQL Server program group to determine what the lock setting is. Query Analyzer can be used to execute and analyze T-SQL commands. A full description on how to use Query Analyzer can be found in Books Online in the SQL Server program group. Log into the server using the "sa" user or another user with administrative rights, and enter the following command:

```
USE master
EXEC sp_configure 'locks'
```

Be sure not to type anything else, or you may accidentally change the locks setting. Press the F5 key to execute the command. A new pane opens showing you the results of the stored procedure. If you receive an error containing the Msg number 15123, your server is not configured to show advanced settings (of which locks is a member). To turn on advanced settings, use the command

```
USE Master
EXEC sp_configure 'show advanced options', 1
RECONFIGURE
```

and then run the command to check the locks. If the numbers in the *config_value* and *run_value* columns is zero, you will not have any problems. A setting of zero means that the number of locks will increase as necessary. If either of the columns is not zero, you should set the locks to zero by running the following commands as one statement:

```
USE master
EXEC sp_configure 'locks', 0
RECONFIGURE
```

In order for this change to take effect, you must stop and restart SQL Server (MSSQLServer service) using the SQL Server Service Manager or Enterprise Manager after running the command. Rerun the first command once SQL Server is back up to ensure that the change took effect. You will still receive an error message about insufficient locks from the Wizard with this setting, but it can safely be ignored because the Wizard does not interpret a value of zero from SQL Server 7 correctly.

ODBC Settings

Another item that needs modification before the Wizard is run is the ODBC time-out settings. These settings determine how long the Jet engine will wait for certain ODBC items to respond to a request before canceling the request in one way or another. Because the Upsizing Wizard uses ODBC connections to transfer all data to SQL Server, ensure that the ODBC timeout specified is sufficient for the task of upsizing a database before the Wizard is run. ODBC settings are managed through the system Registry and must be configured when Access (and all other Jet clients) is not running. To access the ODBC Registry settings, you need to open the Registry Editor application. Select Start➡Run. In the Run dialog that appears, type **regedit**, and click OK. In the Registry Editor, use the tree view on the left to navigate to the Registry key:

```
HKEY_LOCAL_MACHINE\SOFTWARE\Microsoft\Jet\3.5\Engines\ODBC
```

for Access 97 or

```
HKEY_LOCAL_MACHINE\SOFTWARE\Microsoft\Jet\4.0\Engines\ODBC
```

for Access 2000. Once you select the ODBC folder, you should see a list of settings in the list view on the right, as shown in Figure 4-2.

The setting that you want to change is the QueryTimeout setting. This setting determines the number of seconds that the Jet engine will wait for a query to complete before Jet believes that the query has failed. The default setting for this value is 60 seconds. When Jet assumes that the query has failed, it sends a command to the ODBC data source to cancel the operation. When the Wizard transfers the data from your Access tables to SQL Server, the transfer can take a long time. If any of your tables have hundreds of thousands of records, the transfer of this data could easily take more than 60 seconds. If it takes longer than 60 seconds to transfer the data from an Access table to SQL Server, the Wizard will fail if the default Query-Timeout setting is not modified. Because upsizing data can take a long time, it is best to turn off the query timeout feature. To do this, set the value of the Query-Timeout setting to zero. Simply double-click the value name and switch the display to decimal by selecting the Decimal option in the Base options. Change the setting

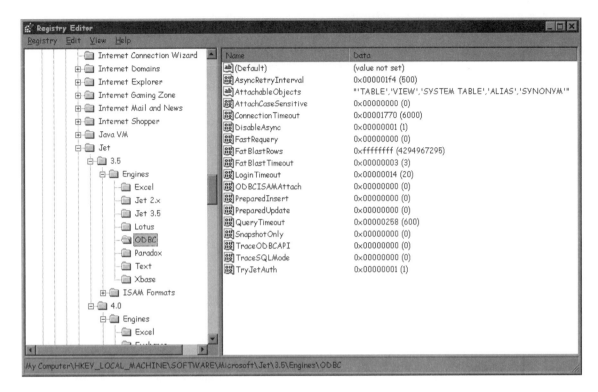

Figure 4-2. Jet ODBC Registry settings

to 0, and click OK. All ODBC queries will then be prevented from timing out while the Wizard is running. However, don't forget to reset this value to its old value when you are done. If you leave this setting at zero, and you then run a query on SQL Server through ODBC that hangs, your application freezes because it does not know to cancel the failed operation.

Date/Time Data

A last step you should take to ensure that the Wizard completes successfully is to check that the dates in any Date/Time fields are not outside of the range that SQL Server can handle. When upsizing these fields, the Wizard translates all Access Date/Time fields into SQL Server datetime fields. This translation may not sound like an issue, but the range of dates that each data type can hold are different. The range of an Access Date/Time field is from January 1, 100 to December 31, 9999. The SQL Server datetime data type has a range of January 1, 1753 to December 31, 9999. Because SQL Server cannot handle dates before 1753, you should check all of your tables to ensure that there are no dates before this time. Check this field even if you do not expect your data to contain any such dates. Typographical errors are very common, especially in fields that might display data differently between computers with different locale settings. Different users may not have their computers configured to display dates in the same way. If a user enters a date of 12/4/10, this date may be interpreted as December 4th, 1910 or October 4th, 1912 or April 10th, 1912, and so on. This interpretation is done by Access, so the user may not notice errors in their own input. These errors can easily cause date information to fall out of the range that SQL Server can handle. If any such data exists when you use the Wizard, you will receive an overflow error and the table will be created, but the data will not be upsized. The rest of the functions in the Wizard will fail, and you will have to delete the objects that the Wizard created on SQL Server, and then rerun the Wizard from the beginning. A quick check of your data prior to using the Wizard can save you from having to restart your migration.

Once you have completed these tasks, you are ready to use the Wizard. Let's take a look at what you can expect along the way.

SQL Server Naming Conventions

Before you run the Wizard, you should also be aware of the naming conventions that you must use when creating SQL Server objects. This affects what you can do when you name objects in SQL Server and could affect how the Upsizing Wizard deals with the names of your objects when it migrates them. In SQL Server, the name of a database object is known as its identifier. The rules for identifiers apply to SQL Server objects, such as tables, views, and stored procedures as well as variables used in T-SQL code. The rules are slightly different for SQL Server 6.5 and SQL Server 7.

SQL Server 6.5 rules are:

- Identifiers must be between 1 and 30 characters.

- The first character of an identifier must be a letter between A and Z or any of the symbols: _, @, #. However, @ and # have special meanings and should not be used for regular database objects.

- Subsequent characters can be any number or letter, or any of the symbols: _, $, #.

- Spaces cannot be used in names (this can be reconfigured, but doing so can cause compatibility issues with other programs so I do not recommend changing this setting).

- The @ symbol used at the beginning of an identifier denotes a local variable name for T-SQL code. The combination @@ at the beginning of an identifier signifies a global variable, but should not be used—it is intended for system use only.

- The # symbol used at the beginning of an identifier signifies a temporary object name. It is visible only to the process that created it. The combination ## signifies a global temporary object, visible to all processes until it falls out of scope.

- The identifier cannot be a Transact-SQL reserved word (for a complete list of these reserved words, see the Transact-SQL Reference in the SQL Server Books Online).

SQL Server 7 rules are:

- Identifiers must be between 1 and 128 characters.

- The first character of an identifier must be a letter as defined by the Unicode Standard 2.0 (A through Z for those of us using English) or any of the symbols: _, @, #. However, @ and # have special meanings and should not be used for regular database objects.

- Subsequent characters can be any number or letter defined in the Unicode Standard 2.0 (0-9, A-Z in English), or any of the symbols: @, _, $, #.

- Spaces cannot be used in names (this can be reconfigured, but doing so can cause compatibility issues with other programs so I do not recommend changing this setting).

- The @ symbol used at the beginning of an identifier denotes a local variable name for T-SQL code. The combination @@ at the beginning of an identifier signifies a global variable, but should not be used—it is intended for system use only.

- The # symbol used at the beginning of an identifier signifies a temporary object name. It is visible only to the process that created it. The combination ## signifies a global temporary object, visible to all processes until it falls out of scope.

- The identifier cannot be a Transact-SQL reserved word (for a complete list of these reserved words, see the Transact-SQL Reference in the SQL Server Books Online).

Running the Wizard

The Wizards in Access 97 and 2000 are very similar and have a familiar Microsoft "look and feel." However, there are some differences between the two versions.

You should be familiar with the Wizard you are going to run, so that you can understand the choices that are available to you in the Wizard and can make informed decisions about what options you should choose. Let's look at each Wizard separately, so that you can make the right choices for your migration.

The Access 97 Wizard

Once you have installed the Wizard using the executable provided by Microsoft, you can start it by selecting the Upsizing Wizard item from Tools➡Add-Ins. The Wizard takes you step-by-step through the information that it requires to do its job.

When you start the Wizard, it asks you whether you want to use an existing database or create a new one, as shown in Figure 4-3.

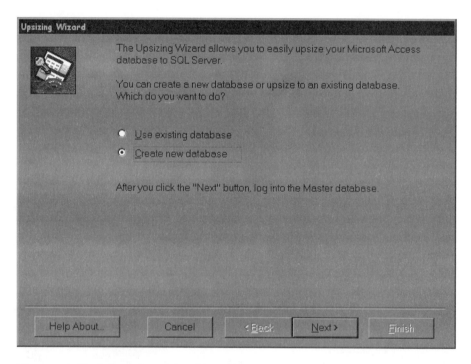

Figure 4-3. Upsizing Wizard database selection

If you have already created a database for your migration, you should select the first option, Use existing database. The advantage of using an existing database is that you can specify where the physical database files will reside on the server when you create the database using Enterprise Manager. If you choose to create a new database, you will be able to specify all of the information necessary to create the database, but you will have no control over where the database files are located. If you do not already have a database set up on SQL Server, you can create one at this time using Enterprise Manager and then continue with the Wizard by selecting to use an existing database, or you can select the Create new database option to have the Wizard help you create the new database.

Create New Database

If you choose to create a new database, after clicking the Next button, you will be prompted to select an ODBC Data Source Name (DSN) that points to the master database on the SQL Server that you want to upsize to. If you do not already have a DSN defined, you can create one at this time (for more information of creating DSNs, see Chapter 10). Once you have provided the ODBC information necessary to connect to SQL Server, you can move on to the subsequent step in the Wizard.

You will then be prompted for the database device names and sizes as shown in Figure 4-4. As described in Chapter 1, devices are the physical files that house SQL Server 6.5 databases and logs. Note that this screen only appears if you are upsizing your database to SQL Server 6.5—version 7 does not use devices. The Wizard only displays this option if you selected a SQL Server 6.5 server in your ODBC DSN. If you are using SQL Server 7, the next screen you see allows you to create the new database. Feel free to skip to the discussion of the database name and size screen shown in Figure 4-5 if this is the case.

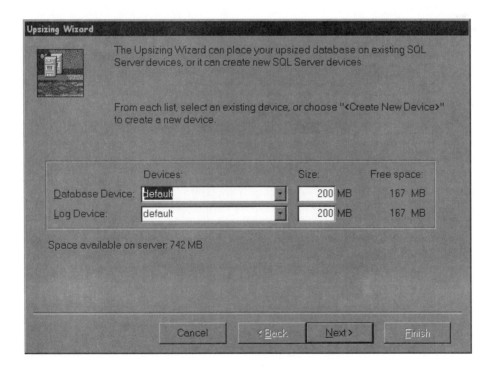

Figure 4-4. Device selection for SQL Server 6.5

Select <Create New Device> to create a new device if you do not already have one designated for your database. You will be prompted to enter a name for the device that conforms to the SQL Server naming conventions. You must also set the size of this device, which requires you to do some calculations.

When creating a database, you should create it so that the size is about twice the size of your current Access database. SQL Server data usually takes less space than the same data does in Access, but you should make the database larger than the Access database to ensure that you do not run into space problems during the upsizing process. Moving the data between Access and SQL Server causes the SQL Server database to use some extra space for processing. If there is insufficient space for this processing when you start the migration, you'll receive an error from the Upsizing Wizard, and you may have to restart the migration from scratch. Giving yourself enough space on the new SQL Server database prevents this error from occurring and allows room for the database to grow in the future. Also, you should make the log about half the size of the new database for the term of the migration just to ensure that you do not run into log problems during the migration. The log tracks all of the data that is inserted into the SQL Server database and grows as the amount of data inserted increases. You should make the device for the log and the log size sufficiently large, so that you do not run into space problems in your migration. Although it can be very hard to resize the database later on, the log can easily be resized in Enterprise Manager.

When creating this database, you will find that you get the best possible performance from SQL Server if you create the database and the log in their own separate devices. You should create one device for your log and one device for your database and not share these devices with other databases.

Set the size of the devices using the guidelines given previously for the separate log and database devices. Click Next when you are done.

The database name and size screen is shown whether you are creating a new database for SQL Server 6.5 or 7. You are prompted for a name for your database and the size of the database and log. This screen is shown in Figure 4-5.

Enter a name for your database or accept the name displayed. You should enter the size of the database and log files using the same values that you used for the devices you created earlier. If you are migrating your database to SQL Server 7, you will not be able to set the size of the database or the log because they will be configured to grow automatically when they are full. As a result, you will not run into the problems that can arise from devices and databases running out of allocated space. Click Next to proceed to the next screen.

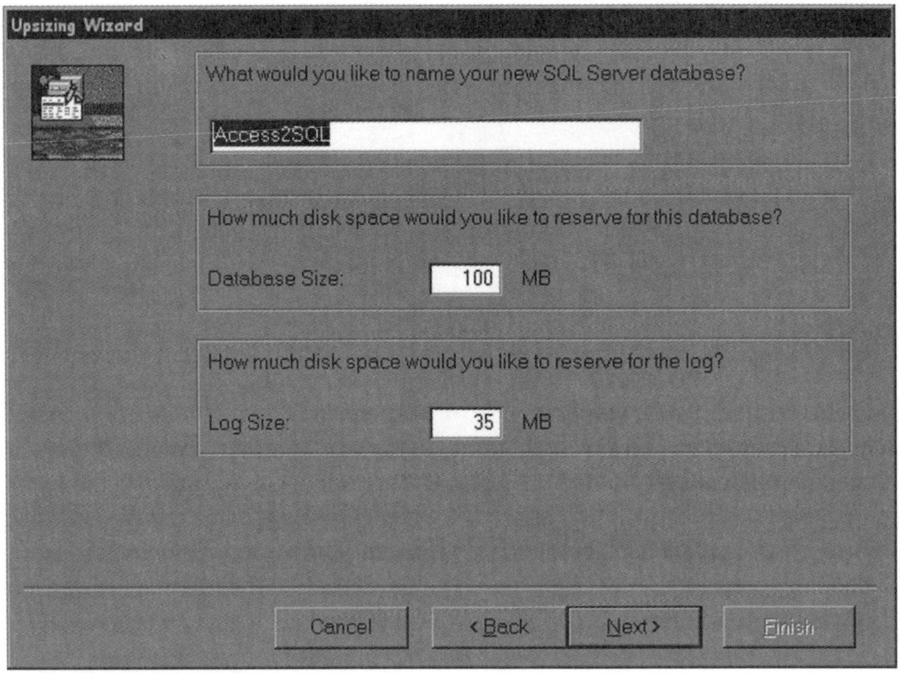

Figure 4-5. Database name and size

Use Existing Database

If you choose to use an existing database, you are prompted to select an ODBC DSN that points to the existing SQL Server database. If you do not have a DSN that points to that database, you can create one by using the New option in the DSN selection screen (a complete description of how to create DSNs can be found in Chapter 10). Create or select a DSN to connect to the existing database. Click OK when you are done to proceed to the table selection screen.

Table Selection

The Wizard will then prompt you to select the tables that are to be migrated (see Figure 4-6). Linked tables are not listed, nor are any tables whose names end in "_local". Tables with names ending in "_local" are not listed because this is how the Wizard renames tables after they have been upsized (if the option to change the local database is selected later on). If you want to migrate tables that are linked into your database, you must run the Wizard from the database where the tables reside.

In this screen, the tables listed on the left side are the tables that are available to be upsized, and the list on the right side shows those tables that have been selected for upsizing. Select the tables on the left that you want to migrate and move them to the list on the right using the arrow buttons. Use the double arrow

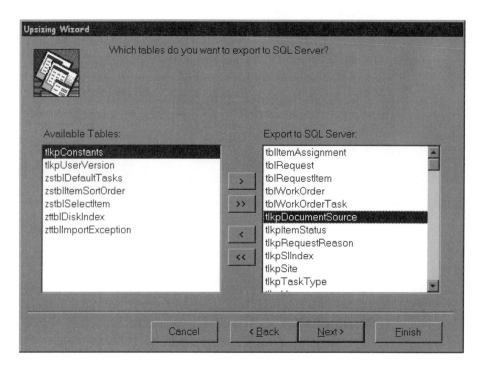

Figure 4-6. Table selection

buttons to copy all tables from one list to the other. If you aren't sure if you want to upsize a particular table, you should probably select it just to be sure that you don't omit any data when upsizing your database. Although including all tables may add to the amount of time it takes for the Wizard to accomplish its job, it is very easy to delete tables in the SQL Server database after the Wizard is finished. Click Next when you are finished selecting your tables.

Upsizing Options

Figure 4-7 shows the Upsizing options screen. This form allows you to select what attributes of the tables will be migrated, what data options to use, and how the current Access database will be modified after the tables are upsized.

There are four table attributes that you can upsize along with your tables. They include indexes, validation rules, defaults, and relationships. Each option is enabled or disabled by selecting one of the checkboxes on the option form.

By selecting to migrate indexes, you tell the Wizard that you want it to re-create in SQL Server all of the indexes that currently exist in the Access database between the tables you chose to migrate.

Selecting to migrate validation rules tells the Wizard to upsize all of the validation rules for tables and fields to SQL Server. Contrary to what you might expect,

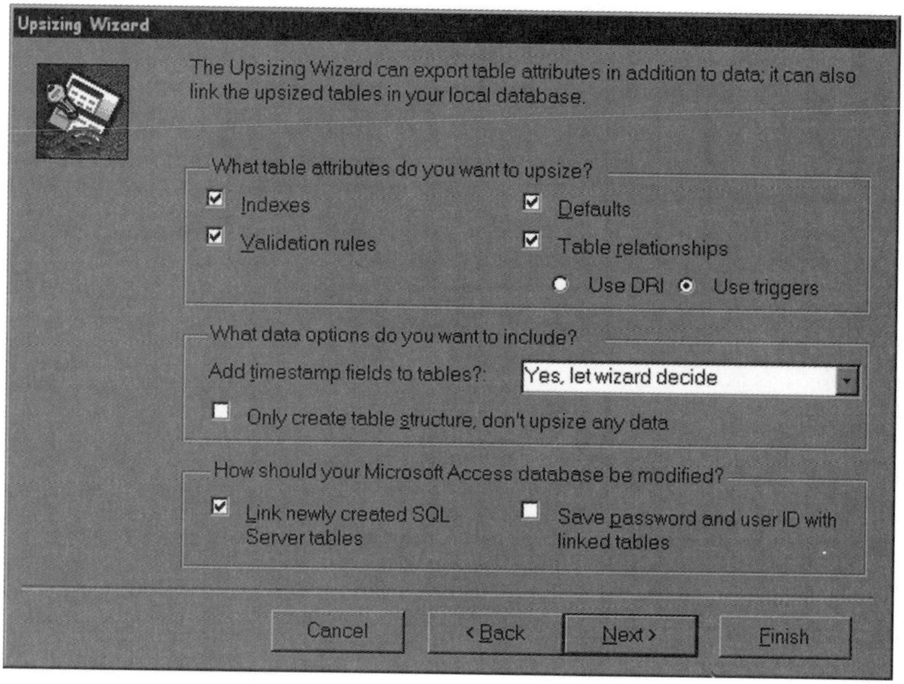

Figure 4-7. Upsizing options

Access validation rules are not converted to SQL Server Rule objects. Instead, the Wizard converts validation rules to triggers on the new SQL Server table. This is due to the fact that SQL Server rules are provided mainly for backward compatibility with older versions of SQL Server.

When you specify that defaults should be upsized, the Wizard creates SQL Server Default objects for each default setting in the Access tables. These defaults are then bound to the fields for which they are required. In only one case, SQL Server creates shared Default objects on SQL Server. This case occurs when zero is used as a default for field values. Only one SQL Server Default object is created (called UW_ZeroDefault) and all fields that have a default value of zero have this default bound to them. In all other cases, default values on each field in your Access tables are migrated to their own Default object in SQL Server. This means that you could potentially end up with numerous Default objects that return the same value. This is something you will have to fix after the upgrade is complete.

The item in the table attributes area on this screen that requires careful attention is the table relationships. Although the other options will, at worst, require you to correct a few errors in your SQL Server database, the options for the table relationships can have a dramatic effect on the performance of your SQL Server database. Table relationships can be migrated using DRI (database referential integrity) or triggers. DRI on SQL Server works the same way as enforced relationships in Access except that you cannot implement cascading updates and deletes. DRI prevents users from deleting records in a parent table while child records exist in another table. DRI also prevents values in parent tables from being updated when related child records exist. If you want to implement cascading updates or deletes, you must not select this option. If you choose to migrate relationships using triggers, DRI is not enforced. Instead, the Wizard creates triggers that return error messages and cancels updates that violate referential integrity rules. Cascade updates and deletes can only be implemented using triggers. Any update that modifies a primary key that has cascading updates defined through triggers automatically updates foreign-key tables to match the data in the parent table. Also, cascading deletes through triggers forces SQL Server to automatically delete any child records in a foreign-key table.

The next set of options you can set on this page are the two upsizing data options. The first of these is the capability to add timestamp fields to tables. As described in Chapter 3, timestamps can be used to make table updates more efficient. There are three choices for this option displayed in the drop-down menu: No, never; Yes, let Wizard decide; and Yes, Always. Selecting the first option—No, never—does not add any timestamp fields to your tables, and you do not get any of the performance improvements that they can give you. Select this option if you want to control how timestamps are added, which is by manually adding them yourself later on. I recommend this option for more experienced SQL Server users who are comfortable designing SQL Server databases. This option is also appropriate for databases that are not regularly updated by users, such as reporting databases.

If you select the second option—Yes, let Wizard decide—timestamp fields are only added to your tables if they contain any fields with data type Currency, Single, Double, Memo, or OLE Object because these fields are often very difficult to compare in SQL statements. In the case of Memo and OLE Object fields, they are often too large to efficiently run queries against. In the case of Single and Double fields, the rounding that takes place in these fields is not always consistent. As a result, the same value can be stored differently each time due to rounding errors. SQL Server may compare these two values and not consider them to be the same, thereby triggering an unnecessary save. This is the best option to choose for most standard databases. Choose this option if you are unsure of which option suits your situation best.

The third option—Yes, Always—adds timestamps to all tables in the migration, regardless of content or size. Choose this option if all of your tables are updated regularly, and the amount of data in the database is large. This option improves response time when data in any table is updated, but increases the overall size of the database.

The second data option allows you to specify that the Wizard upsize the tables and not any of the data. This can be very useful if you do not need to keep your existing data for historical purposes, and you want to start out with a clean database.

Upsizing only your tables can also be a useful way to prototype your SQL Server database, so that you can see exactly how the tables should be created and what data types to use. The tables only option can also be used to create a database that you can use to test your application.

The final options in this step in the Wizard allow you to determine what changes are made to the Access database that is being migrated. You can select whether or not the newly created SQL Server tables are linked into the current database. When you choose this option, all of the selected tables are renamed in the Access database by having "_local" added to the end of their names, and the new SQL Server tables are attached using the old table names. The other modification option, choosing to save the password and login information in your tables, allows you to access the tables without having to log into SQL Server each time the application is started. This option tells the Wizard to save the user ID and password in the connection string for the table. You should be aware that anyone who has sufficient security rights to open the table can use this information to connect to any portion of the SQL Server database to which the login has rights. This option should be used with caution due to the obvious security holes it opens.

Selecting the Next button takes you to the final screen, shown in Figure 4-8, which allows you to create an upsizing report.

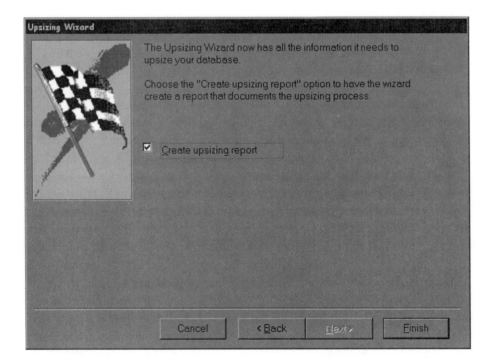

Figure 4-8. Upsizing report option

This report recounts the results of the migration and includes the options chosen as well as the actions taken by the Wizard. This report details what tables were migrated, how field data types were translated, what indexes were created, what triggers were created for the tables and what their definitions are, and any name changes that occurred along the way. When you click Finish, the migration begins. The progression screen, shown in Figure 4-9, relates the progress of the SQL Server upsizing.

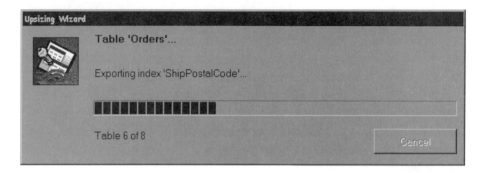

Figure 4-9. Upsizing progression screen

After the migration is complete, the report is displayed in a window for your review. You should immediately print the report or export it to Microsoft Word because there is no way of accessing it again once you close it.

If you are using the Wizard to upsize your database to SQL Server 7, or the Wizard determines that you do not have sufficient locks available on your server, you will see the following message:

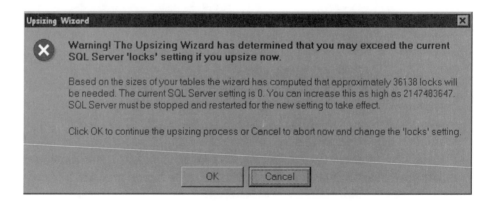

Figure 4-10. SQL Server locks error message

This may not necessarily be an error, but you should pay careful attention to the warning. The message example used in Figure 4-10 occurred in an upsizing to SQL Server 7. It can be ignored because the Wizard thinks that the current SQL Server setting of 0 is insufficient. In fact, it just means that locks are assigned as needed and do not have to be assigned in advance. For SQL Server 6.5, you should pay heed to this warning. Insufficient locks may cause the Wizard to fail. If you are upsizing to SQL Server 7 and this message is displayed but the configured locks are not set to 0, you should also heed this warning. In either of these two cases, you should stop the migration, reconfigure your server as appropriate, and then rerun the Wizard. If you confirm this setting before you run the Wizard, you can save yourself some of the extra time and effort involved in running the Wizard.

The Upsizing Report

Once the Wizard has completed its task, you are presented with the Upsizing Report. As stated earlier, it is imperative that you immediately print or export this report to Word. The Upsizing Report, shown in Figure 4-11, contains information that is extremely important to your migration.

The upsizing report contains an almost complete account of what occurred during the migration. It includes:

- The options you selected in the Wizard.

- Errors that were encountered in the migration, if any.

- Names of the tables before and after migration including if the SQL Server tables were linked into the database and under what name.

- If timestamps were added to tables.

- Indexes migrated to SQL Server.

- Default values assigned to fields.

- Full textual definitions for triggers created to enforce referential integrity or validation rules.

- Relationships created on SQL Server and the details of those relationships.

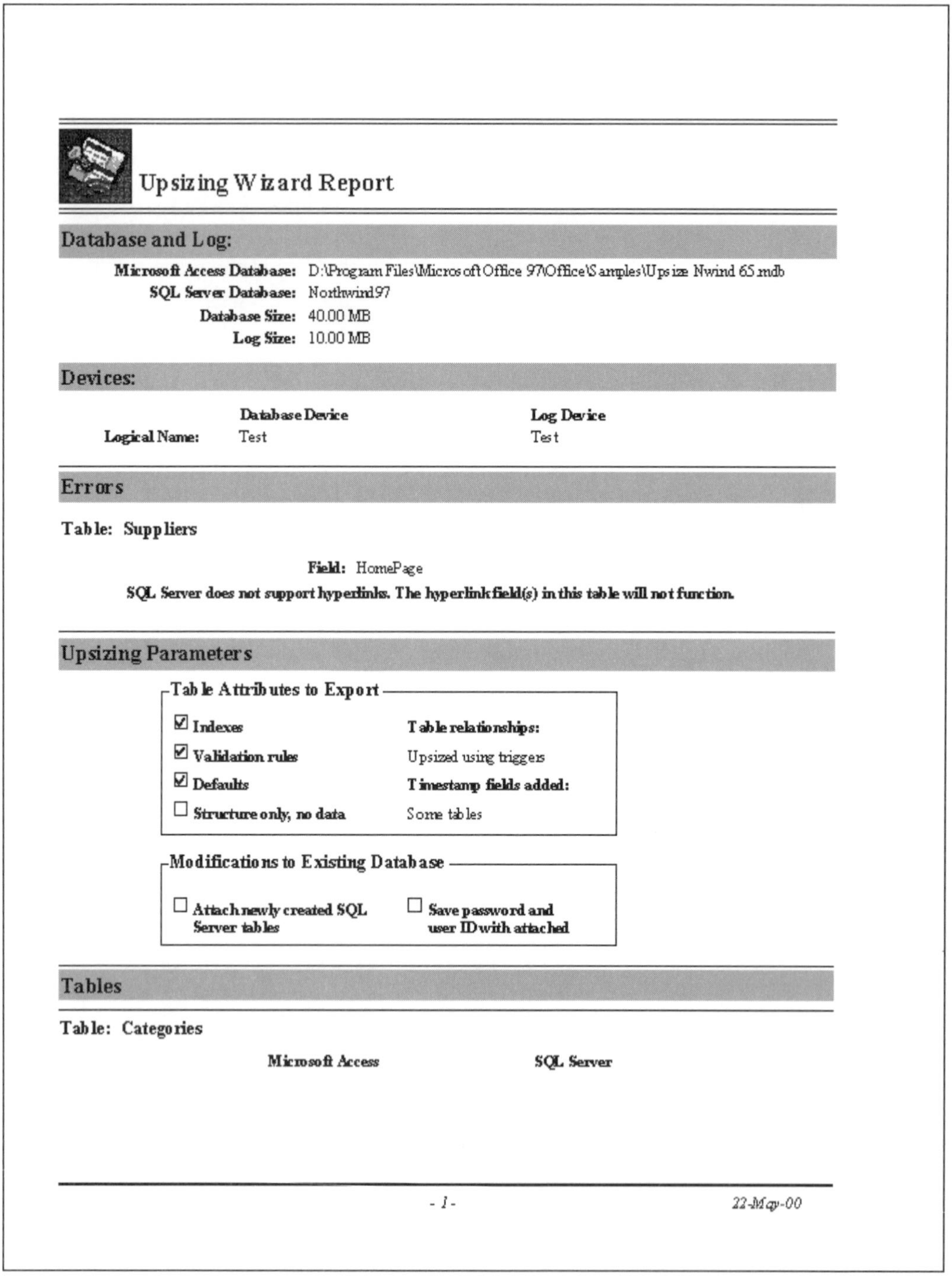

Upsizing Wizard Report

Database and Log:

Microsoft Access Database:	D:\Program Files\Microsoft Office 97\Office\Samples\Upsize Nwind 65.mdb
SQL Server Database:	Northwind97
Database Size:	40.00 MB
Log Size:	10.00 MB

Devices:

	Database Device	Log Device
Logical Name:	Test	Test

Errors

Table: Suppliers

Field: HomePage

SQL Server does not support hyperlinks. The hyperlink field(s) in this table will not function.

Upsizing Parameters

─Table Attributes to Export─

☑ **Indexes**

☑ **Validation rules**

☑ **Defaults**

☐ **Structure only, no data**

Table relationships:

Upsized using triggers

Timestamp fields added:

Some tables

─Modifications to Existing Database─

☐ **Attach newly created SQL Server tables**

☐ **Save password and user ID with attached**

Tables

Table: Categories

Microsoft Access	SQL Server

Figure 4-11. Upsizing Wizard Report

There is one very important item that the report does not tell you—the primary key information for the migrated tables. The Wizard migrates primary keys for tables to SQL Server and adds the characters "aaaaa" to the beginning of the key name, so that it always appears first in a list of indexes and will therefore be used by Access as the main unique index on the table.

The information that is included can be used to determine exactly what happened during the migration. This report should be used to correct a few problems that are commonly encountered in an upsizing.

First, you should check the list of indexes for each table to ensure that duplicate indexes have not been created for the same field. Delete any duplicate indexes from the SQL Server tables. If any indexes are listed that are defined on the Primary Key column, they may all be safely deleted. Because the primary key has been created (but is not listed on the report), you can safely delete any indexes that are set for that field or combination of fields.

Second, you should check the Defaults that were created by the Wizard. In most cases, you can probably delete the Default object altogether and just add a default value to the necessary fields as a literal value. In cases where the default value is a simple value or expression, Default objects should not be used.

Finally, check the Errors section on the first page of the report to see if there were any problems that might be of concern. This section of the report lists any incompatibilities, errors in the migration, or other pertinent information that may not be listed elsewhere. Take action to correct these issues if they are a concern.

Once the migration is complete and you have printed or saved your report, you have completed your work with the Wizard.

The Access 2000 Wizard

The Upsizing Wizard in Access 2000 is very similar to the Wizard in Access 97, but there are some very important differences. One of the primary differences is that the Upsizing Wizard is included with Access and does not have to be downloaded from the Web. However, as mentioned earlier, ensure that you have the most up-to-date version of Access by checking the Microsoft Office Update Web site for any changes to Access.

You can start the Upsizing Wizard by selecting it from Tools➡Database Utilities. You are then presented with the screen shown in Figure 4-12.

This screen is very similar to the first screen that you see with the Access 97 Wizard. The main difference in this version is that the Help button is actually helpful. In the Access 97 Wizard, the Help About button only provides copyright and version information. This Help button takes you to a Help file that details the steps involved in using the Wizard, what preparation is necessary, and what the Wizard does. Explore the Help file because it can guide you through using the Wizard if you have any questions. It also contains some additional information on upsizing,

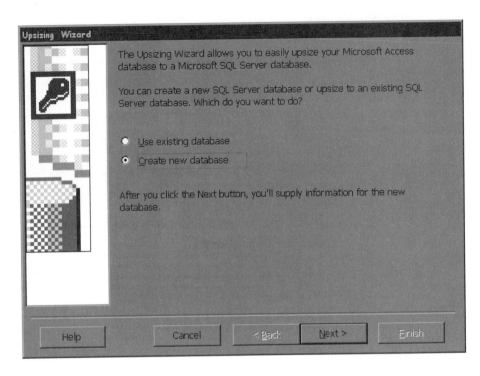

Figure 4-12. Database selection

most of which was already discussed. Once you have looked through the Help file, return to the Wizard and choose to upgrade to a new or to an existing database. If you have already created a database for your migration, select the option to use an existing database. If you do not have a database created, you can create one by selecting the second option. Click Next when you are ready to proceed.

Create New Database

If you choose to create a new database, you see the Create Database screen, shown in Figure 4-13.

Select the server you want to create the database on from the drop-down list at the top of the screen. If the server is not in the list and you have entered the server information into the Client Network Utility or SQL Client Configuration Utility (see Chapter 1), you can simply type it into the box. If you haven't registered the server that you want to use on the computer that you are running the Wizard on, then register it before entering it into the box, so that you can be sure that the Wizard will find the server. However, you do not have to exit the Wizard once the server is registered. You can simply type the server name in the Wizard and the Wizard will obtain the information necessary to connect. In the appropriate boxes, enter the login ID and password of a user who has the security rights to be able to

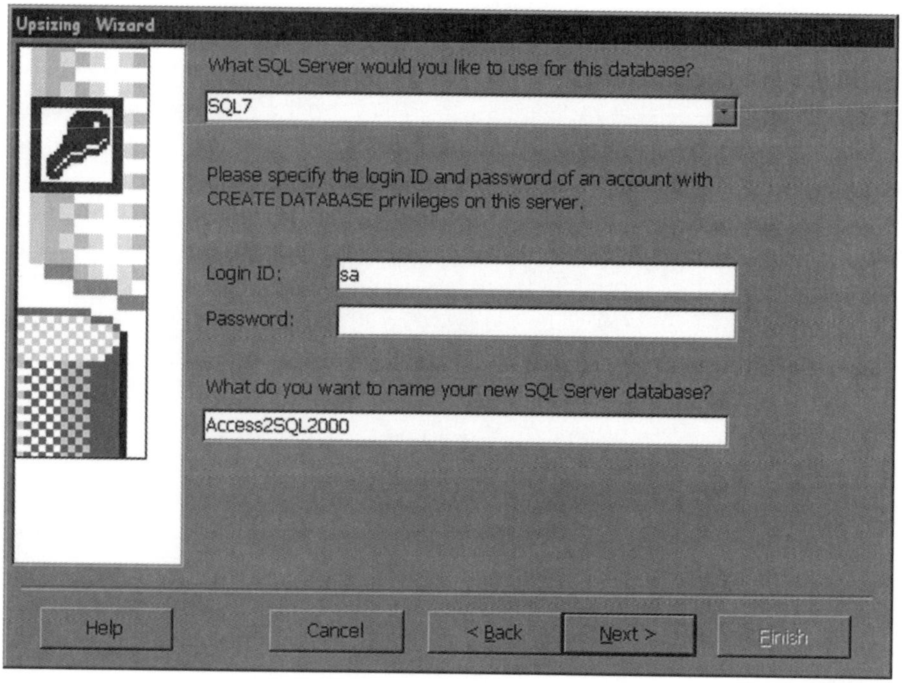

Figure 4-13. Create Database screen

create a database. Finally, enter a name for your new database or accept the default name that is provided. Once this step is complete, you are ready to go on to the next step. If the database name you entered already exists on the server, the Wizard changes the name of the database you entered and displays a message, so that the name is unique for the server. If this message occurs, confirm the new name, and click Next to move on to the next screen.

If you are upsizing to SQL Server 6.5, you will see two additional steps to the Wizard that do not appear when upsizing to SQL Server 7. These steps pertain to device creation and database size. Because SQL 7 databases are sized dynamically and SQL 7 does not use devices, this information is not required.

The first screen you see after the Create Database Screen when upsizing to SQL 6.5 is the device selection screen shown in Figure 4-14.

Select <Create New Device> to create a new device if you do not already have one designated for your database. You are prompted to enter a name for the device that conforms to the SQL Server naming conventions. You must also set the size of these devices, which requires you to do some calculations.

When creating a database, you should create it so that the size is about twice the size of your current Access database. SQL Server data usually takes up less space than the same data does in Access, but you should make the database larger than the Access database to ensure that you do not run into space problems during

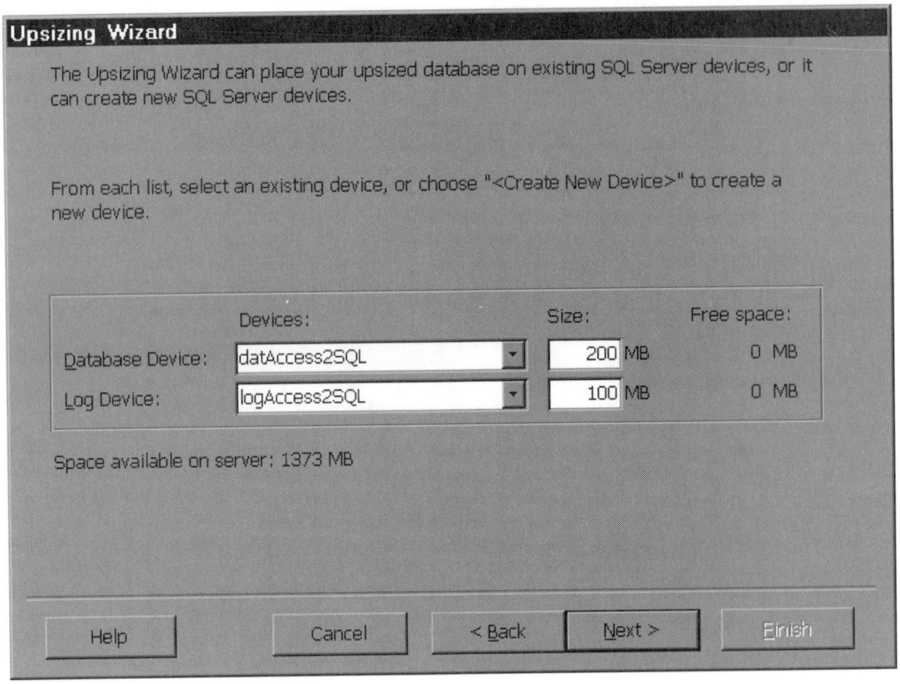

Figure 4-14. Device selection

the upsizing. Moving the data between Access and SQL Server causes the SQL Server database to use some extra space for processing. If there is insufficient space for this processing when you start the migration, you should receive an error from the Upsizing Wizard, and you may have to restart the migration from the beginning. Giving yourself enough space on the new SQL Server database prevents this from occurring and allows room for the database to grow in the future. In addition, you should make the log about half the size of the new database for the term of the migration just to ensure that you do not run into log problems during the migration. The log tracks all of the data that is inserted into the SQL Server database and grows as the amount of data inserted increases. You should make the device for the log and the log size sufficiently large, so that you do not run into space problems in your migration. Although it can be very hard to resize the database later on, the log can easily be resized in Enterprise Manager.

When creating this database, you should create one device for your log and one device for your database and not share these devices with other databases. This will give you the best possible performance from SQL Server. It also allows SQL Server to dedicate the entire device to a single database, thereby eliminating problems if any of the databases on the device need to be resized. With only one database or log on each device, size problems in one database need not affect other databases.

Set the size of the separate database and log devices using the guidelines given in the "Create New Database" section. Click Next when you are done.

This screen also only appears in a SQL Server 6.5 upsizing (see Figure 4-15). This screen prompts you to specify the size of the database and log files.

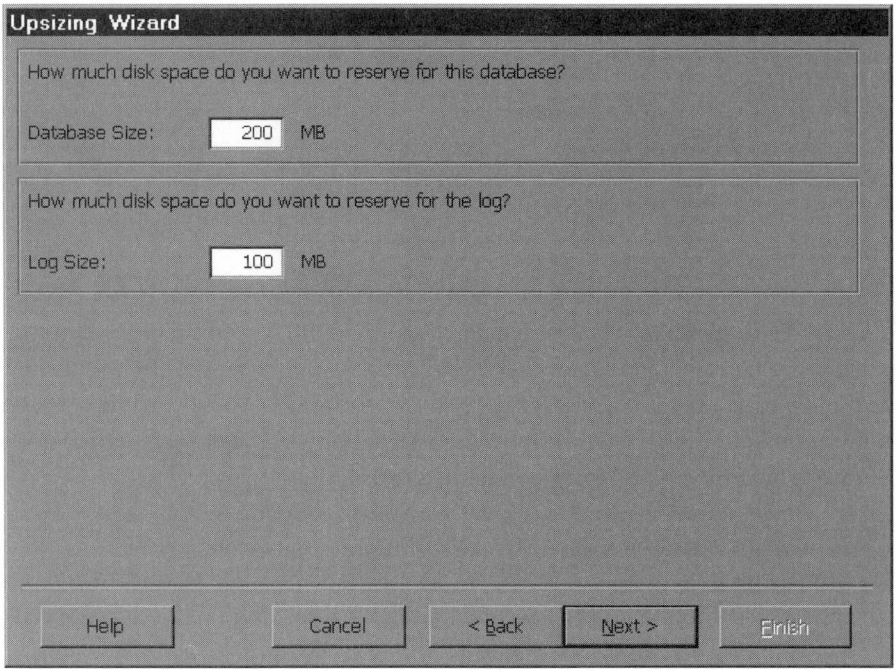

Figure 4-15. Database size

Enter the size of the database and log files, so that they match the size of the devices you created earlier. Once you have entered the necessary information, click Next to proceed.

Use Existing Database

If you chose to use an existing database, you are prompted to select an ODBC DSN from the current ODBC data sources defined on your computer. If you do not already have a DSN defined, you can create one from the selection dialog (for more information on creating DSNs, see Chapter 10).

Table Selection

The Wizard then prompts you to select the tables that are to be migrated (see Figure 4-16). Only those tables that reside locally in your database are listed. If you want to migrate tables that are linked into your database, you must run the Wizard from the database where the original tables reside.

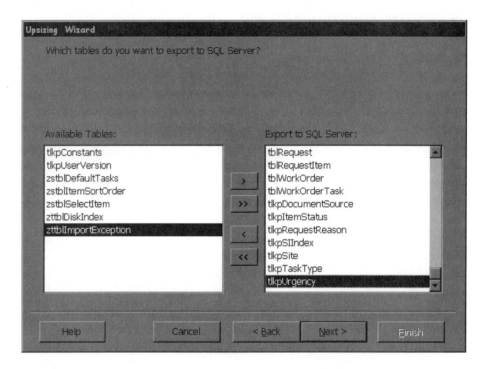

Figure 4-16. Table selection

In this screen, the tables listed on the left side are the tables that are available to be upsized, and the list on the right side shows those tables that have been selected for upsizing. Select the tables on the left that you want to migrate and move them to the list on the right using the arrow buttons. Use the double arrow buttons to copy all tables from one list to the other. If you aren't sure if you want to upsize a particular table, you should probably select it just to be sure that you don't omit any data when upsizing your database. Although including all tables may add to the amount of time it takes for the Wizard to accomplish its job, it is very easy to delete tables in the SQL Server database after the Wizard is finished. Click Next when you are finished selecting your tables.

Upsizing Options

The Upsizing Options screen provides you with the ability to specify what attributes of the tables will be upsized and what data options you can include (see Figure 4-17).

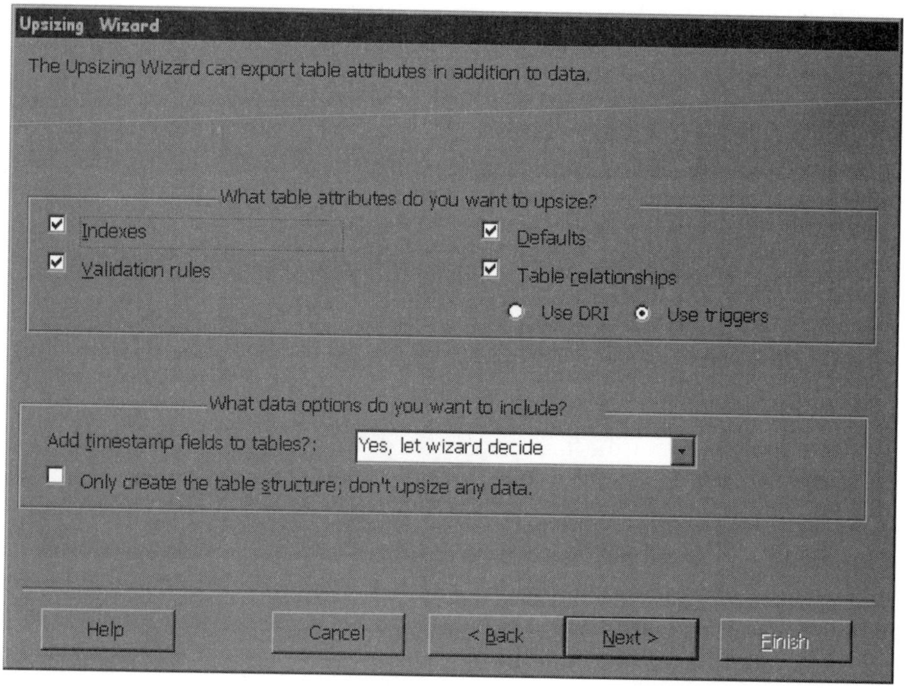

Figure 4-17. Table and data options

There are a number of attributes you can upsize along with your tables. They include indexes, validation rules, defaults, and relationships. A checkbox is provided for each item and the behavior of each object migration is as follows.

By selecting to migrate indexes, you tell the Wizard that you want it to re-create all of the indexes that currently exist in the Access database in the new database on SQL Server.

Migrating validation rules tells the Wizard to convert all of the validation rules for tables and fields to UPDATE or INSERT triggers that validate this data as it is entered.

When you specify that defaults should be upsized, the Wizard sets the Default Value property for the field to the same value or to a SQL Server equivalent function to the Access field's Default Value.

The item in the table attributes area on this screen that requires careful attention is the table relationships. Although the other options will, at worst, require you to correct a few errors in your SQL Server database, the options for the table relationships can have a dramatic effect on the performance of your SQL Server database. Table relationships can be migrated using DRI or triggers. DRI on SQL Server works the same way as enforced relationships in Access except that you cannot implement cascading updates and deletes. DRI prevents users from deleting records in a parent table while child records exist in another table. DRI also prevents values in parent tables from being updated when related child records exist. If you want to implement cascading updates or deletes, you must not select this option. If you choose to migrate relationships using triggers, DRI is not enforced. Instead, the Wizard creates triggers that return error messages and cancels updates that violate referential integrity rules. Cascade updates and deletes can only be implemented using triggers. Any update that modifies a primary key that has cascading updates defined through triggers automatically updates foreign-key tables to match the data in the parent table. Also, cascading deletes through triggers forces SQL Server to automatically delete any child records in a foreign-key table.

The next set of options you can set on this page are the two upsizing data options. The first of these provides the capability to add timestamp fields to tables. As described in Chapter 3, timestamps can be used to make table updates more efficient. There are three choices for this option: No, never; Yes, let Wizard decide; and Yes, Always. Selecting the first option—No, never—does not add any timestamp fields to your tables and you do not get any of the performance improvements that they can give you. Select this option if you want to control how timestamps are added, which is by manually adding them yourself later on. I recommend this option for more experienced SQL Server users who are comfortable designing SQL Server databases. This option is also appropriate for databases that are not regularly updated by users, such as reporting databases.

If you select the second option—let Wizard decide—timestamp fields are only added to your tables if they contain any fields with data type Currency, Single, Double, Memo, or OLE Object because these fields are often very difficult to compare in SQL statements. In the case of Memo and OLE Object fields, they are often too large to efficiently run queries against. In the case of Single and Double fields, the rounding that takes place in these fields is not always consistent. As a result, the same value can be stored differently each time due to rounding errors. SQL Server may compare these two values and not consider them to be the same, thereby triggering an unnecessary save. This is the best option to choose for most standard databases. Choose this option if you are unsure of which option suits your situation best.

The third option—Yes, Always—adds timestamps to all tables in the migration, regardless of content or size. Choose this option if all of your tables are updated regularly and the amount of data in the database is large. This option improves response time when data in any table is updated, but increases the overall size of the database.

The second data option allows you to specify that the Wizard upsize the tables and not any of the data. This can be very useful if you do not need to keep your existing data for historical purposes, and you want to start out with a clean database. Upsizing only your tables can also be a useful way to prototype your SQL Server database, so that you can see exactly how the tables should be created and what data types to use. The tables only option can also be used to create a database that you can use to test your application.

Application Changes

The Application Changes screen in the Wizard prompts you to select the changes that should take place to the current application. See Figure 4-18. This section differs considerably from the Wizard in Access 97 due to the new functionality in Access 2000. The Access 97 Wizard only gives you two options—No changes and Link tables—whereas the Access 2000 Wizard gives you three options, the new one being to create an Access Database Project.

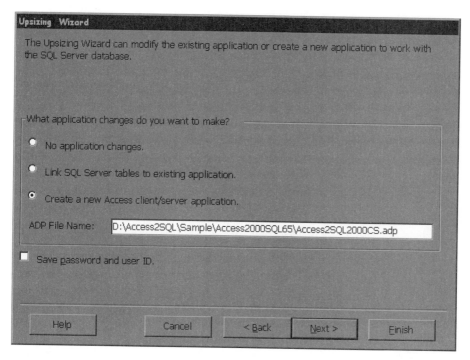

Figure 4-18. Application changes

The first option on this form allows you to migrate the tables with the options you specified without making any changes to the Access application. No tables will be attached from the SQL Server database to the Access database and no changes will be made to any other objects in the Access database. This option allows you to create the SQL Server database you will use in your application, but allows you to maintain the Access database in its current state. This is a good option to choose if you want to control how the Access database is changed to accommodate the new SQL database.

The second option causes the Wizard to link the newly created SQL Server tables into the Access database through ODBC. When you choose to have the Wizard link the newly created SQL Server tables into your database, all of the selected tables are renamed with "_local" on the end of their names, and the new tables are attached using the old table names.

The final option is to create a new client/server application for your database. This option creates an Access database project (ADP) based on your original application. You are prompted to enter a name for the new project. Enter a new name for your ADP or accept the default name provided. When you select the client/server option, a number of changes are made to the database objects as they are moved to the ADP.

The first and most obvious change is that the selected tables are translated to SQL Server tables, as they would be if you selected one of the other application options. All of the options that you selected in the Wizard are used to determine how these tables are translated and in what database they will reside. You should be aware that any tables you did not select in the Table Selection screen are not upsized to SQL Server and are therefore not available in the new ADP that is created. You cannot link tables from multiple databases into an ADP because it is designed to work against a single SQL Server database. You should keep this in mind if you choose not to migrate tables that are used by any Access objects for example, Forms, Queries, or Reports. These Access objects are still migrated, but the record source that the Wizard attempts to provide them with does not exist. When you open these objects in the ADP, you will receive an error message that the source cannot be found.

The next change that takes place is that all queries in your database are translated into SQL Server views (for simple SELECT queries) or SQL Server stored procedures (for action queries) or a combination of the two (for SELECT queries containing ORDER BY clauses). You should keep in mind that any queries that contain VBA functions or Jet functions that do not have equivalents in SQL Server, are not migrated because SQL Server does not know how to parse them.

The Wizard then modifies the record source for each of your forms and reports to new SQL Server views. Record sources for list boxes and combo boxes are also changed to views. These views are created by the Upsizing Wizard and are named *ut_qry##* where ## is a number for the query based on the order in which the queries were created.

If you want the Wizard to save the user ID and password with the database, you can select the item to do so. However, you should use caution when doing this because it is possible for users to employ the user name and password in the connection information to access objects in the database that you may want to prevent them from accessing. If the security of the database or the application is a concern, you should not save the connection password.

The final page in the Wizard, shown in Figure 4-19, is simply a confirmation that you want to run the Wizard.

Click Finish to start the upsizing. The progression screen, shown in Figure 4-20, displays the status of the upsizing as it progresses.

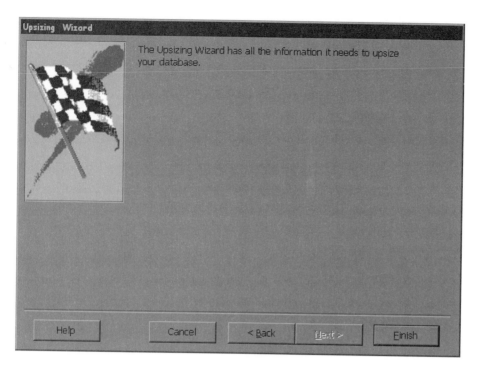

Figure 4-19. Final confirmation screen

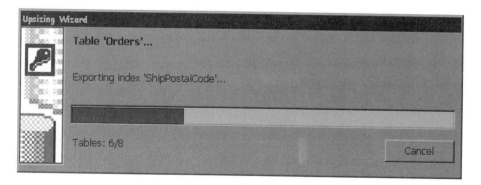

Figure 4-20. Upsizing Wizard progression screen

The Upsizing Report

Once the upsizing is complete, the system automatically opens the Upsizing Report in preview mode. The Upsizing Report, shown in Figure 4-21, contains information that is extremely important to your migration.

Upsizing Wizard Report

Database

Microsoft Access Database: D:\Program Files\Microsoft Office\Office\Samples\Northwind.mdb

SQL Server Database: Northwind2000

Errors

Table: Order Details

Field: Discount

Validation Rule not exported: Between 0 And 1

Field: Quantity

Validation Rule not exported: >0

Field: UnitPrice

Validation Rule not exported: >=0

Table: Suppliers

Field: HomePage

SQL Server does not support hyperlinks. The hyperlink field(s) in this table will not function.

Upsizing Parameters

Table Attributes to Export

☑ **Indexes**

☑ **Validation rules**

☑ **Defaults**

☐ **Structure only, no data**

Table relationships:

Upsized using triggers

Timestamp fields added:

Some tables

22-May-2000

Figure 4-21. Upsizing Wizard Report

The upsizing report contains an almost complete account of what occurred during the migration. It includes:

- The options you selected in the Wizard.

- Errors that were encountered in the migration, if any.

- Names of the tables before and after migration including if the SQL Server tables were linked into the database and under what name.

- If timestamps were added to tables.

- Indexes migrated to SQL Server.

- Default values assigned to fields.

- Full textual definitions for triggers created to enforce referential integrity or validation rules.

- Relationships created on SQL Server and the details of those relationships.

There is one very important item that the report does not tell you—the primary key information for the migrated tables. The Wizard migrates primary keys for tables to SQL Server and adds the characters "aaaaa" to the beginning of the key name, so that it always appears first in a list of indexes and is therefore used by Access as the main unique index on the table.

There is also an error in the upsizing report for the Access 2000 Wizard. If you chose to upsize your database and selected the first option (no changes) in the Application Changes screen, the report will show that you chose to link the newly created tables into the Access database. This is an error and can safely be ignored.

The information that is included in the report can be used to determine exactly what happened during the migration. This report should be used to correct a couple of problems that are commonly encountered in an upsizing.

First, you should check the list of indexes for each table to ensure that duplicate indexes have not been created for the same field. Delete any duplicate indexes from the SQL Server tables. If any indexes are listed that are defined on the Primary Key column, these may all be safely deleted. Because the primary key has been created (but is not listed on the report), you can safely delete any indexes that are set for that field or combination of fields.

Second, check the Errors section on the first page of the report to see if there were any problems that may be of concern. This section lists any incompatibilities, errors in the migration, or other pertinent information that may not be listed elsewhere. Take action to correct these issues if they are a concern.

The Wizard automatically saves this report in Access Snapshot format (if installed) to the directory that is the current working directory (you can determine this by selecting File➡Open in Access—the current directory is the one that the Open dialog starts in). You can access the report at a later time to print it or save it to another location. You should keep a copy of this report handy to ensure that you know all of the actions taken by the Wizard when you start working with the database later on.

Once you have finished viewing or printing the report, you can close it and your work with the Upsizing Wizard is complete.

Evaluating the Wizard

Once you know all of the steps involved in using the Wizard, you may inquire as to how you should use it. In order to make an informed decision about how and where to use the Wizard, let's take a look at what the Wizard does well, and what it does poorly.

What the Wizard Does and Doesn't Do Well

The Upsizing Wizard, be it in Access 97 or 2000, was designed with one concept in mind: move Access tables to SQL Server. This is the reason the process of upsizing appears to be so table-oriented. It is also the reason that most table characteristics are migrated accurately.

The Wizard does an excellent job of translating tables and fields. The main table definition and data types that are used in the upsizing are usually the best possible choices. The Wizard also does an excellent job of creating relationships, whether they are enforced through DRI or triggers. Creating DRI relationships or relationships that use triggers by hand can be very time consuming. The Wizard does this quickly and, in most cases, correctly. When it creates triggers, it adds error messages that are returned to the application when relationships are violated. The messages used in these triggers are often much easier to understand than the normal SQL Server DRI violation messages.

The Wizard is also very good at migrating lots of data. Migrating this data manually can be a difficult and time consuming task. Considering that the Wizard can usually accomplish this using only a few minutes of your time dedicated to selecting the options to run the Wizard, it is definitely worth considering as a tool for migrating data.

One of the most important tasks that the Wizard doesn't do well is manage how data is accessed. As discussed in the previous chapter, there is much more to migrating a database than just converting all of the tables. Views and stored procedures must be created to manage how data is accessed and to make the application more efficient. The only way you can get the Wizard to create these items is if you are using Access 2000 and you upsize from Access to an ADP. Even in this case, the views that are created to replace queries and form and report data sources do not necessarily have the best possible design. In addition, they are named randomly with names like "ut_qry1View", which does not help to discern where they are used in the ADP. When the ADP upsizing Wizard changes all of the report and form data sources, it does not include a list of changes that took place to the forms and reports in the Upsizing report. It is up to the user to figure out which SQL Server views belong to which Access objects. There is no record of this, nor do the names that are used leave any clue as to the purpose of the views or stored procedures.

The upsizing Wizard is also not very good at managing the migration of indexes. This may not pertain directly to the Wizard as some of the issues arise due to the way that Access itself deals with indexes. The first concern is that the Wizard does not cluster primary keys. This can make the table extremely inefficient to update and detrimentally affect the application performance. Although Access automatically clusters primary keys, SQL Server does not. The Wizard, instead of duplicating the Access configuration, leaves it to you to define which key is to be clustered. Letting you choose the clustered index gives you more control over the design and performance of the SQL Server database, but it also makes it harder for a SQL Server novice to create a database that provides the fastest access times for the application that depends upon it.

The Wizard also adds indexes to foreign keys in related tables. This is, again, a function of the way Access works. In Access, all foreign keys are indexed, even though the user is not informed about those indexes. This is intended to ensure that joins between the tables are performed as quickly as possible. However, indexes have a cost associated with them when data is modified in a table. The added overhead that arises when updating the table often outweighs the need to index a foreign key. This is especially true when there are a small number of different values in the index, such as a Gender field that only contains two possible values: Male and Female. Depending on how Access is configured, it is also very common for a field to be indexed more than once unnecessarily. This can occur due to user error or through the automatic indexing that Access can be configured to do for columns with certain characters in their names. When these indexes are migrated to SQL Server, no checking is done for redundant indexes. This results in fields that are indexed multiple times. This also results in SQL Server having to track two identical indexes. Consequently, this adds to the amount of disk space that is used by the database, increases the amount of time it takes to change or add a record in the affected table, and can lead to unnecessary bottlenecks in the application.

Finally, the indexes that are originally created in Access often do not have meaningful names and the Wizard does nothing to improve this situation. This can lead to confusing index names in the SQL Server database that will have to be renamed by the database administrator. However, there is one case where the Wizard modifies index names and it is a useful feature. The Upsizing Wizard renames the indexes created for primary keys, so that when they go to SQL Server the primary key appears first in an alphabetical list of indexes. This is done by adding the characters "aaaaa" to the beginning of the index name. This is beneficial because Access uses the first unique index on a non-native table as the primary key, regardless of what the real primary key is.

The Wizard also seems to have a problem with allowing Nulls in fields. In Access, this can be configured by setting the Required property to True. In SQL Server, this can be done by setting the field's AllowNulls property to False. However, neither the Access 97 nor 2000 Wizard handle this properly. In Access 97, the Wizard creates code in the triggers that enforce the Required setting. In the Access 2000 Wizard, this characteristic is migrated, but there is no information on the Upsizing Report to let you know that it has been done. Using triggers to enforce NULL constraints is not the best way to manage the application because it forces SQL Server to have to run the trigger each time data is updated. This adds overhead to your data changes. SQL Server already has the capability to manage this characteristic with a simple property setting, so why add unnecessary overhead to the application? Adding overhead can make the database difficult to administer and can lead to confusion because the validation you are expecting from your tables may not be in the place you expect to find it.

The Access 2000 Wizard has one very serious problem that arises when tables are not included in the upsizing. If any of your forms or reports or any controls reference the nonupsized tables and you select the option to create an Access database project, the record source for these objects will be changed to nonexistent views or stored procedures and the Wizard will give you an error similar to the one shown in Figure 4-22.

The error, if you are not aware of its cause, can be very confusing. The Upsizing Wizard attempts to modify the record source for a form, report, combo box, or list box to satisfy the changes required to access data in the ADP, but the Wizard does not take into account the fact that the data source for the object was not included in the upsizing and is not available to be modified. The Wizard still changes the data source of the object to the view or stored procedure it is trying to create, and it can be difficult to determine what the original value for the RecordSource property was.

Recommendations

The Wizard is primarily intended to migrate tables from an Access database to a SQL Server database. It is by no means a complete utility for migrating an application. Being aware of this fact, you can use the Wizard to handle some of the more tedious work involved in moving your tables and the data they contain. Knowing the

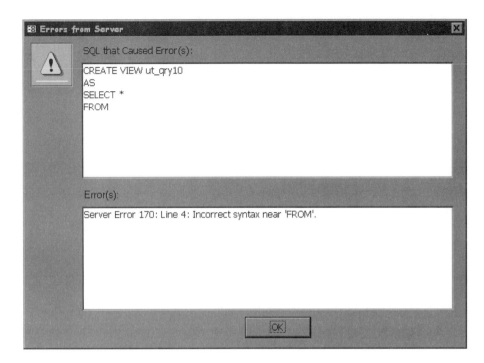

Figure 4-22. Upsizing error

capabilities and the failings of the Wizard, you should consider using the following guidelines when migrating:

- Configure the ODBC Registry settings and SQL Server locks before running the Wizard.

- Separate your devices from all other devices on the server. Keep separate devices for the database and the log files (SQL 6.5).

- Make the size of your database and log files (SQL 6.5) large enough to support future growth.

- Export only those tables to SQL Server that are used to house regular data. Temporary tables are unnecessary as you can create temporary tables as necessary in stored procedures.

- Don't upsize indexes if you are comfortable creating them yourself. The Wizard does not do a good job of migrating indexes and Access's indexing schema does not necessarily scale well.

- Reassess validation rules before using the Wizard to upsize them. You may be better off deleting them and using the Validation Rule properties of controls on a form. This allows you to customize the error message that the user sees. When implemented on SQL Server, the error message that a user sees includes extra text regarding the ODBC provider itself. This can make the error message confusing to a user. Also, the validation will not take place until the whole record is committed to the server. If you want to ensure that users are notified of a validation error as soon as they finish editing a field, build the field validation directly into the Validation Rule for the control on the form.

- Avoid upsizing Default values for fields if you can. Re-create them on the server only for those fields that need a default value when the field will not be shown to a user. ODBC tables linked into an Access database and tables in an ADP do not show the default value of the field. Use the Default property of the Access control that is used to display a default value instead.

- Let the Wizard create the relationships for you. They can be tedious to re-create in SQL Server, especially version 6.5, and you may miss some of the relationships along the way.

- Use triggers to enforce relationships wherever possible. Triggers are much more versatile and allow you to include cascading updates and deletes if necessary. They also provide you with the flexibility to add or remove cascades temporarily or permanently.

- Let the Wizard decide if it should add timestamps, but also add your own timestamps after the upsizing to only those tables that are updated frequently. It can dramatically improve the performance of your application.

- With Access 97, allow the Wizard to upsize your data if you need to retain historical information, but ensure that you have set the correct timeouts in the Registry.

- In Access 2000, avoid using the Wizard to upsize data, but allow it to upsize tables. Use Data Transformation Services (the subject of Chapter 5) to move the data to the server. This allows you greater control over how the data is migrated and also allows you to create a reuseable data migration plan.

- Don't let the Wizard make modifications to your current database. You should always leave the original database as is. Create a new database to use to interface with the SQL Server system and import all of the nonupsized objects, linking in the new tables where necessary. This allows you to back out of the migration if an error occurs. If you allow the Wizard to modify the current database, you may have to do some extra work to reset the Access database to its original state. If you want to upsize a database and have the Wizard make the changes necessary to connect to your SQL Server database, make a copy of your Access database first and upsize the copy, so that you maintain a backup of your original system.

- If you are concerned about security, don't save passwords in the linked tables. Leaving them out causes Access to automatically prompt users to enter this information when they start the application.

- Don't forget to reset any changes you made to SQL Server locks or the ODBC Registry settings once you are done.

- Don't expect the first time you run the Wizard to be the last. There are some items you will find that you have to modify to ensure that the Wizard is optimized. Play with the Wizard and learn as you go. For example, you may want to set the option to have the Wizard enforce relationships using DRI once, and then try the same settings with relationships enforced through triggers. This allows you to see how each type of enforcement can be designed.

The Upsizing Wizard can be a very useful tool in any migration if it is applied properly. It should not be used as the one and only step in migrating an Access application to SQL Server, but it can certainly be very helpful.

CHAPTER 5

Data Transformation Services

AS THE EXISTENCE OF THE UPSIZING WIZARD indicates, developers have needed tools that allow them to migrate data from one system to another. Often these developers have had to build customized solutions to translate data between the various systems. These customized solutions usually involved an investment of a great deal of time and effort on the part of the developers who built the solution as well as the end users who had to oversee the process. This is because these solutions face a major hurdle: They must connect multiple data sources together, account for the major differences between the systems, and integrate the methods used to access the data in the disparate systems. In order to alleviate some of the problems associated with accessing multiple heterogeneous data sources, Microsoft developed OLE DB, a component of Universal Data Access, their new strategy for accessing information across the enterprise. OLE DB provides an infrastructure that allows developers to connect to multiple, unrelated data sources using identical code.

As the next step in the evolution of OLE DB technology, the Microsoft SQL Server development team created Data Transformation Services (DTS) for SQL Server 7.

What Is Data Transformation Services?

The DTS component of SQL Server allows you to—using a wizard, DTS Designer, or code—define how data is passed from one data source to another. DTS was also designed to allow you to reuse this definition. This enables developers and database administrators to easily migrate data between multiple data sources, and even to build a single data warehouse from multiple data sources

DTS provides Access developers with a new choice of methods to use to upsize a database to SQL Server. Using DTS as part of your upsizing solution lets you perform functions that aren't possible with the Upsizing Wizard.

DTS Architecture

DTS allows you to import, export, or transform data between multiple data sources in a single solution. This solution can then be saved in an easy to administer object called a DTS Package. *Packages* are the main objects in DTS. Packages house all of the other objects that DTS uses. Think of a DTS package as an application that brings together all of the functionality you require from DTS. Within each DTS package, there can be any number of each of three object types: connections, tasks, and steps.

Connections are used to define each OLE DB data source used as a source or destination for data in the package, or OLE DB data sources against which actions are run. A package can contain any number of connections, although there is usually at least one. Connections are useful in defining data and object transfers between multiple systems. The valid types of connections a package can use are:

- Data Source Connections (using OLE DB or ODBC)

- File Connections (text files)

- Microsoft Data Link Connections (files with the extension UDL that define an OLE DB connection)

Tasks define units of work within a package. They describe and control what actions are run within the package. There can be any number of tasks within a package. Tasks use connections to connect themselves to the data sources that they run against. The types of tasks that a package can execute are:

- Execute SQL Tasks

- Data Pump Tasks (data transformation)

- Microsoft ActiveX Script Tasks

- Execute Process Tasks (OS-level program or command)

- Bulk Insert Tasks (bcp)

- Send Mail Tasks

- Data Driven Query Tasks

- Transfer SQL Server Objects Tasks (between SQL 7 databases)

- Custom Tasks (COM objects created by developers)

When data is transferred within a task, the data transfer always runs through the DTS Data Pump. The DTS Data Pump is an OLE DB service provider that manages the import, export, and transformation of data between data sources. Data Pump tasks can be straightforward transformations, like a simple transfer of data from one data source to another, or the tasks can be complex operations that call customized transformation algorithms. Other types of tasks, such as Execute Process tasks, ActiveX scripts, mail tasks, and COM-object tasks can be used for cases where the package designer wants to perform non data-related tasks or where the designer wants to customize the Data Pump behavior.

Steps define the relationships between different tasks. They set precedence and manage the flow of control within a package. They can be used to define which tasks will be executed in what order and which tasks will be run based on the results of previous tasks. There are three general flows defined by steps:

- On Completion

- On Success

- On Failure

On Completion steps direct the flow of the package, regardless of the outcome of a task. The next task in the list is run as soon as the previous one completes. *On Success* steps direct the flow when the parent task completes without error. This allows you to ensure that one task that depends on the successful completion of another is only executed if the previous task completed without error. *On Failure* steps direct the flow of control when a task fails and can be used to run tasks that handle abnormal situations. Using a combination of step types allows you to define which tasks will run under different situations.

Relevance to an Access Migration

Where does DTS fit in with an Access migration? Well, DTS is able to transfer data from any OLE DB or ODBC compliant data source to any other. In the case of an Access to SQL Server migration, both Access and SQL Server have OLE DB and ODBC drivers that are provided with Windows free of charge, so you can use DTS to migrate the basic definition of your tables and all of the data they contain from Access to SQL Server.

Using DTS to migrate your data has a number of advantages over using the Upsizing Wizard. One advantage is the capability to save DTS packages. When you use the wizard to migrate data from Access to SQL Server, there is no way to save the definition you use in order to rerun the conversion later or rerun the conversion with modifications at a later date. In order to adjust the settings for a migration, you must start the wizard from the beginning each time and reenter the settings you chose with the mappings. DTS allows you to create a package and save it to be run at a later date. You can also make modifications to the package and run it as often as you like. This can be useful in situations where you want to upsize data more than once, such as once for testing purposes and again later to move the finalized data from your Access databases to your production SQL Server database. It also allows you the opportunity to merge many similar Access databases into a single SQL Server database.

Another advantage to using DTS to migrate your tables and data is that you can customize how data is migrated. The Upsizing Wizard only allows you to define simple copy operations between tables, whereas DTS allows you to transform data using ActiveX scripting. Using a script, you can validate all of your data as it is copied, use lookup tables to obtain missing values, summarize data in multiple rows, or perform just about any other task you need. For example, you might want to validate or change the values stored in a field before each row is added to SQL Server. Using DTS and a script, you can do this in one easily defined process without the need to manually modify the data that exists in Access. With this capability, DTS can help you avoid many of the problems inherent in using the Upsizing Wizard. One of the issues with upsizing data to SQL Server that was discussed in the previous chapter was that the range of valid dates in Access and SQL Server do not match up. Access Date/Time fields can hold data that is outside of the valid range of dates for the SQL Server datetime data type. Using a transformation script, you could check each record just before it is added to SQL Server and modify the data in any Date/Time fields that would cause an error.

One more advantage to using DTS is that you have total control over what is migrated and how it is migrated. Although DTS does not automatically support migrating indexes, rules, defaults, or triggers between databases unless the source and destination databases are both in SQL Server 7 systems, you can customize a package using a combination of scripts and/or Execute SQL tasks to tell DTS how to create these items for you. For example, you could copy SQL Server object definition scripts (Transact-SQL scripts that can be used in SQL Server to create objects) from a database and paste them into DTS. You could then create an Execute SQL task that DTS would run before the data is migrated. This allows you to create an entire SQL Server database from scratch in your package, and then migrate the data from an Access database without having to run multiple tasks.

One final advantage to using DTS is that it does not matter whether you are migrating your database to SQL Server 7 or 6.5. You can use DTS if you have a single copy of SQL Server 7 available. Because Microsoft provides the desktop version of SQL Server 7 with many of its development products, you can use the desktop version of SQL Server 7 running on your own computer to manage your migration to any database system that has an OLE DB driver available including any SQL Server 6.5 systems in your environment.

Before you can use DTS, you must install Microsoft SQL Server 7 Desktop Edition or Server Edition. These versions differ slightly from what you may know as Microsoft Data Engine (MSDE). MSDE does not include any administrative utilities and does not have DTS built into it. If you do not have a Server Edition of SQL 7, you can install the Desktop Edition, complete with administrative utilities, from the MSDE or Office 2000 Developer CD.

Accessing DTS

DTS is installed as a component of SQL Server 7. DTS is accessed from within Enterprise Manager by selecting the Data Transformation Services folder under your registered server in the tree view on the left of the screen. Right-clicking the folder and choosing New Package or double-clicking an existing package in one of the DTS items opens a new window. This provides access to the DTS Designer, which is a robust interface that allows you to define the actions to take place in any package, from simply copying a single table from one data source to another to complex enterprise data transformations.

The DTS Designer is a graphical tool that is quite simple to use once you get some practice with it. However, to make life even easier, Microsoft has included a very good wizard that helps you through the bulk of the work involved in designing a DTS package.

Running the Wizard

There are a three ways to access the DTS Wizard. The first way to access the DTS Wizard is to open Enterprise Manager, select a server (highlight the server name) in the tree view on the right, select Import or Export Data from the Getting Started Task-pad shown in the right pane of Enterprise Manager, and then select either the import or export subfunction shown in the Import or export data taskpad view. The second method you can use to access the DTS wizard is to click the Run a Wizard command from the Enterprise Manager toolbar, and then expand the Data Transformation Services option to display the Import and Export Wizards. The final way to access the wizard is to start the wizard from the command line by running the dtswiz.exe executable, located in the SQL Server BIN directory (usually C:\MSSQL7\BIN).

If you choose to start the wizard from Enterprise Manager using the database Taskpad or the Run a Wizard function, you are presented with two options: run the Import wizard or run the Export wizard. The two wizards contain identical steps with the sole exception being that the appropriate information is filled in for the SQL Server connection in either the source or destination, depending on whether you are importing or exporting data. When you run the wizard from the dtswiz.exe executable, no information is filled in for you. You are able to select any valid OLE DB source and destination that you want to use. Because you are migrating data from Access to SQL Server, you should use either the Import wizard or the dtswiz.exe command-line utility.

Once you start the wizard, the first screen you see is the welcome screen. This screen gives you a quick introduction to the wizard and tells you what the wizard is for (see Figure 5-1).

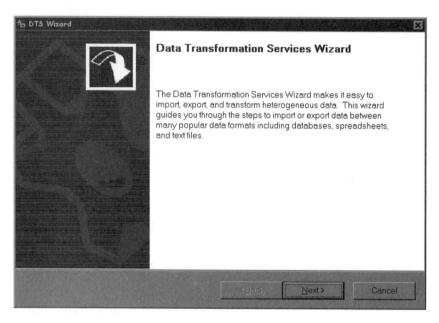

Figure 5-1. Data Transformation Services Wizard

Click Next to begin using the wizard.

Getting Connected

On this wizard screen, you can define your data source (see Figure 5-2). You are presented with the default wizard connection—a connection to the local SQL Server installation—that must be configured.

Because you are migrating data from Access to SQL Server, you must first select a Source data driver that can be used to connect to your Access database. This is the Indexed Sequential Access Method (ISAM), ODBC, or OLE DB driver that you will use for your connection. Select the Microsoft Access item from the drop-down list. This tells the wizard to use the Microsoft Jet 4.0 OLE DB Provider to connect to the database. This driver should be used for the wizard because it can handle Access databases created in Access 2000 or any earlier version. It has more functionality than the Jet 3.5 driver—functionality that is required for the DTS import to run properly. Once you select Microsoft Access as your data source, the form for entering information about the data source changes to the one required by Access. For an Access database, the required information is the file name, user

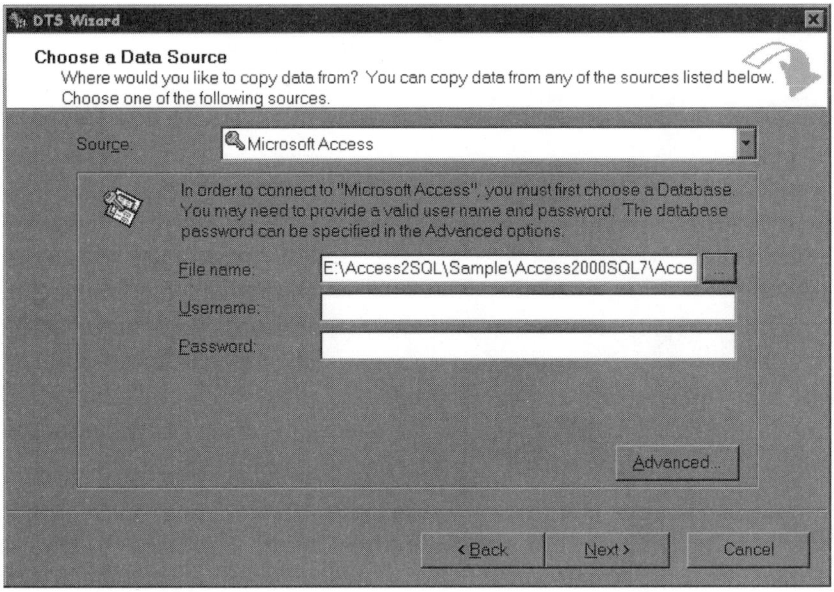

Figure 5-2. Choose a Data Source

name, and password. Select your Access database by browsing your computer using the button to the right of the File Name field. This opens the standard file selection dialog that allows you to select your database. Once you have selected your database, click OK, and the file name is entered into the appropriate box.

If your database is not secured using Microsoft Access security or a database password, you do not need to enter any further information and may proceed to the next step. If your database is secured using standard Access security, you must enter the information necessary to open the database. Enter a user name and password for an Access login that has sufficient rights to view the design of the tables in your database. Click the Advanced button to view the advanced connection information. See Figure 5-3.

There are more settings that you may need to configure. If your database is secured using Access security, you must enter a value for the Jet OLEDB:System database setting. Enter the full path, including the file name, to the MDW file that contains all of your security settings. Typically, this file is located in your C:\Winnt\System32 or C:\Windows\System directory and is named system.mdw.

If your database is secured using a database password, enter that password in the Jet OLEDB:Database password property. The other settings on this screen do not need to be configured in order for DTS to migrate your data. Click OK when you are done to return to the wizard, and then click Next when you are ready to proceed to the next step.

This screen allows you to define the destination data source for the tables and data you are migrating (see Figure 5-4).

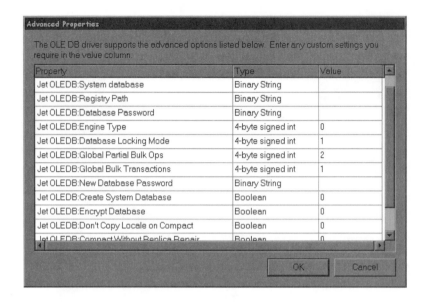

Figure 5-3. Advanced Jet OLE DB Properties

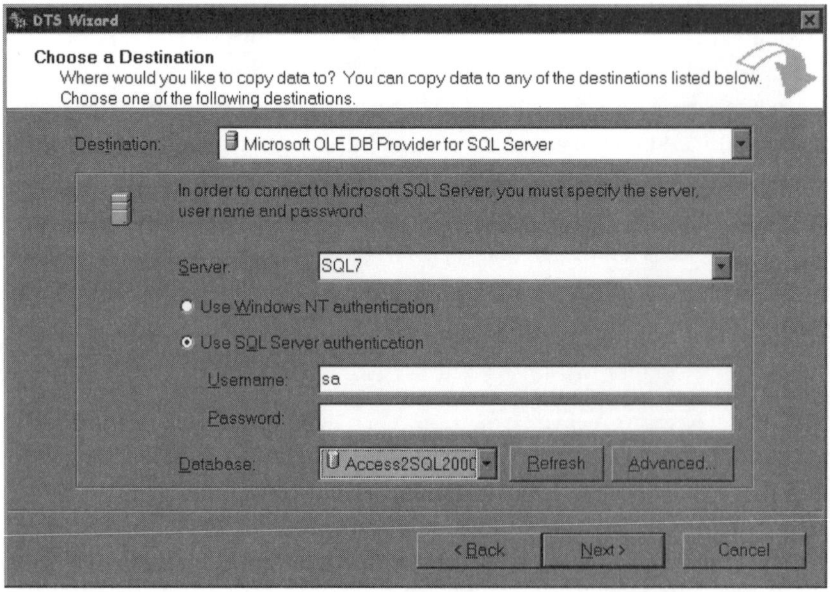

Figure 5-4. Choose a Destination

If you selected the DTS Import wizard from within Enterprise Manager, the Destination, Server, and login information is already set to the same values used to login to the current session that started Enterprise Manager. However, you are not limited to using the userid, password, or destination database presented to you. In fact, you don't even have to use the current server as a source or destination. Being able to select a destination allows you to leverage the abilities of SQL 7 to migrate data to SQL 6.5 databases by specifying a SQL 6.5 database as your destination.

On the Destination Screen, you first need to select a driver for the destination system. Because this setting defaults to the Microsoft OLE DB Provider for SQL Server, you do not have to change it. If necessary, change the server you are migrating your data to by selecting it from the drop-down list. If your server is not listed, you must add it into the Client Network Utility (CNU) described in Chapter 1. Once the server is listed in your CNU, you can switch back to the wizard and type the name of the server into the appropriate box. Next, define the user name and password that will be used when connecting to the server. If you are going to create a new database, the user id must be one that has sufficient rights to be able to create a database. If you are going to use an existing database, the login must have sufficient rights to be able to create tables within that database.

The final step in this screen is to select the database you will be creating or moving your tables to. Once valid security information is selected, click the Refresh button to refresh the list of databases if you want to use an existing database. Some databases may have been hidden from the userid and password used to log on to the system. If you want to create a new database, select the <New> item. If you are using the wizard to migrate data to SQL 6.5, always use an existing database because the wizard is incapable of creating databases on SQL Server 6.5 (create the database beforehand if necessary). You are then prompted for the name and size of the database, as shown in the Figure 5-5.

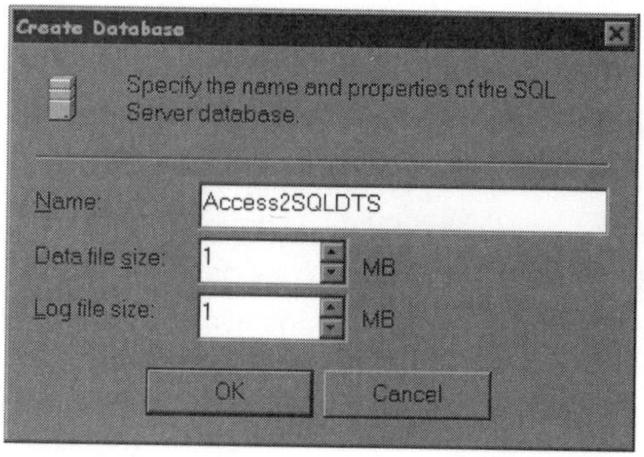

Figure 5-5. Create Database

Enter a name for your new database, and if your destination database resides on a SQL 7 system, accept the defaults for Data file size and Log file size. The files will automatically be configured to grow as needed when they run out of space.

If your destination database resides on a SQL Server 6.5 system, use the guidelines outlined in Chapter 4 under the "Create New Database" section of the Upsizing Wizard. Note that when using SQL Server from the wizard, you probably do not need to change any of the settings on the Advanced tab. However, you may want to have a look at this tab just to see what options can be configured. When you are finished with this screen, click Next to go to the next step.

Designing the Transfer

The screen shown in Figure 5-6 is the first screen that helps you specify exactly how data is to be transferred between the source and destination.

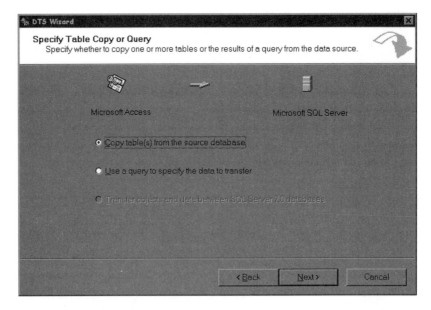

Figure 5-6. Specify Table Copy or Query

Because you are transferring objects from Access to SQL Server, there are only two choices in the list. You can copy tables from your Access database to SQL Server, or you can create a query to transfer customized data. If you select the first item, you are able to transfer tables as they currently exist in your database. If you select the second option, you are only able to transfer data using a single query. However, if you want to transform your data before it is added to SQL Server, a query transfer can be quite useful. Because you are transferring your Access tables as they currently exist, select the first item and go on to the next screen.

You are then prompted to select the tables that will be migrated to SQL Server, as shown in Figure 5-7.

When you select a table, a default destination table name is generated for you. The table is named in SQL Server using the format [*database*].[*user name*].[*table*]. For example, selecting the table tblRequest in database Access2SQL under user "sa"

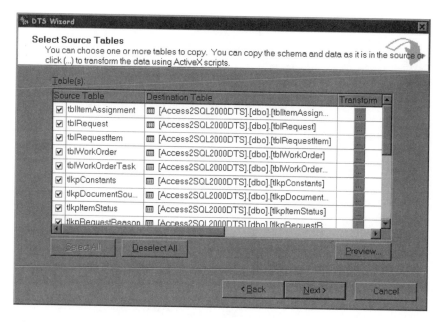

Figure 5-7. Select Source Tables

selects a table called [Access2SQL].[dbo].[tblRequest] (dbo means database owner) . If you are connecting to SQL Server using a login that is not aliased to dbo, the user name portion is replaced with the login you are currently using. For example, if the same table was being migrated under the login "bill", the new table name would be [Access2SQL].[bill].[tblRequest]. If this table does not exist, the wizard assumes that you want to create it. If a table with this name does exist, the wizard assumes that you want to use it as the destination for your data.

A very important section on this screen is the Transform column beside each table. This column provides access to a set of options that you can use to define how your tables and data should be altered. Be sure to verify the information in this section for each table. Selecting the builder (…) button for a table opens the Column Mappings and Transformations screen shown in Figure 5-8.

The Column Mappings tab allows you to define how fields will be copied between Access and SQL Server. The source and destination columns are listed along with the type, nullability, size, precision, and scale of the columns in the destination. There are three options available that determine what will happen to the data in the destination table:

- Create a new destination table.

- Delete all rows from the existing table, and then insert the new data.

- Append the data to an existing table.

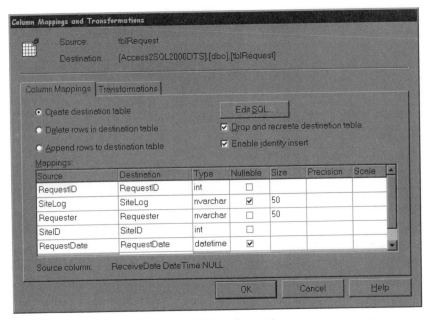

Figure 5-8. Column Mappings and Transformations

If your table does not already exist, you must select the Create destination table option. When you do this, you should check the SQL that DTS will use to create your table by clicking on the Edit SQL button. This displays a window showing the SQL data definition language (DDL) statements that will be used to create the new SQL Server table. The default DDL generated by the wizard to create your table is a very simple statement to create the table without any indexes, relationships, or constraints.

If you know how to write DDL, you can easily modify these statements to create a more complex table that includes indexes, relationships, and other SQL Server table characteristics. Alternatively, you can use the script generator from SQL Server to generate these scripts and copy the text generated by SQL Server script generator into the appropriate table definition statement in DTS. You can reset the DDL to the default definition provided by DTS at any time by clicking the Auto Generate button. Generating these definition scripts will be discussed further in Chapters 6 and 7.

Two other options are available for the translation. By selecting the Drop and recreate destination table option, you can have the wizard delete the existing destination table, and then re-create it before the data is inserted. This option is only available if you select the option to create a new table. It can be useful if you plan on running the DTS package more than once as part of the testing stage during the development of your application.

The other option, Enable Identity Insert, can be used in situations where your table contains identity fields (autonumber fields). This option allows you to insert data into identity columns while specifying the value to insert for that column and bypassing the standard functionality that has the server create the identify column values. This option is automatically selected for you if you are migrating your data to an existing table and that table has identity columns. This setting has no effect if the destination table does not have an identity column.

Once you have set all of your options, you need to define how your fields will be translated. Generally, the wizard does a good job of translating data types. One data type you should watch for, though, is a Date/Time field. The wizard initially translates these to the SQL Server smalldatetime fields. However, this is often inadequate for the data that is contained in these fields because the smalldatetime data type is only accurate to the minute and does not store seconds. It also only covers date ranges from January 1, 1900 to June 6, 2079. If this is not acceptable for your data requirements, change the data type to datetime to allow a broader range and more precision.

You should also ensure that the wizard translates text data types appropriately for your situation. If you have fixed-length text fields where all of the characters are filled in, you should use nchar rather than nvarchar data type. The nvarchar data type does not pad the text to the full length of the string, whereas nchar always does. Not padding adds a small amount of overhead to the processing of this field when used in SQL Server. Because of this, you may prefer to use nchar because it always fills the full extent of the field with spaces even if some of the string is left blank. However, as was pointed out previously, this overhead disappears in fields over approximately eight characters.

The other tab on this screen, shown in Figure 5-9, allows you to create your own customized script for the data translation.

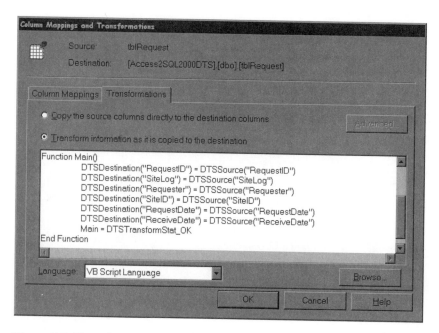

Figure 5-9. Transformations tab

The Transformations tab gives you two options. You can copy the source columns directly to the destination columns as defined in the Column Mappings, or you can define your own customized transformation script.

When you copy the columns directly, DTS inserts the data into the destination table in bulk groups. This means that large quantities of data are inserted in a single action, which results in a much faster transformation of data from one system to another. With the copy columns directly option, no changes are made to the data except for translating data types to larger or smaller data types (data type promotion and demotion).

If you choose to transform the information as it is copied, you must define your own script to handle the transformation. DTS allows you use a variety of scripting languages, but the default is VBScript. The language you want to use can be selected from the drop- down list. Scripting can be used for any number of functions including validating data, modifying data, splitting fields, and combining fields as well as for most data functions you may find necessary to perform. Refer to the "Scripting DTS" section for further discussion of this topic.

Click OK to save your changes and return to the wizard. Click Next to proceed to the next screen.

Saving the Package

On this screen, you must enter the schedule and save options of the DTS Package, as shown in Figure 5-10.

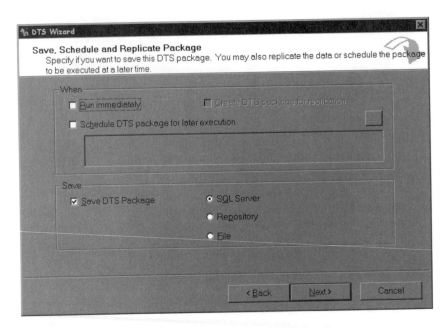

Figure 5-10. Save, Schedule and Replicate Package

There are three options that can be selected in the When section on this screen. The first option is to run the package immediately. This means that the package will run as soon as you are finished with the wizard. Although you can select this option, it is better to disable this option and run the package later, after you have had some time to explore the package in the DTS Designer to see how it works and to ensure that it performs as you expect it to. The second option, Create DTS package for replication, allows you to define this package as a replication method for your originating data source. Because you are migrating an application from Access to SQL Server, this is not necessary. If you want to configure Access as a replication partner with SQL Server, you could create a DTS package, created for replication, to replace the default behavior of the SQL Server replication engine. The third option, Schedule DTS package for later execution, allows you to schedule the package to run at a later date or even multiple times. This option does not need to be selected for your purposes because you will be running the package manually at a later date.

The save options allow you to save the package in one of three areas: SQL Server, Microsoft Repository, or to a File. The first option is the one that you should choose. It saves the package to the msdb database with all of the information you have selected. Because the package is stored in msdb, the person creating the package must have the ability to write to the sysdtspackages table in that database or the package cannot be saved. Your package is then accessible through Enterprise Manager in the Local Packages section under Data Transformation Services for your server. The second option allows you to save your packages to the Microsoft Repository. This is a technology that Microsoft has developed to manage large, interrelated systems through a common interface and is beyond the scope of this book. However, if you want to find out more about it, check out the Repository Web site at `http://msdn.microsoft.com/repository`. The final option is to save the DTS Package as a file. The advantage of this option is that it can be emailed, copied, or otherwise distributed to other people or servers for execution at a later date. However, these packages are not listed in Enterprise Manager and must be loaded from disk as needed.

Because you chose to save the package in SQL Server, you are prompted to enter some information about the package and the necessary SQL Server information. See Figure 5-11.

On the Save DTS Package screen, you must give your package a name. The name that you use must be unique to the server. You should then enter a description of the package because this information, along with the creation date, will be displayed to a user when the user looks at the local packages for the server. Be as descriptive as you can and include information such as what project the package is to be used with as well as what the purpose of the package is.

There are two passwords that you can assign to your package: owner password and user password. The owner password is the password that must be entered for

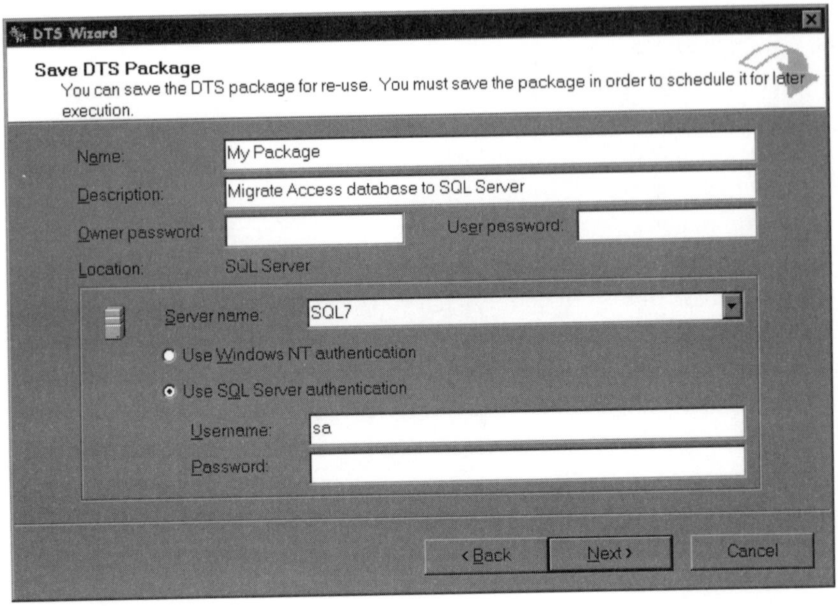

Figure 5-11. Save DTS Package

a user to be able to view and edit the definition of the package. If you do not set a password, anyone with rights to create packages will be able to modify your package and view its definition. This includes access to sensitive information, such as login names and passwords necessary to connect to the Access and SQL Server databases. You should set an owner password for your package if anyone else has access to your server. The user password is the password that allows another user to run your package. This password does not allow other users to modify the package or view its definition, but they will be able to execute it using SQL Server. This password can be useful if someone other than the package's creator will be running the conversion.

In order to save your package to SQL Server, you must provide the information necessary to connect to that server. This information defaults to the context under which you started the wizard. Select the server and enter the appropriate login information. Remember that the login used must have sufficient access to write to the sysdtspackages table in msdb. Click Next to proceed.

Wizard Summary

The final screen of the wizard, shown in Figure 5-12, displays a quick summary of the options you chose and allows you to finish your work with the wizard.

Review the information in the summary to confirm your choices, and then click Finish to have the wizard save your package. A progression screen is displayed showing the progress and success status of the save.

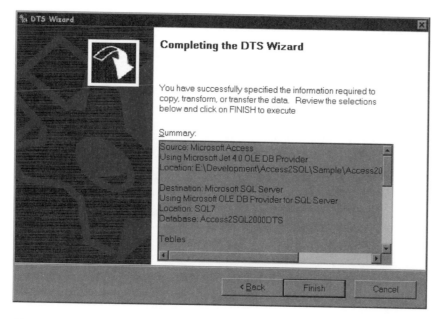

Figure 5-12. Completing the DTS Wizard

Using the DTS Designer

Creating a DTS package using the wizard is reasonably simple. However, you may run into difficulty when you want to do more than just a simple data transfer. This becomes more apparent when you want to define complex transformations for your data as it moves to SQL Server. The wizard does not include the best tools for writing transformation scripts. You only have the ability to edit the scripts as free-form text, and you cannot validate the script before it is run. Making an error in the script means that the transformation of a whole table can fail. Fortunately, there is a more robust scripting tool: the DTS Designer. The DTS Designer is the graphical tool within Enterprise Manager that is used to create and design DTS packages. It can be a little clumsy to work with at times, but is actually a very good tool for creating data migration processes.

One of the reasons that I recommended that you save your package instead of running it from the DTS wizard is that the package you created using the DTS wizard makes a very good example for demonstrating DTS Designer. It is much easier to understand the designer if you look at a package that you built because you already know what you wanted that package to do.

In order to access the designer, open Enterprise Manager, expand the Data Transformation Services folder under your server, and select the Local Packages item, as shown in Figure 5-13.

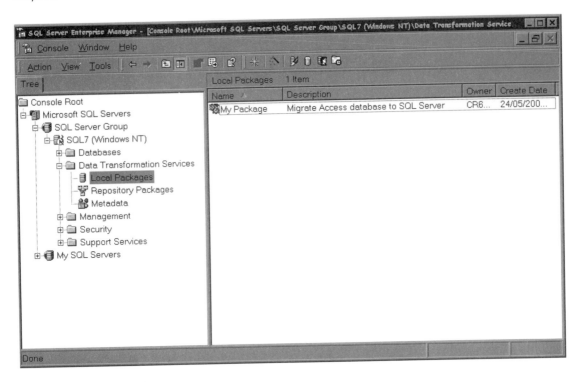

Figure 5-13. Local Packages

    The packages that currently exist on your server are listed in the right pane. If you saved your package earlier, it should be listed. Open it by double-clicking it or by right-clicking it and choosing Design Package from the context menu. You can also create a new package by right-clicking the right pane or by clicking on any of the DTS items and selecting New Package from the menu. Either way, one of these options will open a DTS Designer window within Microsoft Management Console (MMC). Open your migration package and look at it in the Designer. With a bit of reorganization, your package will look something like the one in Figure 5-14. The package is usually arranged automatically by SQL Server to show each item in a straight line. The layout can be a little puzzling, so you may want to reorganize the package as I have. You can do this by simply dragging items around in the DTS Designer using your mouse. I have also renamed a number of the objects to make the package easier to understand.

    This may look a bit confusing at first, but there is logic to it. Figure 5-14 illustrates a complete data transfer process from Access to SQL Server including the creation of objects as necessary in SQL Server. Each group of three objects is a single flow. These flows currently do not depend on each other, so they can be considered separately. To make this easier to analyze, let's look at only one flow shown in Figure 5-15.

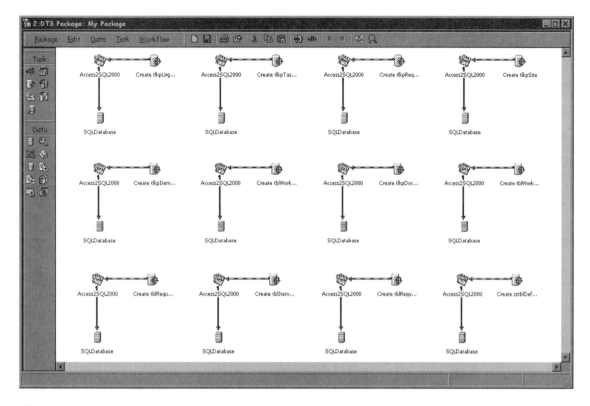

Figure 5-14. Package in DTS Designer

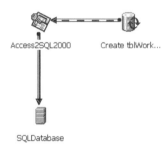

Figure 5-15. Single DTS Flow

The flow in this illustration includes two tasks, two connections, and one step. Let's first look at the item with the caption "Create tblWork…", which is the first task. Tasks define units of work within the package. As described earlier, there are many functions that you can use a task to accomplish, such as executing an application, running a script, or modifying data. In this case, the task is an Execute SQL task.

This type of task executes a SQL statement against one of the providers in the package. To see the properties of this item, simply double-click on it or right-click on it, and select Properties from the menu. The Properties of this particular task are shown in Figure 5-16.

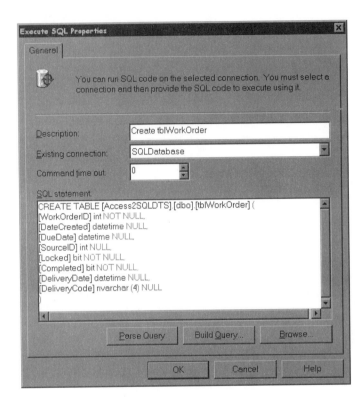

Figure 5-16. Execute SQL Properties

The task is set up to run against a connection called SQLDatabase (yours may be called something like "Connection2"), which we will look at shortly. The actual SQL statement that the task will run is a DDL statement that creates the table into which the data will be migrated. This was the option that was chosen when the wizard was run. Click Cancel to leave the definition.

The blue and white dashed arrow leading from this task is a step. Steps help define the flow of control within a package. The fact that the arrow is blue specifies that this is a completion step. This means that the next item in the flow takes place no matter what the result of the previous task was, but it is not initiated until the task is complete.

The step indicates the flow of control to a connection. This particular connection is to the Microsoft Access database being migrated. Because the Access OLE DB driver is used, the connection is represented with an Access icon. The icons used to represent different connections in the DTS designer will change depending on the type of data source they point to. This makes finding the right connection in your package much easier.

When you view the properties of the connection, as shown in Figure 5-17, you will notice that they look very similar to the properties that you set when the wizard was used. The options at the top of the property sheet allows you to specify that this is a new connection, or allows you to reuse one of the other connections that already exists in the package. You can click the Advanced button to view extended driver properties as you did in the wizard.

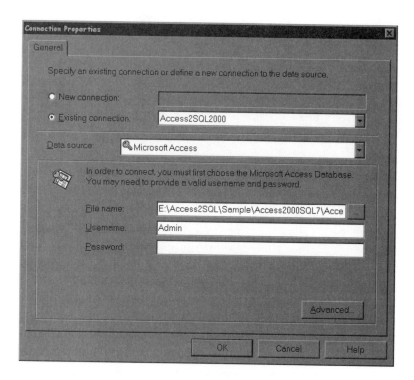

Figure 5-17. Access Connection Properties

The Access connection is linked to a SQL Server connection by a Transformation task. This task, represented by a solid black arrow, is where the actual importing of data occurs. Transformation tasks must be linked on each end to connection objects. You can view the properties of this transformation, as shown in Figure 5-18, by double-clicking the task arrow.

The properties of a transformation are quite numerous and are organized into four tabs. The Source tab contains information on the source of the data. The source connection is set to the connection at the beginning of the step's arrow and can only be modified by changing the connection in the Designer's main window.

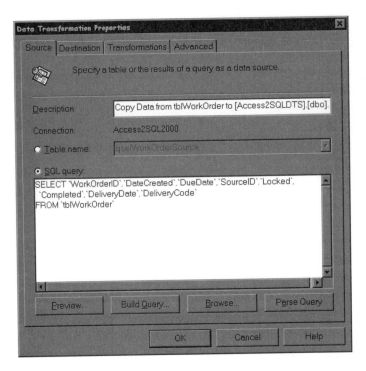

Figure 5-18. Source Transformation Properties

The source of the actual data is set to a table in the database to which the connection is linked or a valid SQL query. Commands are available from this screen to preview the results of the query, build it graphically, load a previously defined SQL file, or check the syntax of your SQL statement for errors.

The Destination tab displays the destination of the transformed data. See Figure 5-19.

If you attempt to view this tab before the table has been created, you will experience errors. However, you can create the table at this time using the Create New button or simply cancel your changes when you leave the properties dialog. Despite the messages you receive due to this problem, no changes will be made to the transformation if you leave the dialog by clicking the Cancel button. The only exception is that if you chose to create a table by clicking the Create New button, it will exist on SQL Server, so you should delete it from the SQL Server database if you want your package to run successfully. This is one of the small annoyances caused by the DTS Designer. However, if you create your tables in advance, this type of error will disappear.

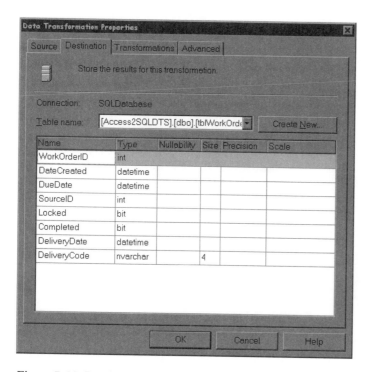

Figure 5-19. Destination Transformation Properties

The Transformations tab, shown in Figure 5-20, specifies the column mappings and transformation details that will be used. Once again, if the destination table does not already exist, you will receive an error, and you will be prompted with three choices:

- Remove invalid transformations

- Change source/destination

- Remove all transformations and redo auto mapping

Each of these choices sounds a little drastic. They all seem to ask you to throw away all of your work. Fortunately, as long as you cancel your changes to the transformation when you close the dialog box, no changes will be made. These three options only apply to the current transformation and not to the package as a whole (although the wording does make it seem that way).

The graphic on the Transformations tab displays the fields that will be mapped from the source to the destination. On this tab, you can define one of two transformation types: Copy Column or ActiveX Script. By choosing Copy Column, you specify that you want data directly copied from the source to the destination. No changes will be made to the data (other than changes due to data type differences, if they exist). If you select ActiveX Script, you must write a script that transforms the data

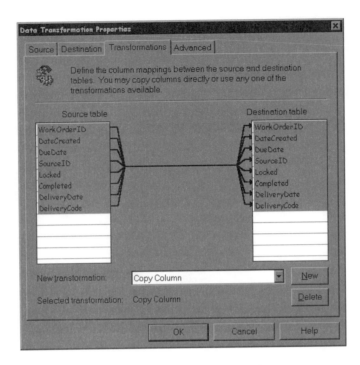

Figure 5-20. Transformation Column Mappings

as it is moved from the source to the destination. The script may be a simple copy operation, a very complex translate, summarize, and validate script, or any other action you can define using the scripting languages that DTS supports

To create a transformation, select the columns in the source and destination that you want to map to each other. If they already participate in a transformation, you must delete the transformation first. A transformation can be deleted by selecting the connection line (or lines) and clicking the Delete button. If there are multiple transformation lines shown between the source and destination tables, you must delete each one separately in order to clear the transformation for these fields. Select the necessary columns, and then select the transformation type that you will be running. Note that you do not have to select all columns on each side. If your migration requires it, you can choose to transform one field into many others, or vice versa. Click the New button to create the transformation.

If you selected Copy Columns from the New Transformation drop-down list, you should check the details of the transformation to ensure that the field mapping that DTS chose for you is correct. Double-click the transformation line to open the Column Order screen shown in Figure 5-21.

This screen allows you to choose the selected columns from the source table on the left and match them with the destination columns on the right. If the mapping shown is not the mapping you want, modify the mapping using the drop-down list of fields in the source or destination column. Click OK when you are done to save your changes.

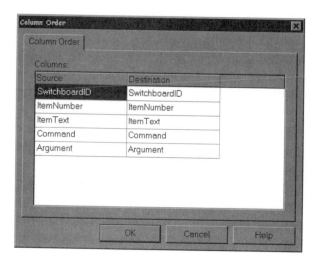

Figure 5-21. Column Order

If you selected ActiveX Script from the New Transformation drop-down list on the Transformations tab, you must now write a script to handle the transformation of the data. The screen that allows you to do this opens once the New button is pressed (see Figure 5-22).

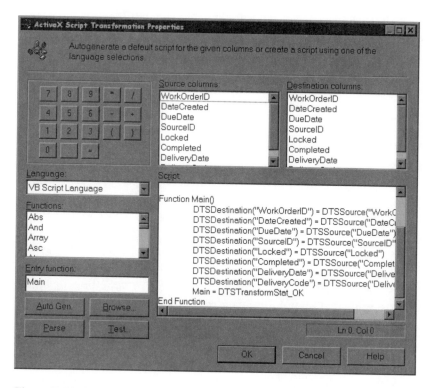

Figure 5-22. Transformation Script Editor

The script editor gives you a simple interface to create a script to translate your data. It provides access to all of the scripting functions and all of your source and destination fields. The default script presented simply copies data from one table to another. This form allows you to select functions or fields from your source or destination and copy them to the script. Double-clicking an item in the Functions, Source columns, or Destination columns list adds the code to refer to the column at the current cursor position in the script. Four command buttons are available on this screen.

The Auto Gen. button restores the original code created by DTS for a transformation. This can help you revert your script to a standard field by field copying of the data if you run into problems with your script.

The Browse button allows you to select a script file that you have already written and saved to disk. This button opens a standard Open dialog, so that you can browse to the location of the script file.

The Parse button checks your script for any scripting syntax errors. You should run this command each time you make changes to a script. It ensures that there are no obvious problems with your code.

The Test button allows you to test the script to ensure that it behaves as you expect it to. This button tests up to the first 200 records in your source data. A progression screen appears showing you the progress of your testing. When the test is complete, click on the View Results button on this dialog to view the data that resulted from the test. This data is not actually sent to the destination data source. It is only intended as a small sample of data to ensure that your transformation will succeed. Keep this in mind because it means that any database validation that takes place when the data is inserted into the destination database does not take place when the script is tested. You may still run into problems when the data is inserted into the real destination. Click Done to leave the test results screen when you are finished.

Once you have completed editing your script, you can return to the transformation properties and save your changes by clicking OK.

The final screen in the transformation properties gives you access to the more advanced properties of the transformation (see Figure 5-23).

The Advanced tab has three areas that can be customized for a transformation. The first defines how errors are handled. The Max error count allows you to define how many errors need to occur before the transformation is terminated. This can be useful if you are migrating a large table and don't want to worry about missing a few rows because their transformation caused errors. Setting the Max error count to a value that is appropriate for your transformation can help you to avoid canceling the transformation if a number of errors you specify occur. You can also have rows that caused errors logged to a file by entering the file name into the Exception file name box. The delimiters selected in the Row and Column drop-down lists are added to the end of each record as it is written to the error file.

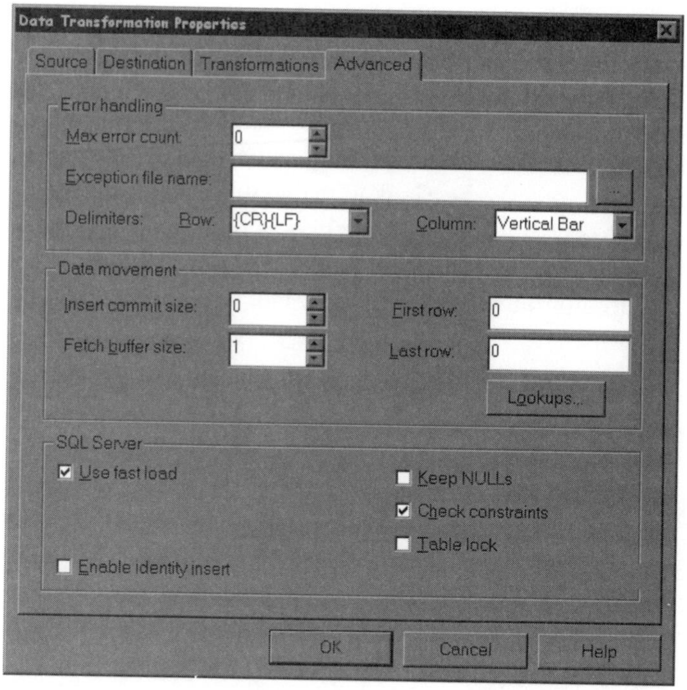

Figure 5-23. Advanced Transformation Properties

The default delimiters ({CR}{LF} for a row and vertical bar [|] for a column) put each record on a separate line and separate fields with a vertical bar when the exception file is read in a text editor like Notepad.

The next section on this tab, Data movement, allows you to define how data is transferred. By setting a value in the Insert commit size, you define how many rows are transformed before they are committed to the destination database. The default setting of 0 states that commit does not occur until all rows are transformed. If you set this to another value, new rows will be committed each time the number of rows you enter are transferred. This means that if you set this value to 100 and the transfer fails on the 203rd record, the transformation would stop, but the first 200 records would remain in the destination database.

The Fetch buffer size determines how many rows are fetched from the source at a time. You do not need to modify this setting when migrating Access data to SQL Server.

The First row and Last row settings allow you to define where the transformation starts and stops in the source. These can be useful for rerunning transformations that failed when the Insert commit size was set, so that you can bypass data that has successfully been loaded to the system.

A very important feature of the Data movement section is Lookups. Lookups are SQL queries that you can access from a transformation script to find information in the source or destination database. For example, suppose you are appending records from an Access table that contains autonumber fields. If you want to migrate these tables to SQL Server and you want SQL Server to rebuild the numbering from scratch, any records in other tables that have a foreign key relationship with this field will no longer be valid. The IDs associated with the parent table will have changed, and you will not be able to update the foreign tables with the IDs that SQL Server created. However, you can use a lookup to find the new ID in SQL Server as part of the script to migrate your foreign tables. This ID can then be used to set the new value of the foreign key column as part of a transformation script. When you click the Lookups button, the Data Transformation Lookups screen shown in Figure 5-24 appears.

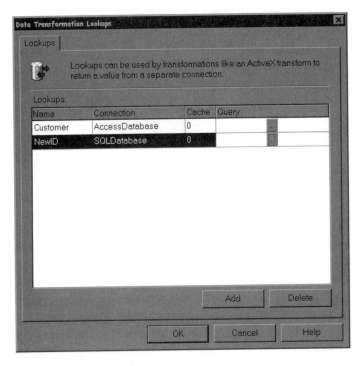

Figure 5-24. Data Transformation Lookups

Each lookup that you need for your script must be defined separately. To add a lookup to the list, click the Add button. A new row will appear in the list for which you must enter information. The first required piece of information you need to enter is a name for the lookup. This name must be unique for each transformation and is the name you will use in your script to refer to the lookup. Next, select a connection from the list to define which connection the query will take place against. The next item to set, Cache, allows you to optimize your lookup. This value sets the number of lookup results that DTS keeps in memory while the script is running. If the lookup you are using can only possibly return a few records, set the cache to the number of records your lookup can return. This allows DTS to perform a lookup for a value the first time the lookup is called, and then retain that value for future calls. If a result is cached, DTS uses the result in memory rather than rerunning the lookup. This process can dramatically improve the speed of a transformation. However, you should not use too high a number as the more items you have cached, the more memory the DTS package will require. I would recommend that you do not set this value higher than 20.

When you have entered all of the required information, click the builder (...) button in the row to build the query for your lookup. The builder opens the Data Transformation Services Query Designer shown in Figure 5-25.

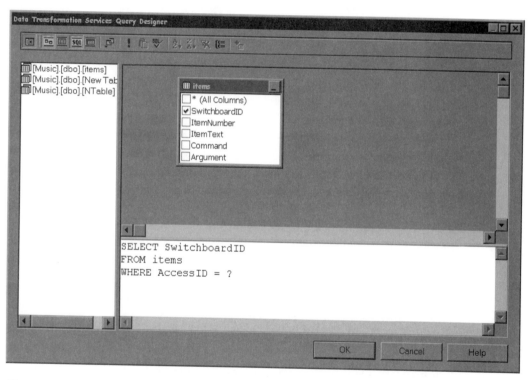

Figure 5-25. Data Transformation Services Query Designer

The query designer is very similar to the SQL Server Query Analyzer described in Chapter 1. You can drag a table from the list on the right to add it to the query, and select fields to include in the results by checking their names in the table details. Before you begin to build your query, however, you should know one very important detail about lookups—they can only return one row and one field to your script. This means that you can only select one field for your output, and that you must filter the results so that only one row is returned. You can define a query that returns multiple rows using this tool; however all but the first row and column will be ignored by your scripts.

You may be wondering how you can use a lookup to return the value you want if you are limited to a single item of data. The answer is that you can use parameters with lookups, just as you can with normal queries. However, lookups run using ADO. This means that you must use the ADO syntax for parameters, which is to use a question mark (?). The order in which you must provide these parameters to your lookup is the same as the order in which they are listed in the SQL pane. For example, if you want to obtain the new SQL ID from a table called tlkpDocumentTypes that contains two columns—TypeID and TypeName, you would need to provide the lookup with the TypeName in order to lookup the TypeID. The SQL string

```
SELECT TypeID
FROM tlkpDocumentTypes
WHERE TypeName = ?
```

could be used to define this lookup. You can test the query by clicking the Run function on the toolbar. You will then be prompted to manually enter the parameter value. We will look at how to use lookups in your scripts in the "Scripting" section later in this chapter.

Click OK when you are finished editing your lookup query to return to the Data Transformation Lookups screen. You can then add other lookups to your transformation if necessary or delete existing ones by highlighting them and clicking Delete. Click OK when you are done to return to the Advanced tab of the Data Transformation Properties screen.

The final section on the Advanced tab defines the SQL Server options that can be used with the transformation. The first selection, Use fast load, only applies if your destination connection is a SQL Server OLE DB connection. It allows faster inserts into SQL Server by turning off SQL Server logging. This means that data is inserted into the tables without maintaining the transaction log. This increases the speed of the inserts, but you should be careful because it also means that if your server crashes while the package is running, any changes you made to the database from the package will be lost. When you select the Use fast load option, three other options are enabled: Keep Nulls, Check constraints, and Table lock.

Keeping Nulls allows you to leave empty fields as nulls. Normally, these fields might be converted to zero-length strings, especially when imported from text files. This option is best left on, so that if Null values are found in the data you are importing, they will not be changed when they are imported.

Selecting Check constraints tells the import to enable table constraint checking. By turning this option off, constraints are not validated against the data and some data may not meet the requirements you have defined for your SQL Server tables. Turning this option off increases the speed of the inserts, but your data may not meet the requirements of your database.

Table lock specifies that the fast load operation should lock the entire table, so that no other users can access it until the operation is complete. If you can be sure that no other users will need to access the table when your package is running, enable this option. It reduces the amount of lock tracking that SQL Server must handle. Instead of having to lock each record as it is accessed, SQL Server can lock the entire table in a single operation and unlock it when the work is done.

The last option, Enable identity insert, is similar to the same option in the DTS wizard. It allows you to insert your own numbers in identity columns for the duration of the transformation. It can be useful for migrating Jet AutoNumber fields to SQL Server while preserving their values.

When you are finished working with your transformation, click OK to save your changes and return to the DTS Designer, or click Cancel if you want to cancel transformation changes made if an error occurred.

In addition, the transformation has another set of properties that can be accessed by right-clicking on it and selecting the Workflow Properties. A full understanding of these properties is beyond the scope of this book, but feel free to explore the two tabs on this screen and consult the Help for information on what each option does. Return to the DTS Designer when you are done.

The final item in this workflow is a connection to SQL Server. You can view the properties of this item by double-clicking on it. The Connection Properties screen shown in Figure 5-26 appears.

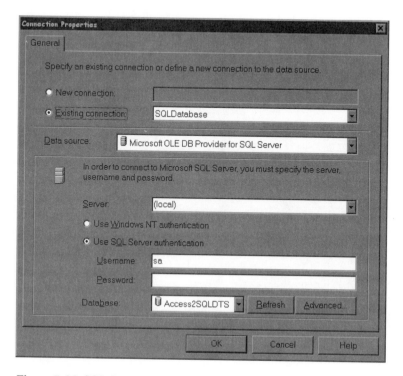

Figure 5-26. SQL Connection Properties

The connection name is similar to the name used for the Access connections. The data source selected defines what information is necessary to be filled in. This information should be identical to the information you entered when using the wizard.

Defining Precedence

One of the main issues in using the DTS wizard is that it does not check relationships when it builds a package. Because of this, the package attempts to load all tables simultaneously. And, because your database may contain relationships, this is not the desired behavior. Using the DTS designer, you can set up your package so that the loading of data into child tables is dependent on the successful loading of the parent tables. The easiest way to do this is to first select the last connection in the parent table load, and then select the first step in the child table load while holding down the control key. Then, from the Workflow menu, select On Success. This will create precedence for the selection actions. With all of the necessary precedence set for the example in Figure 5-14, the new package might look like Figure 5-27.

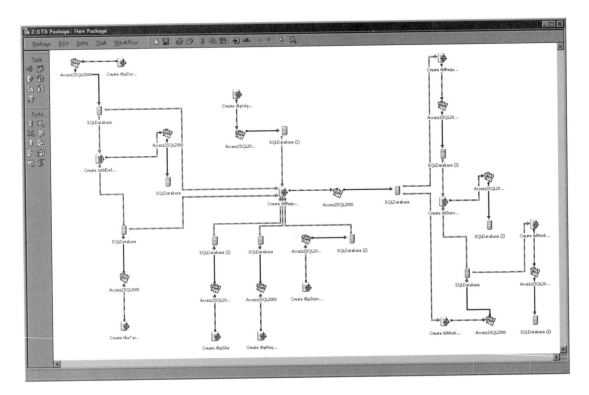

Figure 5-27. Package with precedence

This new package ensures that all parent tables are loaded before child tables are loaded. These settings are a very good idea when the tables you are loading your data to are already created with relationships that prevent child tables from being loaded before parent tables.

Relationships are not the only place that precedence can be used. You could use precedence to handle cases where errors occur during your load. You could use an On Failure step to run a cleanup of all the previously completed steps. Or, you could also have a step direct the flow to run a task that calls an executable. The definition of the precedence is really up to you, and it can be customized as much as necessary.

Let's look at a simple example to help you understand how steps can be useful to you in migrating Access data to SQL Server. In this example, you have three tables that must be migrated:

- *tblCustomer*: Contains a list of customers and some information about them.

- *tblOrder*: Contains a list of orders placed by customers.

- *tblOrderDetail*: Contains the detail information for each order.

In this scenario, the primary key in tblCustomer (CustomerID) is related to a foreign key in tblOrder. This means that in order for the data in tblOrder to mean anything and in order to avoid referential integrity problems, tblCustomer must be loaded before tblOrder is loaded. Also, the primary key in tblOrder (OrderID) is related to a foreign key in tblOrderDetail. This relationship means that tblOrder must be loaded before tblOrderDetail. One of the problems you have when you are creating this package is that you are not allowed to load the data while any users are in the system. This restriction means that you must run the package after hours. You really don't want to stay after work (you have an important dinner to attend), so you must schedule the package to run while you aren't at work. Because this is a very important job and it must be done that evening, you need to be notified if the job fails. Fortunately, you have a cell phone that has email capabilities. You'll need to have SQL Server email you if anything goes wrong. You'll also want to know at exactly what point the migration failed, so you can decide how long you will need to fix the problem (maybe you can even sleep in). And just for good measure, you want to receive notification that the job completed successfully. Finally, if the job fails, you want to lock out all users until you can fix the problem. The logic for the package you want to create might look like the following pseudocode:

```
LOCK database
LOAD tblCustomer
if tblCustomer loaded successfully
    LOAD tblOrder
    if tblOrder loaded successfully
        LOAD tblOrderDetails
        if tblOrderDetail loaded successfully
            UNLOCK database
            SENDMAIL "Success!!!"
        else (tblOrderDetail load failed)
            SENDMAIL "Loading of tblOrderDetail failed :-{"
        end
    else (tblOrder load failed)
        SENDMAIL "Loading of tblOrder failed :-("
    end
else (tblCustomer load failed)
    SENDMAIL "Loading of tblCustomer failed >8-@"
end
```

Analyzing this logic, you will find that there are a number of tasks you need in your package:

- *2 Execute SQL Tasks*: To lock and unlock the database using a SQL command.

- *3 Transformations*: One for each table load.

- *6 Connections*: One Access and one SQL Server for each transformation.

- *4 Send Mail Tasks*: One for each email that could be sent.

Once you know the logic of your package and what objects you need, creating the package is reasonably simple. The end result should look something like Figure 5-28.

The flow of this package runs clockwise starting at the top left. You can see from this package exactly how you would define precedence using steps. This example is quite simple. Your real-world situation is likely much more complex. However, understanding how to use steps in your package can help you to build a complex package that handles the logic of your application.

Scripting

One of the most powerful functionalities of DTS is its capability to use scripting to manage the transformation of data. Scripts can be built using any ActiveX compliant scripting language. However, because Microsoft Access uses Visual Basic for

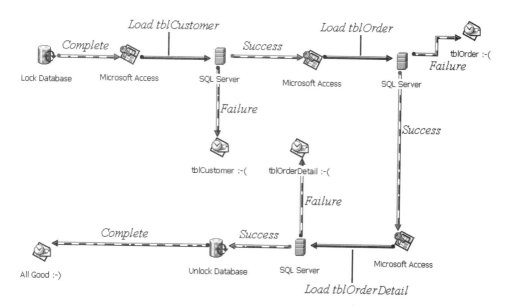

Figure 5-28. Linked DTS package

Applications (VBA) as its native language, you are probably already familiar with the VBA syntax and language constructs. VBScript and VBA are very similar, so you can leverage your background in VBA to get a jump on VBScript. VBScript, originally designed for use over the Internet, is a scripting language based on Visual Basic . It can be used in DTS to define how data is transformed between a source connection and a destination. VBScript can be used to run a customized function outside of the DTS environment. And, it can be used to automate the process of creating DTS packages from outside of SQL Server, although a discussion of this capability is beyond the scope of this book. Let's look at the more common uses for scripting in a simple transformation.

There are three main collections within a DTS transformation that are used by scripts. Table 5-1 lists these collections and their purposes.

Table 5-1. DTS Transformation Collections

COLLECTION	PURPOSE
DTSSource	Provides access to the source fields in the DTS transformation.
DTSDestination	Provides access to the destination fields in the DTS transformation.
DTSLookups	Provides access to the lookups defined for a DTS transformation.

In order to understand how these objects are used, take a look at a relatively simple transformation script that uses each of these objects:

```
Function Main()
    DTSDestination("ItemID") = DTSSource("ItemID")
    DTSDestination("RequestID") = DTSSource("RequestID")
    DTSDestination("UrgencyID") = DTSSource("UrgencyID")
    If DTSSource("DueDate") < #01/01/1753# Then
        DTSDestination("DueDate") = #01/01/1900#
    Else
        DTSDestination("DueDate") = DTSSource("DueDate")
    End If
    DTSDestination("DocumentNumber") = DTSSource("DocumentNumber")
    If Not IsNull( DTSSource("ReasonID") ) Then
        DTSDestination("RequestReason") = _
            DTSLookups("Resn").Execute(DTSSource("ReasonID").Value)
    End If
    DTSDestination("Comment") = DTSSource("Comment")
    DTSDestination("SourceID") = DTSSource("SourceID")
    DTSDestination("AssignedTo") = DTSSource("AssignedTo")
    Main = DTSTransformStat_OK
End Function
```

This function, partially created by the wizard, copies the data from an Access database to SQL Server, ensures that the dates in Access do not cause errors, and uses a lookup to update the RequestReason field with data from another table.

The basic language used to access a field in a DTS source connection is DTS-Source("FieldName"), where FieldName is the name of a field in the source table. Likewise, the language used to access the data in or set the value of a field in the destination connection is DTSDestination("FieldName"). These constructs are the basis for all DTS VBScript transformations. If you examine the sample code, you will see that most of the fields are directly copied from the source to the destination using the code

```
DTSDestination("FieldName") = DTSSource("FieldName")
```

because they do not require validation or modification of any kind. However, two cases in this example use customized code instead of the default direct mapping. The first case is used on the DueDate field, which is an Access Date/Time field. Because you cannot store dates before January 1, 1753 in a SQL Server datetime field, a few lines have been added to verify that the data being transformed does not cause the transformation to fail. The code

```
If DTSSource("DueDate") < #01/01/1753# Then
    DTSDestination("DueDate") = #01/01/1900#
Else
    DTSDestination("DueDate") = DTSSource("DueDate")
End If
```

checks the value in the field and replaces it with a default value if the date is earlier than the range that SQL Server can handle. Otherwise, it directly copies the data from the source to the destination as with the other field.

The second case, where a lookup table is not being used in SQL Server, is handled with the code:

```
If Not IsNull( DTSSource("ReasonID") ) Then
    DTSDestination("RequestReason") = _
      DTSLookups("Resn").Execute(DTSSource("ReasonID").Value)
End If
```

This piece of code performs a couple of functions. First, it checks to ensure that the field is not null. This is necessary because DTSLookups cannot handle null values in their parameters. Second, it retrieves the value from the lookup query passing in the current ID used for the field in Access. The SQL for the lookup "Resn" is

```
SELECT ReasonDesc
FROM tlkpRequestReason
WHERE ReasonID = ?
```

When you create a lookup for a DTS transformation, you usually want to use parameters for that query. Any parameters you want to use must be represented by question marks. A lookup query can have as many parameters as necessary, but when you call the lookup in your code, you must provide the necessary parameters in the order they appear in the query. The language used to run a lookup and return its value is DTSLookups("LookupName").Execute([Parameter1], [Parameter2],…, [ParameterN]). If your lookup returns more than one field, you must assign it to a variable. This variable then becomes a zero-based array that you can use to access the values of the various fields in your lookup query.

Each item within the DTSSource and DTSDestination collections also has its own properties. These properties, outlined in Table 5-2, are based on ADO Field object properties and expose some useful information for each field.

Table 5-2. DTS Field Properties

PROPERTY	PURPOSE
ActualSize	Actual length of the data contained in a field.
Attributes	Extended properties of the field: combination of `FieldAttributeEnum` constants.
DefinedSize	Maximum defined length of the field in the database.
Name	Name of the field.
NumericScale	Number of decimal places to which a number in a field will be resolved.
OriginalValue	Value originally stored in the field when the data was retrieved from the database.
Precision	Maximum number of digits that are used for a number in a field.
Recordset	A recordset object that the current record belongs to.
Type	Data type of the field: one of the ADO `DataTypeEnum` constants.
UnderlyingValue	Value currently stored in the database for a field.
Value	Value assigned to the field object in the current context.

In addition to these properties of each field, the collections themselves have one property: Count. The Count property returns the number of fields in the collection. Incorporating some of these properties, you could build a simpler generic script for direct copying of fields, as shown in the following code:

```
Function Main()
    Dim varI
    For varI = 1 To DTSSource.Count
        DTSDestination(DTSSource(varI).Name) = DTSSource(varI)
    Next
    Main = DTSTransformStat_OK
End Function
```

This script uses the Count property to loop through each of the fields in the source connection. It then uses the name of that field to set the value of a field with the same name in the destination connection. This code works if the names of the fields in each database are identical. However, it fails if a field name in the source does not exist in the destination connection.

At this point, you may notice that there is one portion of all of these scripts that we have not looked at, and that is the return value. What is it and what does it do?

DTS provides a number of constants that you should use when you want to change how the transformation of a record occurs. Some of these constants are useful in scripting transformations. These constants, listed in Table 5-3, can be used as return codes from a transformation script to tell DTS what the status is of the row that is being transferred to the destination connection.

Table 5-3. Selected DTS Transformation Return Values

CONSTANT	PURPOSE
DTSTransformStat_OK	Processed successfully, continue as necessary.
DTSTransformStat_SkipRow	Do not commit changes to destination and continue on next source record.
DTSTransformStat_SkipFetch	Do not fetch the next row. Use this same source row for the next run of the transformation, but go on to a new destination row.
DTSTransformStat_SkipInsert	Do not advance to the next destination row in the next run, but do use the next source row.
DTSTransformStat_Error	Error occurred, handle according to package/task error settings.
DTSTransformStat_ErrorSkipRow	Same as DTSTransformStat_Error except row is not logged to file if task is configured to do this.
DTSTransformStat_AbortPump	Error occurred, abort current task entirely and roll back all changes since last commit.
DTSTransformStat_NoMoreRows	Do not process subsequent rows.

These codes can be very useful for ensuring that only the data that is necessary for the system is transformed and that critical errors in the data are not committed to the server. They can also be used to control the flow of the package. By defining whether your task completes with or without an error, steps will send the flow of control in the package in the appropriate direction.

It is likely that you can see a situation in which you might want to use most of these constants. The two that may not seem to have an easy application are DTSTransformStat_SkipFetch and DTSTransformStat_SkipInsert. For this reason, they require a bit more explanation. They both affect how the transformation will change records on the next run against a row in the database.

The first constant, DTSTransformStat_SkipFetch, performs two functions. It tells DTS to commit the changes made to the current destination record and open a new destination record on the next pass, as normal execution would. It also tells DTS not to advance the current source record. This means that you can create multiple records in your destination based on a single source record. In an Access to SQL migration, this may not be very useful.

The second constant, DTSTransformStat_SkipInsert, works in the opposite way to DTSTransformStat_SkipFetch. It tells DTS to commit the changes to the current destination record, but not to advance to a new record on the next pass. It also tells DTS to advance the current source record, as normal. This means that you can create aggregate rows on SQL Server that are comprised of multiple Access records. All you have to do is use the value of the field in the DTSDestination collection with values in the DTSSource collection and assign those values to the destination.

These two constants can lead to some very complex situations, and I would recommend that you only use them if you are very comfortable with DTS. Otherwise, try to create SQL statements in your tasks that achieve the desired effect.

Using DTS with the Upsizing Wizard

At this point, you know all that you need to in order to use DTS properly. But you may be wondering where DTS fits when performing an Access to SQL Server migration. DTS can take over a large part of the functionality previously provided in the wizard, especially if your database design has some changes that must take place along the way.

The best way to use DTS in a migration is as a tool to move your data into tables already created on SQL Server. DTS is not a robust tool for analyzing and migrating table definitions. However, creating and migrating table definitions can be easily managed with the upsizing wizard. By using DTS to manage your data transfer, you can save and rerun packages without losing table definitions. You can also automate the clearing of tables through DTS, so that the data will be upsized without duplication, and control the order in which tables are populated.

You can use DTS to modify data as it is inserted into SQL Server to conform to new rules you may have created in the SQL Server database. It is also the best tool to use if your table structure changes in any way. If you know how your data needs to be modified in the migration, you should be able to program those changes into your DTS packages.

One of the true strengths of DTS is its capability to define an order of execution. Using steps, you can ensure that the package flows as you need it to, accounting for restrictions in the database design.

If you are in doubt as to how a portion of a DTS package will perform, create a simple package and try it out with a test database. This type of action can often tell you more about DTS than the documentation does.

A Final Word about DTS

DTS is an extremely powerful tool. It is designed to manage the process of moving data between different data sources. But that is only the beginning of what it can do. If you want to make historical data available for reporting purposes, but do not need to retain this information in your application database, you can use DTS to automate the process of migrating archive data to a data warehouse. Reports can then be designed to run off the warehouse database, so that the performance of your application database is not affected.

DTS can also be used to handle migration of data from SQL Server to an Access database. This allows you to disconnect your data from the server, so that mobile users can run reports without being connected to your network. You can even design a DTS package to run the other way and allow users to update data and synchronize it with the SQL Server database when they reconnect to the network (although you would normally use SQL Server replication for this).

Your real need for DTS arises when you want to migrate an Access database to SQL Server. By combining the strengths of DTS with the strengths of the Upsizing Wizard, you can design a powerful tool to aid in your migration.

CHAPTER 6

Using SQL Server 6.5

THE DIFFERENCES BETWEEN SQL Server and Microsoft Access result in not being able to just jump from one system to another very easily. Consequently, you need to understand how to use SQL Server.

SQL Server can be administered using text-based SQL commands. These commands can be extremely difficult to master and are aimed at users that have extensive knowledge of the system as well as a full understanding of what these commands are capable of (i.e., trained database administrators). Fortunately for us Access users, SQL Server has graphical interfaces to perform many of these administration tasks. These interfaces can make administrative functions accessible for just about anyone. Because these utilities can handle most of what we need to do to migrate to and maintain an application in SQL Server, I will concentrate on the graphical, rather than on the textual commands, that are available to you.

No single chapter can do the administrative functionality in SQL Server justice. Because there is so much that can be done within SQL Server, I can only hope to introduce you to some of the basic concepts you will need to know for your migration. This chapter introduces you to the core concepts of how to manage the different objects within SQL Server 6.5 and how this management pertains to you, the developer.

Using SQL Server 6.5

The graphical administration utility for SQL Server 6.5 is called SQL Enterprise Manager, and it can be found in your SQL Server Utilities group on your Start menu. When you start Enterprise Manager, the application automatically opens the Server Manager window (see Figure 6-1), showing you a list of each of the server groups you have created and all of the servers registered within each group.

To see the different categories of administration within a particular server, you can expand the server name by clicking on the plus (+) sign beside it, as you would with any other tree view component in Windows. For a description of each area of administration and instructions on how to add your server if it is not already listed, see "Using Enterprise Manager (SQL 6.5)" in Chapter 1.

Within Enterprise Manager, you have the ability to create all of the objects that your database requires. You also have the ability to fully administer your servers and any databases that they contain.

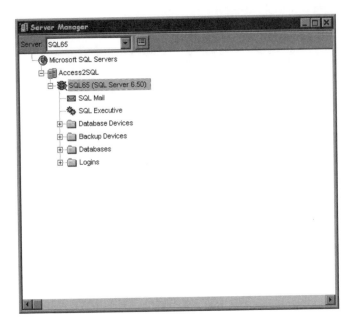

Figure 6-1. Server Manager

Managing Devices

Before you can create a database or back up an existing database, you must create the devices that will house these databases and backup objects. Devices are operating system-level files that contain a database, its logs, or a database backup. There are two types of devices that you will find in SQL Server 6.5:

- *Database devices* are used to hold database and transaction logs. Each database or transaction log can be spread over multiple devices. A single device can also house multiple databases.

- *Dump devices* are used to store database backups. A single backup device can house multiple backups from multiple databases.

When you create a device, SQL Server creates a physical file on disk according to the specifications that you provide. The size of a device, as far as SQL Server's automated tools are concerned, is static and can only be changed with user intervention. Although you can enlarge a device if necessary, you cannot reduce the size of a device. You should ensure that you make the devices large enough for the data being housed on them, but not so large that they interfere with other system requirements. For a complete discussion on choosing a device size, see "Device Selection" in Chapter 4.

Database Devices

There are two ways to administer database devices in Enterprise Manager. The first option is to choose Database Devices from the Manage menu. This displays the database device manager shown in Figure 6-2.

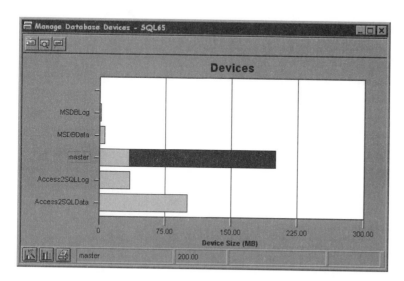

Figure 6-2. Manage Database Devices

This utility shows the devices that are currently configured on the system and their implementation. By hovering the mouse over the different devices (represented as bars), you can see the configuration of that device including how much of the device is already allocated to databases. Used space is represented in blue on the left side of the graph's bar and unused space on the device is represented in brown on the right side of the bar. The layout of the graph can be changed or the whole graph printed using the command buttons at the bottom left of the screen. Three buttons in the toolbar allow you to administer the database devices. The first button allows you to create a new device, the second allows you to edit the definition of the selected device, and the third allows you to delete a device.

The other method of administering database devices is through the right-click menu from items within the Database Devices group in the Server Manager window. You can create a new device by clicking on any item within the group or the group itself and selecting New Device from the right-click menu. You can edit or delete an existing device by selecting the device from the list in Server Manager and choosing the appropriate option from the right-click menu. You can also bring up the device manager window by selecting Edit from the right-click menu for the Database Devices group.

Creating a Database Device

When you choose to create a device, you are presented with the screen shown in Figure 6-3.

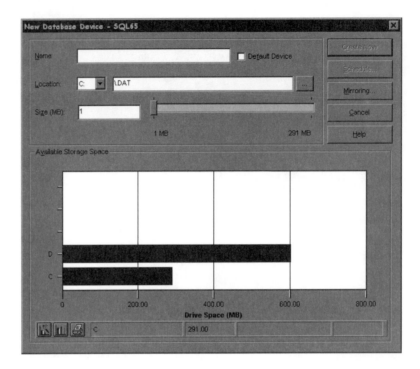

Figure 6-3. New Database Device

The first piece of information you need to provide is the device name. This is the name that will appear in Server Manager under the database devices and is the name that you will use to refer to this device for all actions against it. Selecting the Default device option makes this database the default device, which is automatically selected when a database or transaction log is created and no device name is specified. Do not set this option unless you are experienced with SQL Server and understand the implications of this choice.

Next, you must enter a location for the database device as a complete path name. By default, the device file has a DAT file extension, and the file name is the same as the device name you selected. Select the drive you want to use, and enter the folder or file name. The location you select is the location relative to the SQL Server installation. If you are administering a remote server, these locations are on the remote server, not the local computer.

The final piece of required information to create the device is the size of the device. When the device is created, the file created will automatically take up that amount of space on disk. Therefore, you should use the graph at the bottom of the screen to ensure that you are leaving sufficient free space on a drive for other devices or for operating system use. You can set the size of the device by typing in the size in megabytes in the appropriate box, or you can set it by moving the slider.

Before you create the device, there is one last option that should be addressed: Mirroring. The Mirroring button allows you to mirror a database device in a MIR file. Selecting this option creates an exact duplicate of your device in another location, including any databases placed on the device and any of the data they contain. This is used to ensure that a database can be recovered, even in a case of hard disk failure, provided of course, that you create the MIR on a different physical drive than the device. By mirroring your device on another physical drive, you can ensure that your database will not be corrupted if one hard disk fails. The server will use the mirror device instead (assuming the disk that fails is not the one SQL Server is installed on). Mirroring is a very basic way of ensuring that your system can always be recovered in case of error.

When you are finished specifying your options to create the device, you can then create the device immediately, or schedule the creation of the device to occur later. Scheduling the device to be created later allows you to avoid taking up valuable server resources while users are online. If you choose to schedule the process for a later time, the server opens a window, allowing you to specify when this action should occur (see Figure 6-4).

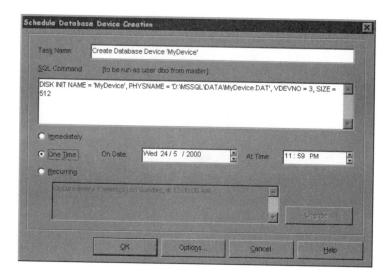

Figure 6-4. Schedule Database Device Creation

Scheduling the device creation creates a new SQL Executive scheduled task. This task can be set to occur once or multiple times. Because you only want to create a device once, you should set the scheduling option to One Time. The text that appears in the SQL Command text box shows the actual Transact-SQL statement that will be used to create the device. This command is the SQL command for creating the device with the options that you specified.

Editing a Database Device

When you edit a database device, only a few of the device properties can be modified (see Figure 6-5).

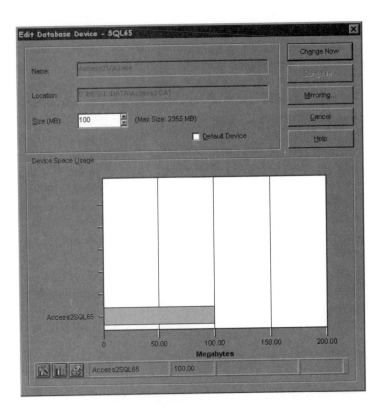

Figure 6-5. Edit Database Device

The name and location of the device cannot be modified after the device has been created. The only way to change this information is to delete the device and create a new one.

You can change the size of the device by entering the new size in the size box or by using the scrolling arrows to change the value. However, keep in mind that you cannot reduce the size of a device; you can only make it larger. You can change whether or not this device is the default device and mirror or unmirror the device. As with the creation of the device, you can schedule these actions to be implemented later.

Deleting a Database Device

When you delete a device, you are automatically prompted to confirm the deletion. If your device does not contain a database or transaction log, you are prompted with a simple Yes/No dialog. If your device contains any databases or logs, you are prompted to delete the entire database or databases held on that log (see Figure 6-6).

Figure 6-6. Delete Non-Empty Device

Databases cannot survive without their devices, so when you delete a device, any databases that use that device are removed from the system. Be extremely careful when you use the Delete Device function.

When you delete a device, the physical file that the device is stored in is not removed from the operating system. This can cause your hard disks to fill up with unused files. When you delete a device from SQL Server, ensure that you delete the physical file in which it was stored.

Backup Devices

Backup devices are managed directly from Server Manager. All actions that you want to perform against them are available by right-clicking a backup device or the Backup Devices folder.

Creating Backup Devices

You can create a backup device by selecting New Backup Device from the right-click menu (see Figure 6-7).

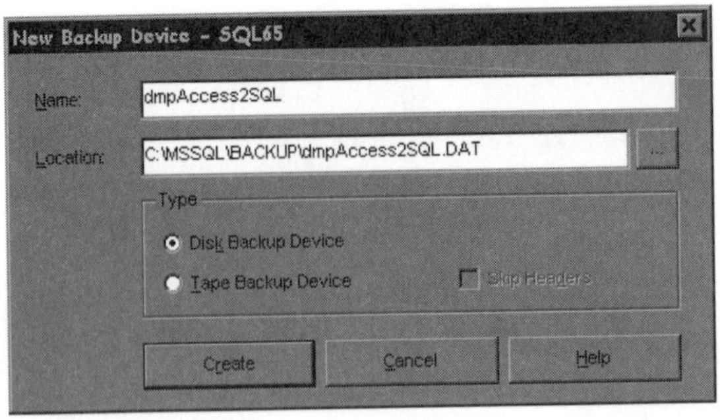

Figure 6-7. New Backup Device

You will be prompted to enter a name for the device. This name will appear in the Backup Devices folder. You must also specify a path to the file in which this device will be stored. A default path and file name are listed for you, but you can select a different directory on the server by browsing the folders using the button to the right of the Location box. When you select a location for your backup device, it is best to place it on a drive other than the one that holds the database you are backing up. This reduces the risk of losing your database due to a hard disk failure. If the drive that houses your database fails, you can still restore your database from the backup drive. And if the drive where your backups are located is damaged, your database will continue to function.

You are also prompted for the type of backup device—disk or tape. Disk backups store the file directly on a hard disk. Tape backups are designed to back up SQL Server data directly to a tape backup system. However, there are problems with tape backups in SQL Server 6.5, so I recommend that you do not use them. Instead, you should back up to disk, and then use a separate utility to copy the disk devices to tape.

Once you have entered all of the necessary information, click Create to create the device immediately.

Managing Databases

Each SQL Server system can house up to 32,767 databases. Each of these databases must be stored on the computer (or computer cluster) on which SQL Server is installed. This should satisfy the requirements of most Access programmers who are moving an application to SQL Server.

Before you begin your migration, you should understand how to manage your databases. As with database devices, there are two ways that databases can be managed in SQL Enterprise Manager. The first is by selecting Databases from the Manage menu. This displays the Manage Databases graphical interface, shown in Figure 6-8, which allows you to manage all of the databases on your server.

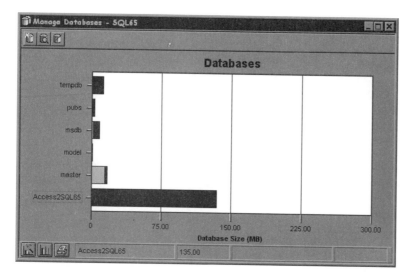

Figure 6-8. Manage Databases

This window is very similar to the window for managing devices. A number of options appear at the bottom of the screen to configure how the graph is shown. Moving your mouse over bars representing the different databases shows you the amount of space used and the amount of free space in those databases. You can create a new database using the New Database command on the toolbar. You can edit a database and its properties using the Edit Database command on the toolbar. You can delete a database using the Delete Database button on the toolbar.

The other method of managing databases is through the Server Manager window. By expanding the Databases section, you are able to manage all of the databases on the selected server through the right-click context menu items.

Creating a Database

When you choose the command to create a database, the Create Database window, shown in Figure 6-9, appears.

This screen shows two main sections. The top section is where you define the main properties of your database. The bottom section shows you the database devices that are configured on your system and how much space is available on each device. It will also show you how your selections will affect these devices.

You must first provide a name for your database in the Name field. This name must follow the naming conventions for objects in SQL Server. This name will appear in Server Manager under the Databases section. The option listed beside the name—Create for Load—is used if you are creating a database that is designed solely for restoring a backup. Only one user can use this type of database at a time,

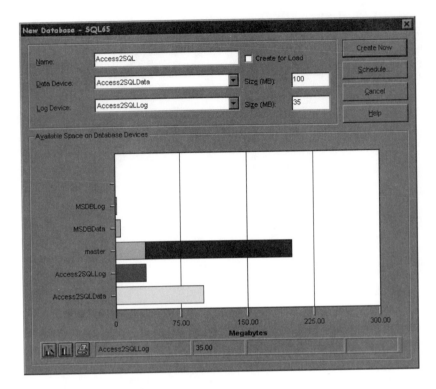

Figure 6-9. New Database

and that user must be the database owner. Do not select this option if you are creating a database for normal use.

The next two settings that you must fill in define the devices that should be used for the database and the transaction log. If you have not created the necessary devices, you can do so at this time by selecting the <new> item in the drop-down list. This will display the Create Database Device window described earlier. Once you have selected a device for your database or transaction log, the size of the database or log will automatically be configured to the same size as the amount of unused space on the selected device. You can change the default size by manually editing the value in the Size field.

The Log Device drop-down list includes a "(none)" option, which is not included in the Database Device drop-down list. Selecting this choice causes the database and transaction log to share the same device. However, placing the log on the same database on the same device isn't a good idea because the log cannot be backed up separately from the database and performance can be adversely affected because SQL Server cannot optimize the log and database individually. It is always best to keep your database and transaction log on separate devices.

Once you have configured the settings, you can create the database immediately by clicking Create Now, or you can schedule the database creation for a later time by selecting the Schedule button. Scheduling a database creation displays the same window as the scheduler used in creating a device. See Figure 6-4. The Transact-SQL statement that is used to create the database will be shown in the schedule window when the schedule dialog displays.

Editing a Database

The edit database dialog is divided into three tabs: database size and device configuration, database options, and database security permissions. See Figure 6-10.

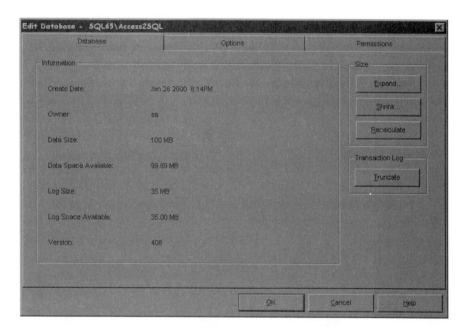

Figure 6-10. Database tab in Edit Database

On the Database tab, you can see when the database was created and who owns it as well as the size and amount of free space for the database and the log. From this screen you can resize the database and manage the log. All of the database information is shown in the box on the left. The size information on this screen can be refreshed using the Recalculate button if necessary.

It is likely that one of your databases will grow to where the size of the database is insufficient for your data. When this situation arises, you can use the Expand button on this screen to increase the size of your database. You will then be prompted for the device information, much as you were in the Create Database window. Keep in mind that you do not need to store the entire database on one device. A single database can reside on as many devices as are necessary. You can also use this command to expand the size of the transaction log if necessary.

Despite the fact that there is a Shrink button on this tab, you cannot shrink your database. When you create a database on a database device, the size of that database can never be reduced. If you need to make the database itself smaller, you must create a new, smaller database, copy the old database over, and then delete the old database. The Shrink button allows you to reduce the amount of space allocated to the transaction log. This does reduce the total disk requirements of your database, but only by making the log smaller. The log also cannot be resized below 1MB.

The final option on the tab allows you to truncate the transaction log. This means that the log is cleared of all entries and space in the log is freed up. This function is useful when the log is getting full. If the log fills up without being truncated, the database stops and users are not able to access it until the log has been cleared. When you truncate the log, you lose the ability to restore your database properly. For this reason, you should ensure that you back up your database immediately after running this command.

The Options tab in the Edit Database window allows you to set different database options (see Figure 6-11).

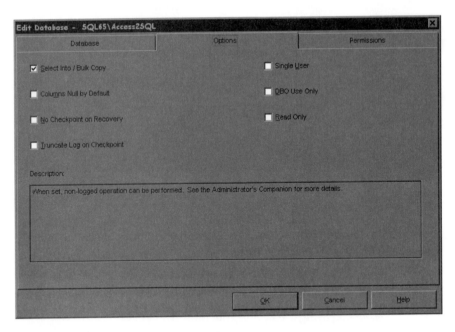

Figure 6-11. Options tab in Edit Database

There are seven configurable options for the database. When an option is selected on this screen, a description of the purpose of that option is shown in the box at the bottom. Usually, you will not have to change the default settings. The main option that you may want to configure from this screen is the DBO Use Only option.

This tells SQL Server that only the database owner can use the database. This is a very good way to ensure that users cannot get into the database if you are modifying objects or running maintenance.

The final screen in the Edit Database window, the Permissions tab, allows you to define the database security permissions (see Figure 6-12).

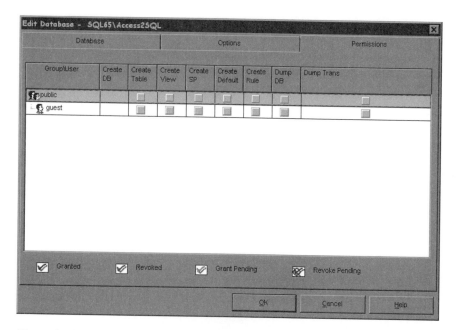

Figure 6-12. Permissions tab in Edit Database

This tab allows you to define the rights users have for creating objects within the database and whether they can back up (dump) the database and transaction logs. These rights can be assigned or revoked on a group and/or on a user basis. You can allow a group certain rights, but explicitly grant or revoke those rights for individual users within that group. Unless specified, a user's rights are the same as the rights of the group of which they are a member. You cannot grant rights for a user to delete objects within a database. Only the object owner, database owner, or system administrator has the rights to delete individual objects in the database.

Deleting a Database

When you choose to delete a database, that database is permanently removed from the system. You are given only one chance to stop the deletion. Use the function to delete a database with caution. If you have a valid backup of the database, it may be possible to restore the database. However, all changes that you made to the database between the time you backed it up and the time you deleted it are lost.

Managing Logins

Security in SQL Server can be configured to use one or both of two authentication methods: SQL Server authentication or NT authentication. SQL Server authentication requires that you create users within SQL Server and configure them using the utilities in Enterprise Manager. NT authentication uses Windows NT login information to validate users entering the database and is configured using SQL Security Manager. However, in SQL Server 6.5, NT authentication is not fully integrated into the system. Changes to NT groups are not propagated to SQL Server, so if anyone is added or deleted from an NT group, his or her rights will not change on SQL Server. For this reason, I recommend that you avoid using NT authentication if possible.

SQL Logins

SQL Server logins are all managed through a single interface. This interface is accessible through the context menu when you right-click on a login or in the Logins group, or by selecting Logins from the Manage menu. Either of these methods opens the Manage Logins screen shown in Figure 6-13.

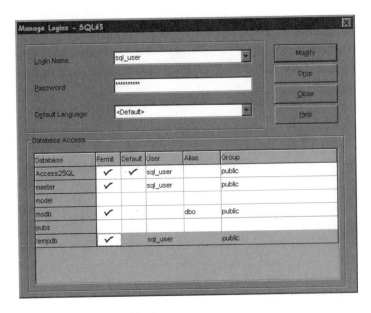

Figure 6-13. Manage Logins

This screen allows you to create new logins, delete (drop) existing logins, and configure each login and the access that it has to the various databases on the system.

Creating a SQL Login

In order to create a SQL Server login, you must select the <new> item from the
Login Name drop-down list in Manage Logins. This clears the form so that you can
fill in the information to create a new user. Enter a name for your new login in the
Login Name field. This is the name that the user will enter when connecting to
SQL Server. You can then enter a password for this user. SQL Server permits the
use of blank passwords, but I do not recommend this practice. Creating a user with
no password essentially nullifies the security that you are trying to configure.

The next piece of required information is the language that the user works in.
The default setting is to use the language that was configured as the default when
SQL Server was installed. It is very unlikely that you will need to change this, so
you can skip this field.

The final piece of information that SQL Server requires from you is what access
the user has to which databases (see Figure 6-14).

Database	Permit	Default	User	Alias	Group
Access2SQL	✓	✓	sql_user		public
master	✓		sql_user		public
model					
msdb	✓			dbo	public
pubs					
tempdb	✓		sql_user		public

Figure 6-14. Database Access

The user's access to each database is configured separately. The Permit column
defines whether the login can access the database. If this setting is turned off, the
user cannot access the database, and no other settings can be configured. The Default
column defines which database the user will be automatically logged in to if no
database is specified when they log in. Only one database can be the default for
any one user. The next column, the User column, defines the name that appears
for the user when they are logged into the database. This does not change the
user's rights within the database and is provided for convenience in cases where
you might want to log user information to a table, so that you can track what
changes were made by which users.

The Alias column provides access to a very useful feature. It can be used to
allow the user to take on another user's identity within the selected database. For
example, you can allow a user to login, but be aliased to the dbo (database owner),
so that the user can administer the database with the same rights as the dbo. This
way, you don't have to reconfigure each user to have the rights needed to use the
objects in the database.

The final column, the Group column, defines what group the user belongs to
within the database. This can save you from having to configure this information

within the database itself. By default, the user is added to the *public* group. You can change this by selecting a different group from the drop-down list.

Once you have entered all of the information for the login, click Add to add the user as specified. If you entered a password for the user, you are prompted to confirm it at this point.

Editing and Deleting SQL Logins

In order to edit a login in the Manage Logins screen, you must first select the login name from the drop-down list. This updates the screen with the information for that user, and you can then make changes as necessary. Once you have made all of your changes, simply click Modify to commit your changes. If you have created a login in SQL Server and have created customized permissions for that user within a database, removing the user's access permissions for that database permanently removes all object-level security settings for that user from the database. For this reason, you should be very careful when modifying existing logins.

You can delete a login from Server Manager by right-clicking a login and choosing Drop from the menu, or you can do it by selecting the Login Name in Manage Logins and clicking the Drop button. Either action permanently removes the user from the system. Any security settings you created for this user are lost and can only be re-created manually. Exercise caution when using this functionality.

Managing Database Objects

The objects in the database are divided into two sections: Groups/Users and Objects. The Groups/Users section allows you to create groups, set permissions, and generally configure the security within the database. The Objects section allows you to create, modify, drop, and otherwise administer the individual objects within the database.

Managing Groups and Users

When you expand the Groups/Users section, you will see the groups within the database. You can further expand each group to show the users that are members of that group. See Figure 6-15.

Each database always contains at least one group, the public group. This group cannot be deleted, but there is no reason you have to add users to it or grant the group any rights. However, it can be useful if you want to set the default security rights for users who have access to your database. Any user that has access to a database must be assigned to a group. If they are not assigned to a group explicitly, they are added to the public group. By granting rights to the public group to use objects within your database, you can ensure that every login that is added to the

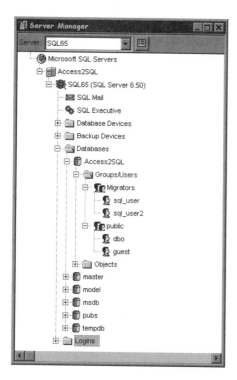

Figure 6-15. Database Groups/Users

database can gain at least a minimum of functionality. Groups within a database can be managed through the right-click menu from Groups/Users section or through the Manage menu once the database has been selected. The same applies for users.

When you choose to manage groups, you are presented with the Manage Groups dialog, as shown in Figure 6-16.

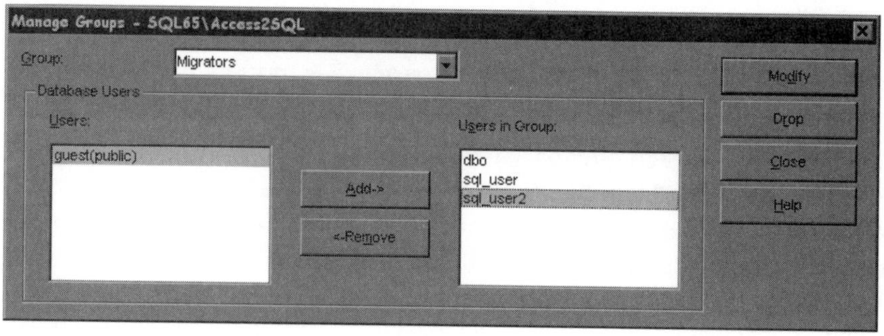

Figure 6-16. Manage Groups

This screen is similar to the other screens within SQL Server for adding or modifying objects. Select the group you want to modify from the drop-down list or type in a new group name. You can then select the users from the list on the left and add them to the group selected in the list on the right using the command buttons between the two lists. Note that users can only be members of a single group within each database. Consequently, the group that the user currently belongs to is shown, in brackets, in the Users list.

You can modify or add your group using the Modify button, or drop it entirely using the Drop button. When you drop a group, any users that are members of that group are reassigned to group public.

Users are managed through the Manage Users dialog, shown in Figure 6-17.

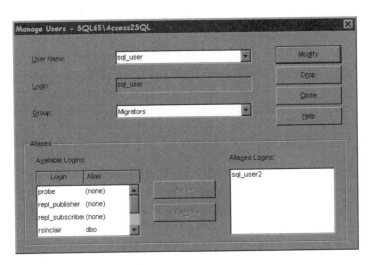

Figure 6-17. Manage Users

This screen allows you to manage the users that have access to the database and the group they belong to as well as control aliases. If you create a new user, you must select the login with which that user will connect to the database. You must also select the group the user belongs to (each user must belong to a group in the database). You can then set which logins are aliased to this user in the database. Only those logins that do not currently have access to the database or those that are already aliased to another login are shown in the list. You can move logins between the lists by selecting the login and choosing Add -> or <- Remove. Finally, select Add or Modify as appropriate to commit your changes. You can also drop a user by selecting the Drop button.

By right-clicking a group or user and selecting Permissions, you can set the rights that person or group has for each object in the database. This dialog is also available from the Permissions item on the Object menu. Figure 6-18 shows the dialog that you will see when you start this function.

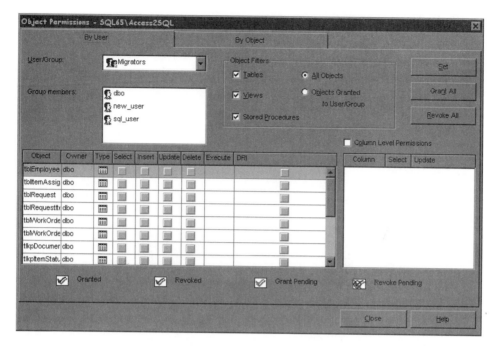

Figure 6-18. Object Permissions By User

Permissions may be set based on a user or a group. The User/Group drop-down list contains a list of all of the groups and individual users who have access to the database. Users that are aliased to other users (including those aliased to dbo) are not listed in this drop-down list because they do not need to be modified. The dbo's permissions cannot be altered, and aliased users will be assigned the settings of the user to which they are aliased.

Each table, view, or stored procedure within the database is shown in the list at the bottom. User or group rights to perform particular functions against an object can be granted or revoked using the appropriate checkboxes. The legend at the bottom of the screen shows what each checkmark color represents. The permissions shown on this screen pertain to the data within each object, not the actual object itself. You can grant Select, Insert, Update, and Delete permissions on a view or table, allowing the user or group to perform these functions against the data. With a stored procedure, you can grant a user or group the rights to execute that procedure. With tables, you can also grant users the rights to reference a table using database referential integrity (DRI) (if they are creating their own tables), and you can even grant permissions on a column-by-column basis, allowing a user to view or update only certain columns within a table.

The Object Filter section allows you to filter the objects that are shown in the list. This can be useful if your database has many objects, and you don't want to have to see them all.

The By Object tab allows you to set object permissions by object, instead of by user (see Figure 6-19). This is often a much better way to set permissions because setting permissions by user does not show you which permissions each user may already have from being a member of a group. Permissions for a group can be overridden for a user, so this screen allows you to see just how the inheritance of permissions is set.

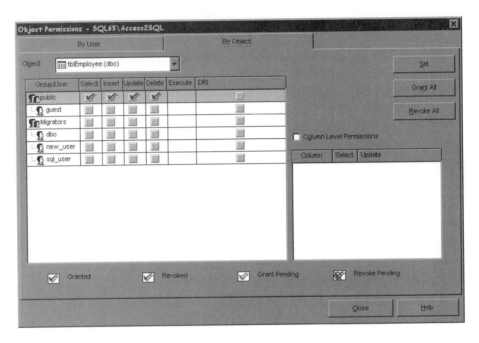

Figure 6-19. Object Permissions By Object

When you have set all of the necessary permissions, you can implement your changes by clicking the Set button. Until you do so, no changes are made.

Managing Database Objects

Within each database there are six object types, each listed within their own folders under the Objects section within the database (see Figure 6-20).

Each object section allows you to create, drop, rename, or otherwise modify objects through the context menu for each item.

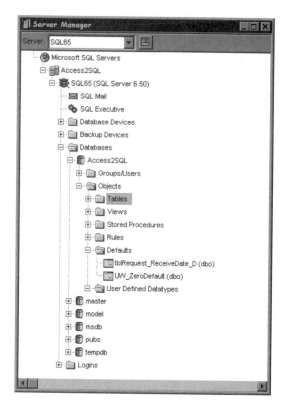

Figure 6-20. Database Objects

Shared Functionality

There is some SQL Server functionality, accessed through the object menus, that is common to all SQL server database objects. One is the capability to set permissions for database objects. In order to set the permissions for an object, select the object, and then select Permissions from the Object menu, or right-click the object and select the Permissions item from the right-click menu. Either of these menu selections will open the Object Permissions dialog with the current object selected. This can be very useful if you want to quickly open the Permissions dialog to a particular object.

Another shared menu item is the Dependencies context menu item. This displays a list of all of the objects that the selected object depends on and all of the objects that depend on it (see Figure 6-21).

This functionality can be very useful if you want to drop an object from the database. Before you drop the object, you can determine whether dropping it will affect other objects in the database. You can also use Dependencies to determine what objects have to be moved if you want to move an object to another database. For example, if you have a table named tblOrder that is related to a customer table

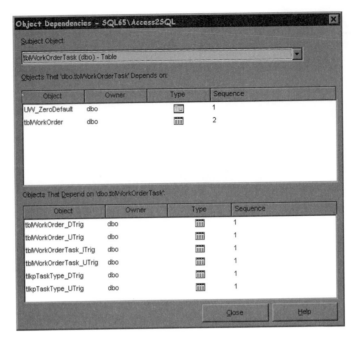

Figure 6-21. Object Dependencies

named tblCustomer as a foreign table in the relationship, and tblOrder is also related to tblOrderDetail as a primary table in the relationship, the Object Dependencies screen will list tblCustomer as an object that tblOrder depends on and tblOrder-Detail as an object that depends on tblOrder.

The final shared menu item for all objects is Generate SQL Scripts. This function displays the Generate SQL Scripts dialog shown in Figure 6-22.

This dialog allows you to create a script that can be used to re-create a database object (or objects) or even an entire database. This script can be saved to a file, and then run against another database to re-create an identical structure. This script is saved in a file using a SQL extension. This functionality can be very useful if you have created your database and want to have different versions for testing, development, and production.

Once you select the objects to script and save them to a script file (.SQL), you can then modify the script using a text editor. Or, you can open the script using ISQL/w and execute the script to re-create all of the objects in the database.

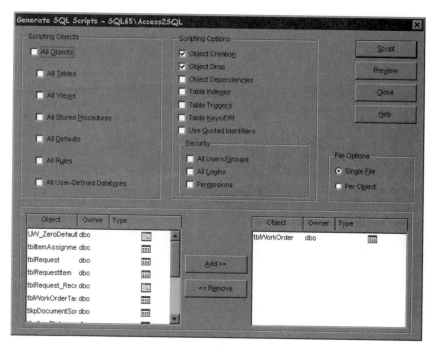

Figure 6-22. Generate SQL Scripts

Managing Tables

Tables within SQL Server are managed using the Manage Tables dialog. This dialog allows you to create or modify a table and can be accessed from the Tables item on the Manage menu. It can also be opened by selecting New Table or Edit from the right-click menu for a table. The Manage Tables dialog, shown in Figure 6-23, starts by only showing the list of fields in the table.

If you want to modify any keys or constraints, you must select the Advanced Features button from the toolbar at the top of the screen.

You can change the definition of or add new fields using the grid at the top of the screen. Drop-down lists and checkboxes help you to create your fields. You can also define default values for your fields by entering a value or system function that returns a value.

The Primary Key/Identity tab allows you to define the primary key for the table. To do this, select a field from the drop-down list. Only those fields that qualify for use as a primary key are listed (fields that allow nulls cannot be a part of primary key). You can then set whether the primary key is clustered or not. Clustering is recommended if you often reference data using the primary key, or you regularly join the table on the primary key in queries. You can also remove a primary key if necessary by clicking the Remove button.

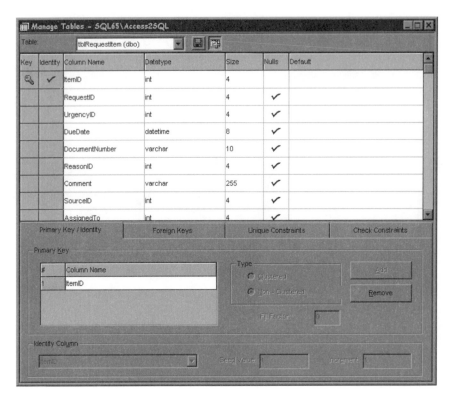

Figure 6-23. Manage Tables

If you are creating a new table, you can set the Identity Column for your table, specifying a seed value and an increment value. This section is not available after a table has been created.

The Foreign Keys tab allows you to define the foreign keys that your table depends on (see Figure 6-24).

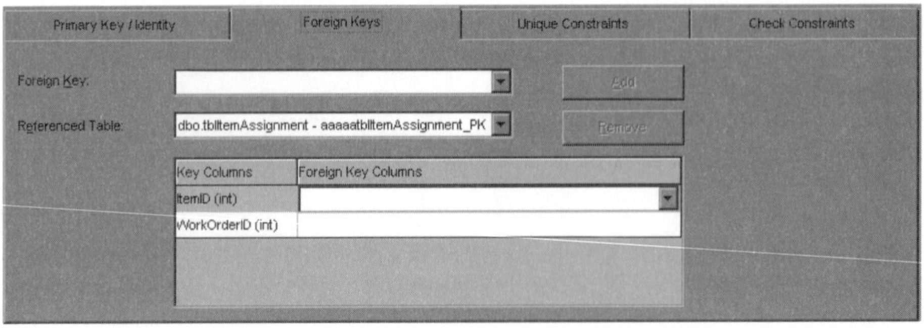

Figure 6-24. Table Foreign Keys

You can edit an existing foreign key by selecting it from the first drop-down list, or create a new one by entering a new name. You set the primary key it references in the parent table by selecting the table/index name from the Referenced Table field. Finally, you set the fields in your table that relate to the parent by selecting fields for the Foreign Key Columns in the grid at the bottom.

The Unique Constraints tab allows you to define unique indexes (unique constraints) within the table. If you have made a field the primary key, it is not necessary to add it to this tab (see Figure 6-25).

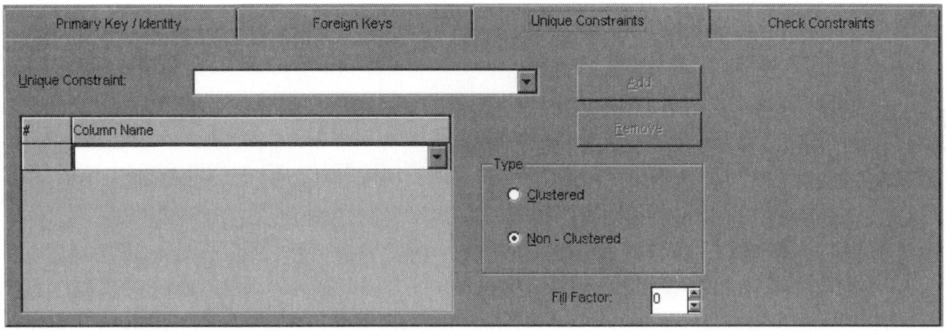

Figure 6-25. Table Unique Constraints

You can edit an existing unique constraint by selecting it from the drop-down list, or create a new one by entering a new name. You then set the columns that are members of this unique index and whether the index is clustered. If you already have a clustered primary key or other clustered index, you must set this index to Non-Clustered. Click Add or Remove as appropriate for the situation.

The Check Constraints tab allows you to define check constraints for your table (see Figure 6-26).

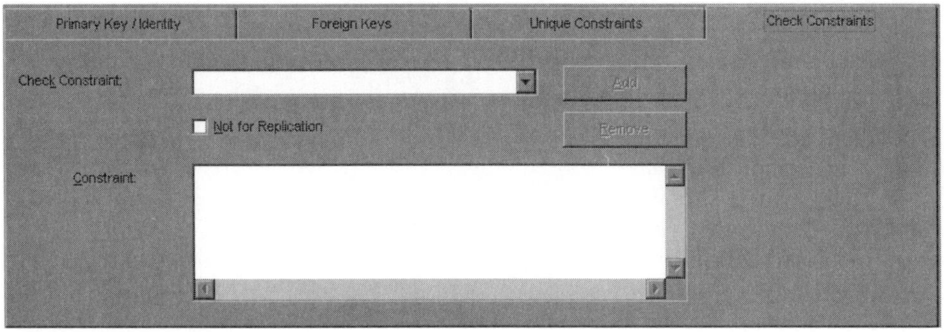

Figure 6-26. Table Check Constraints

As with the other items, you can create new or edit existing constraints. These constraints define rules for data within the table. They are similar to Access's validation rules. However, there can be multiple constraints in a table and each of those constraints can reference as many fields in the table as necessary. The Transact-SQL validation code for the constraint is entered into the Constraint field, and the constraint is added or removed with the appropriate button.

Once you have completed creating your table, you can save your changes by selecting the Save button on the toolbar. You can then create another table or edit another table by selecting the appropriate option from the drop-down list in the toolbar.

Managing Indexes

Indexes can be managed by right-clicking a table and choosing Indexes or by selecting Indexes from the Manage menu. Either one of these actions opens the Manage Indexes dialog, shown in Figure 6-27, which allows you to manage all of the nonprimary indexes in the database.

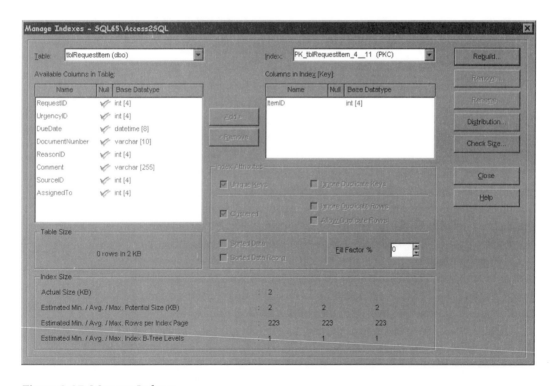

Figure 6-27. Manage Indexes

Before you create or edit an index, you must select the table that has that index from the Table drop-down list. You can then edit or create a new index by selecting an index from the Index drop-down list or by typing in a new index name. Add the fields that will be included in your index by selecting them from the list on the left and using the Add -> button or remove them using the <- Remove button. You can then define whether they are unique or clustered using the appropriate options and specify the characteristics of the clustering. You can also remove or rename indexes using this screen. Primary keys cannot be edited from this screen; they should be created using the Manage Table dialog described earlier.

Managing Triggers

Triggers on tables consist of Transact-SQL code that runs when some action is performed against data in a table. The Manage Triggers dialog, shown in Figure 6-28, is available by selecting Triggers from the Manage menu or by right-clicking a table and choosing Triggers.

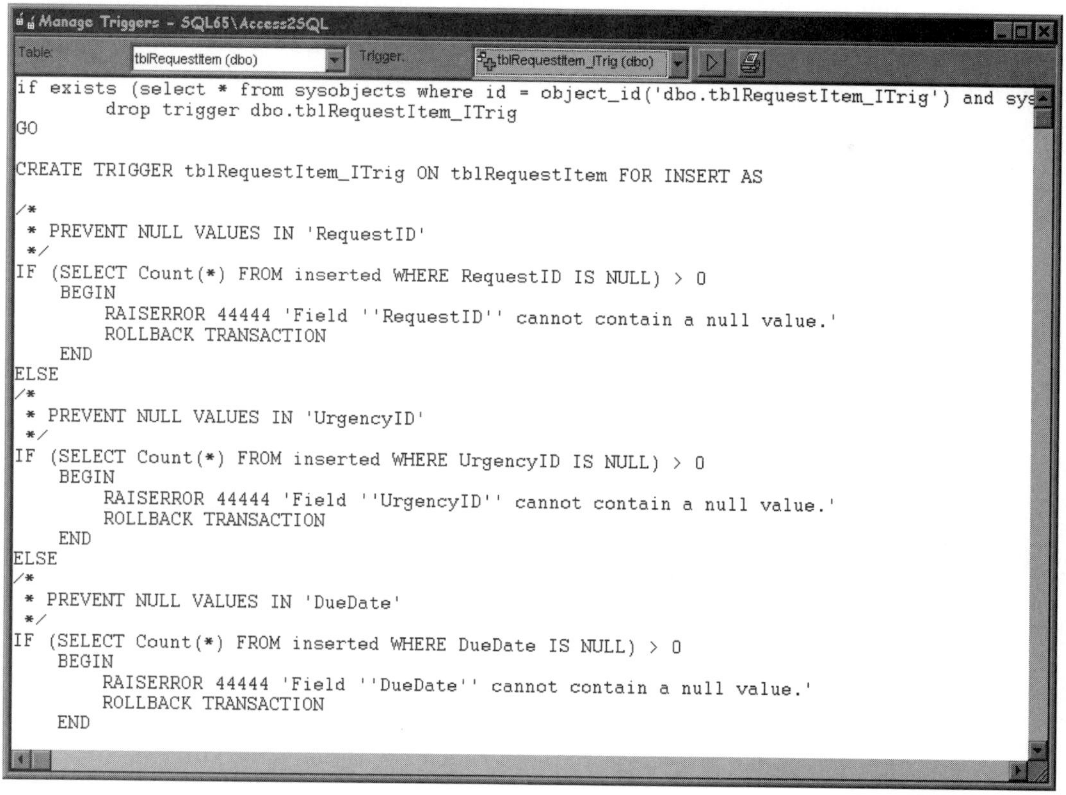
Manage Triggers - SQL65\Access2SQL
Table:
tblRequestItem (dbo)
Trigger:
tblRequestItem_ITrig (dbo)
if exists (select * from sysobjects where id = object_id('dbo.tblRequestItem_ITrig') and sys
drop trigger dbo.tblRequestItem_ITrig
GO
CREATE TRIGGER tblRequestItem_ITrig ON tblRequestItem FOR INSERT AS
/*
* PREVENT NULL VALUES IN 'RequestID'
*/
IF (SELECT Count(*) FROM inserted WHERE RequestID IS NULL) > 0
BEGIN
RAISERROR 44444 'Field ''RequestID'' cannot contain a null value.'
ROLLBACK TRANSACTION
END
ELSE
/*
* PREVENT NULL VALUES IN 'UrgencyID'
*/
IF (SELECT Count(*) FROM inserted WHERE UrgencyID IS NULL) > 0
BEGIN
RAISERROR 44444 'Field ''UrgencyID'' cannot contain a null value.'
ROLLBACK TRANSACTION
END
ELSE
/*
* PREVENT NULL VALUES IN 'DueDate'
*/
IF (SELECT Count(*) FROM inserted WHERE DueDate IS NULL) > 0
BEGIN
RAISERROR 44444 'Field ''DueDate'' cannot contain a null value.'
ROLLBACK TRANSACTION
END

Figure 6-28. Manage Triggers

Select the table for which you want to administer triggers from the Table drop-down list. You can then select an existing trigger or create a new one by selecting the appropriate item from the Trigger drop-down list. Three types of triggers can be created: Insert, Update, or Delete. Each type of trigger is represented using a different icon, and selecting the <new> item allows you to create new triggers for appropriate actions. The code to create the trigger is shown in the dialog. Edit this code as necessary, and save your changes by clicking the Save Object button on the toolbar.

If you are editing an existing trigger, SQL Server automatically adds code in the first few lines of the trigger to drop it from the database before it is re-created. This is necessary because you cannot overwrite a trigger by creating a new one. It must be deleted and re-created using the new code.

Managing Views and Stored Procedures

Views are managed through the Manage Views dialog. This dialog is accessed from the Manage menu or by right-clicking in the Views section. This displays a window similar to the Manage Triggers dialog where you can add, edit, or delete a view using the appropriate Transact-SQL.

Stored procedures are managed in a similar dialog accessible from the Manage menu or by right-clicking in the Stored Procedures section.

Managing Rules

The Manage Rule window, shown in Figure 6-29, can be opened from the Manage menu or by right-clicking in the Rules group. This window contains three tabs.

The Rules tab allows you to create a definition for your rule. Enter a name in the Rule field, and then enter a definition for this rule in the Description field. You cannot edit an existing rule using this tool. You must drop the rule and re-create it.

From this tab you can also quickly check the columns and data types that are bound to this rule. The Bindings button opens the dialog shown in Figure 6-30.

Although you cannot add bindings from this screen, you can unbind selected items using the Unbind button. Bindings can be added using the next tab.

The Column Bindings tab in the Manage Rules window allows you to set the columns in which tables are bound to the selected rule. Simply select a table and bind a rule to a column in that table by selecting the rule from the drop-down list beside the field name. Any existing rule may be bound using this tab, not just the one selected in the Rules tab.

The Datatype Bindings tab allows you to bind your rule to a user defined data type (UDDT). This can make implementing a rule much easier if you implement all fields that require this rule with a UDDT.

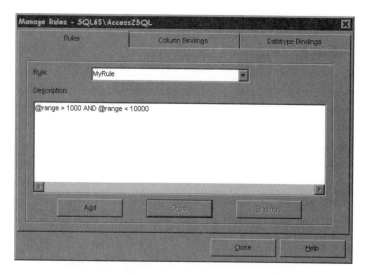

Figure 6-29. Manage Rules

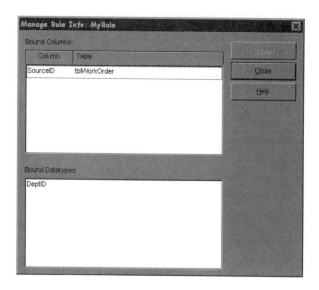

Figure 6-30. Manage Rule Info

Managing Defaults

The appearance and behavior of the Manage Defaults screen is identical to the Manage Rules screen. The only difference is the information entered in the Description. Follow the guidelines for managing rules when managing defaults.

Managing User-Defined Datatypes

UDDTs are the final items in a database that can be managed from Enterprise Manager. When you choose to manage these objects, you are presented with the Manage User-Defined Datatypes screen shown in Figure 6-31.

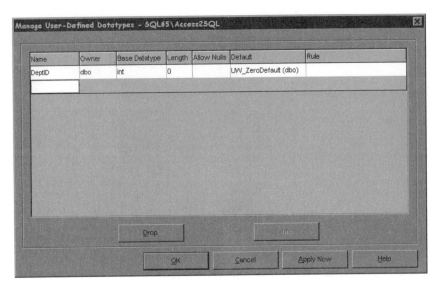

Figure 6-31. Manage User-Defined Datatypes

When you create a UDDT, you must first enter a name for the new UDDT you are creating. This name is selected when designing tables as the data type for fields that use this UDDT. The owner is automatically set to the current context under which you are logged into Enterprise Manager, usually dbo. You must then select the SQL Server base data type that the UDDT is based on, set the length and nullability, and then select a default and/or rule to use with this data type, if necessary.

You can also check the binding of the data type to table columns by clicking the Info button. In addition, you can delete a data type by selecting it and clicking the Drop button.

Other Tools

Although you can administer SQL Server using Enterprise Manager, there are a few other ways of administering a database. If you have downloaded the Upsizing Wizard for Access 97, the installation of this wizard adds a menu item to the Tools➡Add-Ins called SQL-Server Browser. This tool, shown in Figure 6-32, can be used to administer most of the objects in a SQL Server database and is designed to look like the regular Access 97 database window.

Figure 6-32. SQL Server Browser

This tool will ask you if you want to link a table to the current database as soon as you create it. It also provides quick access to a SQL Server database without having to start Enterprise Manager.

If you do plan to use SQL-Server Browser, keep in mind that it does not provide the full functionality of what can be done in Enterprise Manager. You cannot bind rules directly when you create them. You must open the table that they are based on before you can do so. You also cannot bind defaults when you create them, and you cannot create user defined data types. Additionally, you cannot configure security from this utility.

The browser does not properly format items that are not created within it. If you create views or rules in Enterprise Manager, they might not show up properly in the browser. You may also find that you cannot design tables in this browser that were not created in it to begin with.

Access 2000 has completely changed the way that databases are administered by introducing the concept of Access Data Projects (ADP). By creating your application as an ADP, you can directly manage SQL Server tables, diagrams, stored procedures, and views. However, you cannot manage security, rules, defaults, or UDDTs from an ADP. You must use Enterprise Manager to do this.

For these reasons, your best bet is to use Enterprise Manager to manage your database.

A Special Note on Security

One property of SQL Server that hasn't been discussed much is how the security you design on your server affects the names of objects. I have left this subject to the end of the chapter because I think it deserves special attention, especially for people who are used to creating database objects in Microsoft Access.

When a user creates an object in SQL Server, the name of that object is actually made up of two pieces of information. The first piece of information that is used to define the object is the owner name. If the login is aliased in the current database, this owner name is the alias for the login. If the login does not have an alias for the database, the login name is used to create this piece of information. The second piece of information that goes into the object name is the name of the object as supplied. For example, if a user connecting to a database under the alias of "application_user" creates a new table named "tblMyOrders", the fully qualified SQL Server name of this object becomes "application_user.tblMyOrders"—the owner of the table followed by the table name. This naming may lead to some confusion when you attempt to access objects in your database. SQL code that references a table named "tblMyOrders" may not reference the table you expect. The convention of adding the owner name before the object name means that there can actually be many tables with the same name, but created by different users. A user named "admin_user" might have a table named "tblMyOrders" as well, and this could be the table that you actually reference.

So how does SQL Server decide which table you are referencing if there are multiple tables with the same name but with different owners. The first table that SQL Server returns is the table owned by the person who is requesting the information. So if "application_user" logs in to the database and requests data from "tblMyOrders", SQL Server first looks for a table with the fully qualified name of "application_user.tblMyOrders". If this table is not found, SQL Server then searches for a table that is owned by the dbo user: "dbo.tblMyOrders". If no matching table name is found under the user's name or under dbo, the table will not be found.

The affect that security has on object names means that you must be careful when you create objects that other users need to access. Unless you fully qualify the name when you call the object, it must belong to the current login or dbo.

Moving On

I hope that the information provided in this chapter helps you to understand how to use SQL Server a little better. I have tried to cover as much information as a single chapter allows. There is much more information available if you want to get a more in-depth understanding of how to use SQL Server. The SQL Server Books Online in your SQL Server program group on the Start menu is a good place to begin. The information contained in these books is complete and can tell you just about anything you need to know about SQL Server.

However, the Books Online probably have far too much information for most users, and the information may not be organized in a fashion that you find easy to read and understand. If you really want to find out more about SQL Server, there are plenty of good books on the subject that can help you find your way in SQL

Server. My personal favorite is *Microsoft SQL Server 6.5 DBA Survival Guide* by Mark Spenic (Sams Publishing, June 1996). It contains a great deal of information not covered by some of the more basic books.

CHAPTER 7

Using SQL Server 7

SQL SERVER 7 AND MICROSOFT ACCESS are very different systems, so in order to make your migration go as smoothly as possible, you should have a solid understanding of the basic functions you can use to manage SQL Server. Although Access 2000 allows you to manage portions of a SQL Server database through an ADP, and Access 97 allows you to manage some SQL Server database objects through the SQL Server Browser, neither version of Access gives you access to all of the capabilities of SQL Server. You should understand the tools available to you and how they can help you to manage your SQL Server databases.

SQL Server 7, like version 6.5, can be administered using text-based SQL commands. These commands can be extremely difficult to master and are aimed at users that have extensive knowledge of the system and a full understanding of what these commands are capable of (i.e., trained database administrators). Fortunately for us Access users, SQL Server has graphical interfaces to perform many of these administration tasks. In SQL Server 7, these interfaces are easier to use than ever before. Microsoft has enriched the administrative tools in SQL 7 beyond what they were in SQL 6.5. These utilities can handle most of what we need to do to migrate to and maintain an application in SQL Server, so I will concentrate on the graphical, rather than on the textual commands that are available to you.

Because there is so much that can be done within SQL Server, I can only hope to introduce you to some of the basic concepts you will need to know for your migration. A single chapter cannot fully describe all of the functionality that is available to you. This chapter introduces you to the core concepts of how to manage the different objects within SQL Server 7 and how this management pertains to you as an Access developer.

Using SQL Server 7

The new version of Enterprise Manager that is included with SQL Server 7 is so different from the one in version 6.5 that it is often difficult to believe that they are different versions of the same program. Microsoft has made some incredible improvements that make it much easier for the "common person" to understand the interface. Although the administrative program for SQL 7 is still called Enterprise Manager, it is in fact a different executable, completely unrelated to the executable used with SQL Server 6.5.

SQL Server 7 is administered through a plug-in that is added to Microsoft Management Console (MMC). MMC is a standard application that Microsoft uses to consolidate the management of its enterprise products. Other products that are managed through this application include Transaction Server, Internet Information Server, FrontPage Server Extensions, and all Computer Management for Windows 2000 PCs. Undoubtedly, there is a lot more to come. Microsoft's intention is to put the administration of all of its enterprise applications under one roof.

All this being said, you can still access this management system from the Enterprise Manager shortcut in the SQL Server 7 group on your Start menu. This displays MMC with the Enterprise Manager plug-in loaded. If you expand your server within the server group, you will see the different categories that can be administered for the server, as shown in Figure 7-1.

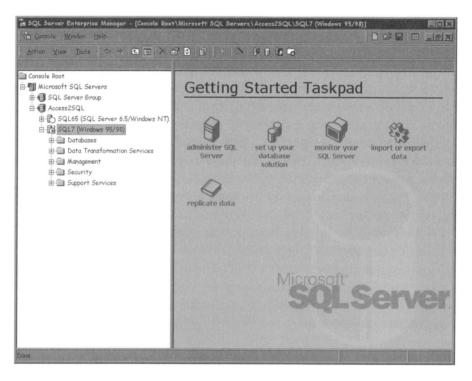

Figure 7-1. Enterprise Manager

One of the features that you are sure to notice is that when you select a server, the Getting Started Taskpad is automatically displayed to provide quick access to some of the most common functions you need to administer your server.

You may also notice that any SQL Server 6.5 system that you have registered in the SQL Server 6.5 Enterprise Manager shows in the list. This does not mean that you can use this tool to administer a 6.5 server. Instead, when you click on the server, Enterprise Manager for version 6.5 is automatically launched.

Almost all aspects of SQL Server 7 can be managed through wizards. Many of these wizards are available from the Getting Started Taskpad. Simply hover the mouse over an item in the Taskpad to display a tooltip that describes what you can do in that task. Some items take you to other Taskpads that allow you even more choices. The wizards that these functions present can be very useful for quickly creating items or for determining how an item should be implemented. However, the choices they give you are often simplified and do not show the true capabilities of SQL Server. For this reason, I will bypass the wizards and concentrate on the base functions for managing SQL Server. Keep in mind that if you want to understand how to do something, you can always use the wizards to create an example that you can use as a base for your understanding.

Managing Databases

Before you can create a database in SQL Server 6.5, you must create the devices necessary to house the database and the log. In SQL Server 7, database devices no longer exist. This makes the job of creating a database much simpler. A database can easily be created in a single step with only a few pieces of information that are necessary to get a database up and running quickly.

You can create a database using a wizard or using the standard interface. Both methods give you the same options, but with slightly different interfaces. To create a database using the standard interface, right-click any database in the Databases section in the left window of Enterprise Manager or on the Databases folder itself, and select New Database from the menu. When you want to edit an existing database, right-click the database you want to edit, and choose Properties from the menu. To delete a database, right-click the database name, and select Delete from the menu.

Creating a Database

When you choose to create a database from the New Database command, SQL Server opens the Database Properties dialog shown in Figure 7-2 (in this figure, all of the required information has already been entered).

A name is required for your new database. Enter a name in the Name field at the top of the dialog. When you do so, a new file name and location is automatically filled in for you. This is the location of the MDF file in which the database will be housed. The default name for the data file is the name you gave the database followed by "_Data". The default location for this file is in the Data subdirectory under which SQL Server was installed. You can easily change this by selecting the browse button (…) and selecting a new location. The location specified in this section is relative to the machine on which SQL Server is installed, which may not be the same as the machine from which you are working. Set the initial size of the

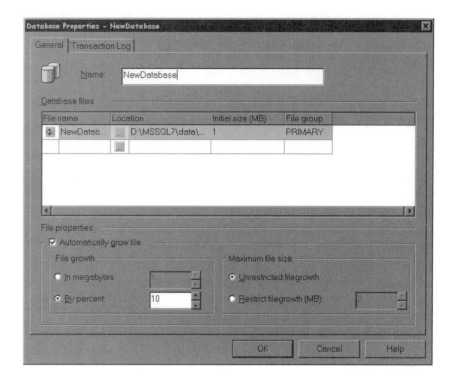

Figure 7-2. Database Properties

database. The size can change after the database has been created, depending on the selections you make in the file properties. You can also assign your files to a particular file group. File groups are a named collection of files that allow DBAs to manage multiple database files as if they were a single unit or distribute database processing across multiple files. They are intended to be used with VLDBs, so you should not change this setting unless you have a solid understanding of how they can affect your database.

At the bottom of the screen, you can set the resizing options for the selected file. By selecting to automatically grow the file, you are telling SQL Server that it should increase the size of the data file whenever it runs out of space. This offers a huge advantage over SQL 6.5, where database size had to be configured manually. With restricted file growth, databases tend to run out of size at inconvenient times.

You can choose to allow your database to grow based on a percentage of its size when it needs to grow or you can fix the growth in megabytes. Also, because you usually don't want your database to accidentally fill up the whole hard drive, you may want to restrict the file growth to a particular size by selecting the appropriate option under the Maximum file size group and entering a maximum size in megabytes.

If necessary, you can create multiple files for your database and locate them anywhere you like on the computer where SQL Server is running. This allows you, if necessary, to spread the database over multiple drives. This can be very useful for ensuring that database access is optimized and that you won't run out of hard drive space on any particular drive. The settings for each of these files are independent, and you must select the file from the grid before setting its properties at the bottom of the screen.

The Transaction Log tab is where you configure the transaction log. It looks virtually identical to the General tab with the exception that there is no place to put the database name. This information should already have been entered. The Transaction Log tab allows you to specify the location and properties of the transaction log file. The default name for this file is the name of your database followed by "_Log" and an LDF extension. The default location for this file is the Data subdirectory below the SQL Server program directory.

The rest of the characteristics of the log files are identical to the characteristics of the database files. You can restrict file growth and create multiple files in exactly the same way that you would for a database file.

When you are finished entering all of the information necessary to create your database, click OK to return to Enterprise Manager.

Changing Database Properties

When you select the Properties menu item from the database right-click menu, the interface you are presented with is similar to the interface for creating a database with the exception that there are two extra configuration tabs. The first two tabs specify the name of the database and the size, location, and growth characteristics of the database and log files. Once a database or file has been created, you cannot rename or move the database and log through this interface. However, you can add files to each section or modify the growth attributes of the files.

The Options tab in the Database Properties window allows you to set the database options (see Figure 7-3).

Database options are divided into two sections. The Access section allows you to define the access options for your database. These can be used to control who can access your database and what access users will have, regardless of the regular security that is configured. These options do not take effect for each user until that user disconnects from the database. Active users are able to continue to use the database until they disconnect or until they attempt to change the context under which they are logged in. Table 7-1 shows a complete description of each option.

These access options can be very useful if you want to prevent users from entering the database but allow those users who are already in to finish what they are working on. You could then do any necessary administration tasks once all users have left the database.

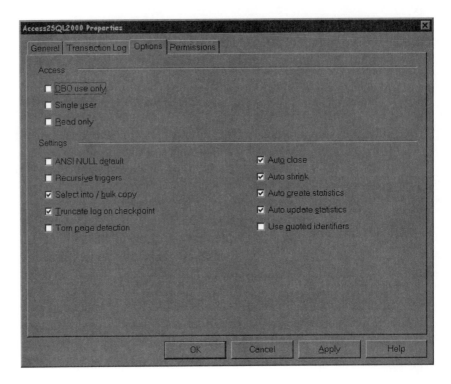

Figure 7-3. Database Options

Table 7-1. Database Access Options

OPTION	DESCRIPTION
DBO use only	Only users aliased to dbo or belonging to db_owner role can access the database.
Single user	Only one user can access the database at a time.
Read only	Data cannot be written to the database. This can dramatically speed up queries because locking does not need to take place.

Below the access options is the Settings section, which contains a number of database settings that define the behavior of the database. Table 7-2 shows a description of each option.

Table 7-2. Database Properties

OPTION	DESCRIPTION
ANSI NULL default	Defines default behavior for data types and columns as to nullability. Turning this option on makes columns nullable by default. Turning it off sets columns to not nullable by default.
Recursive Triggers	Defines whether triggers that update other tables can invoke the triggers on the tables they update. Turning this option off forces only the trigger on the originally updated table to fire.
Select into/bulk copy	Allows the database to perform non-logged operations. These non-logged operations cannot be reversed, and a backup of the transaction log cannot be created.
Truncate log on checkpoint	Committed transactions are removed from the log whenever a checkpoint occurs. This usually occurs when the log becomes 70% full or when a checkpoint is called explicitly.
Torn page detection	Allows SQL Server to detect incomplete input/output operations on the hard disk and raise an error if they are found.
Auto close	Causes the database to close and shutdown when all users have left the database and all operations are complete. This frees server resources for other tasks, but results in more overhead because the server must close and reopen the database file each time it is accessed.
Auto shrink	Allows SQL Server to automatically shrink the database and log files when more than 25% of the file is unused space.
Auto create statistics	Defines whether statistics are automatically created for table columns to ensure optimal performance of queries. Leave this option enabled unless you are fully aware of the implications of changing it.
Auto update statistics	Defines whether statistics are automatically updated when they become out of date due to changes in data content of tables. Leave this option enabled unless you are fully aware of the implications of changing it.
Use quoted identifiers	Defines that all object references can be enclosed in double quotes and literals must be enclosed in single quotes. Otherwise, standard Transact-SQL naming is used.

These properties can be modified to ensure the optimal performance of your database. Consult the SQL Server documentation for more information on what setting you should use for your situation. Usually, you will not have to change them from the default setting. However, you may want to enhance the performance of your database as it grows by modifying some of these settings. For a full description of the effect they have and how they can be used to modify database performance, see the Books Online.

The Permissions tab in the Database Properties, shown in Figure 7-4, allows you to set the database permissions.

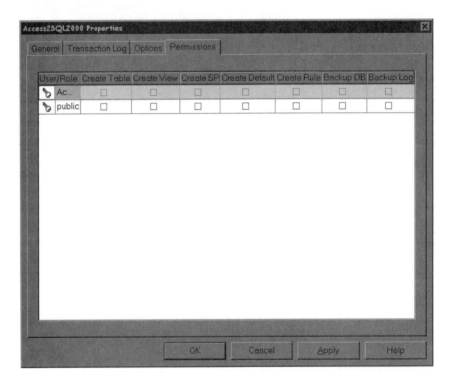

Figure 7-4. Database Permissions

The main purpose of these permissions is to administer user rights relative to creating objects and backing up the database or transaction log. Users generally do not have the ability to create objects within a database unless they are administrators for that database. They also usually do not need to be able to back up the database. However, if you want certain users to be able to perform these functions, you can configure the necessary access from this screen. To add rights for a user or role to perform a task in the database, simply select the checkbox in the row for that user that corresponds to the rights you want to add. To remove the rights, clear the checkbox.

Deleting a Database

When you delete a database, the database and the files that it is stored in are permanently removed from the server. This option should be used with extreme caution. However, it is much easier in SQL Server 7 to restore a database that has been deleted. If you do delete a database accidentally, you may be able to restore it using backups if they exist. However, it is best to use caution when deleting databases, so that you don't delete a database accidentally.

Managing Logins

The security model in SQL Server 7 has changed dramatically from the model used in version 6.5. The security is better integrated into the operating system, and groups have been replaced with SQL Server roles. Roles allow you to define a particular set of rights for various functions that a user can inherit. Before you can add a user to a role, you must create a login for that user.

All SQL Server logins are managed using the Logins item under the Security section for a server. You can create a new login by right-clicking the Logins item and choosing New Login. You can edit a login by double-clicking it or by right-clicking it in the right pane of the MMC and selecting Properties. And, you can delete a login by right-clicking it and choosing Delete from the menu.

Creating or Editing a Login

The choices you are presented with when creating or editing a login are identical. The only difference is that you cannot rename or change the authentication method of the login.

The first screen you are presented with when creating or editing a login, the General tab, allows you to set the name, authentication method, password, and defaults for the login (see Figure 7-5).

Enter a name for your user if you are creating a new one. If you want to use Windows NT authentication, you must enter a user or group name that is currently in use on your domain. You can then select the domain from the drop-down list. With NT authentication, you can deny users access if that is your intention by selecting the Deny access option. If you are using SQL Server authentication, you must supply a password for the user. You will be prompted to confirm this password when you save the login.

Finally, set the default database and language for the user. The default database is the one that the user will automatically be connected to if they do not specify what database they want to connect to. If the login is intended for a program that uses a particular database, select the correct database. You can set the default language if necessary or leave it as the one that SQL Server is configured to use.

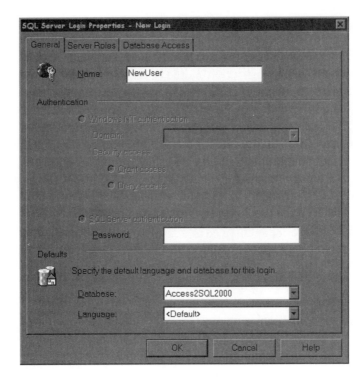

Figure 7-5. General tab of Login Properties

The basic information for connecting with your login is now entered. You must then set the server roles and database access for your login. Select the second tab, Server Roles (see Figure 7-6).

By selecting the checkbox next to a role, you grant the user the rights associated with a particular server role. A short description of the role is available at the bottom of the screen when a role is highlighted. To see which logins are currently members of the server role and what permissions that role has, highlight the role, and click Properties. Server roles cannot be deleted and their rights cannot be modified.

Go to the Database Access tab to set what databases the login can access and what role it will assume in that database (see Figure 7-7).

Specify which databases the login has access to by selecting the Permit checkbox option for the database in the top list. If you want your user to assume a different name in that database, simply change the information in the User column by typing in a new name.

Within each database to which the user has access, you should set what database roles the user can assume. Choose the appropriate roles for the user by selecting the checkboxes. If you want to determine what other users are included in a role, highlight the name of the role, and click Properties.

When you are finished setting the properties of the new login, click OK to save your changes and return to Enterprise Manager.

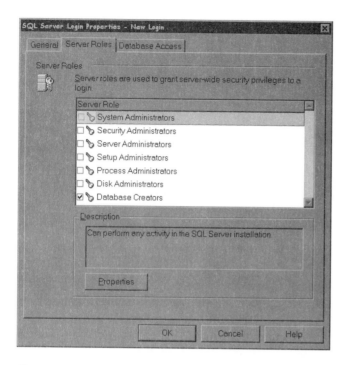

Figure 7-6. Server Roles tab of Login Properties

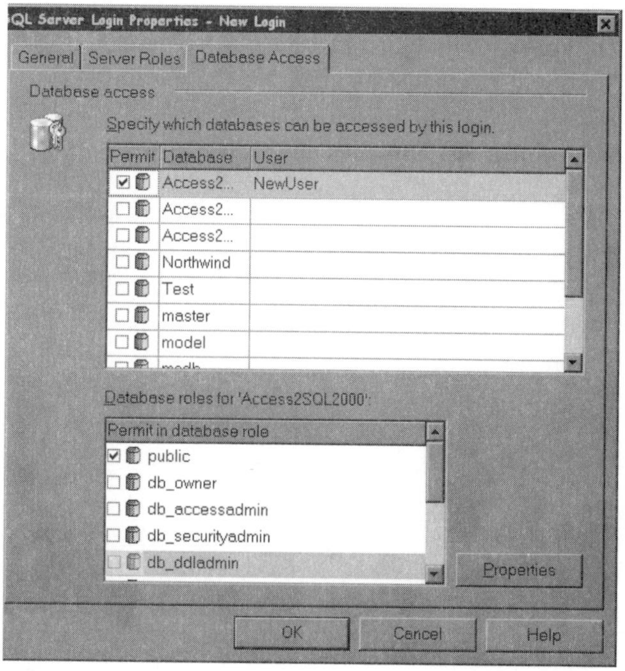

Figure 7-7. Database Access tab of Login Properties

Deleting a Login

When you delete a login from SQL Server, you delete all of the rights that you have assigned to that user. This information cannot be recovered. If you are unsure as to whether the login should be deleted, it is best not to delete it. Change the password so that users who know the login can no longer use it. Delete a login only if you are sure that it is no longer required.

To delete a login from SQL Server, open the Security section in MMC for your server and select the Logins subsection . Right-click the login you want to delete, and select Delete from the right-click menu. You are prompted to confirm the login deletion. Answer Yes to delete the login permanently.

Managing Database Objects

You can manage all of the objects that each database contains by expanding the database name in Enterprise Manager. In addition to the database objects, you can manage some aspects of the database by selecting the database itself and using one of the wizards available in the Taskpad view for the database. The Taskpad appears in the right pane when a database is selected.

Shared Functionality

Each object in a database can be managed by right-clicking the object itself in the list view on the right side in Enterprise Manager and choosing the appropriate management command from the menu. For each object that can be created, the menu allows you to create a new one by selecting the New Object item from the menu (where "Object" in the menu is replaced by the name of the object type). All of the objects of a particular type (diagrams, tables, views, stored procedures, roles, rules, defaults, and user defined types) are listed in the right pane when the object group is selected in the tree view in Enterprise Manager under the database name. You can then delete or modify the properties of an individual object by right-clicking it and choosing the appropriate option.

Object permissions can be managed by right-clicking the object in the list view on the right side in Enterprise Manager, and selecting All Tasks ➠ Manage Permissions. This menu item opens the dialog shown in Figure 7-8.

This screen allows you to configure the security permissions for users and roles within the database. To grant a user the ability to run selects, inserts, updates, or deletes of the data in a table or view, select the appropriate option. To allow a user to execute a stored procedure, select the checkbox in the EXEC column (this option is only available with stored procedures). If you want your user to be able to reference this table in a relationship when the user creates other tables, select the

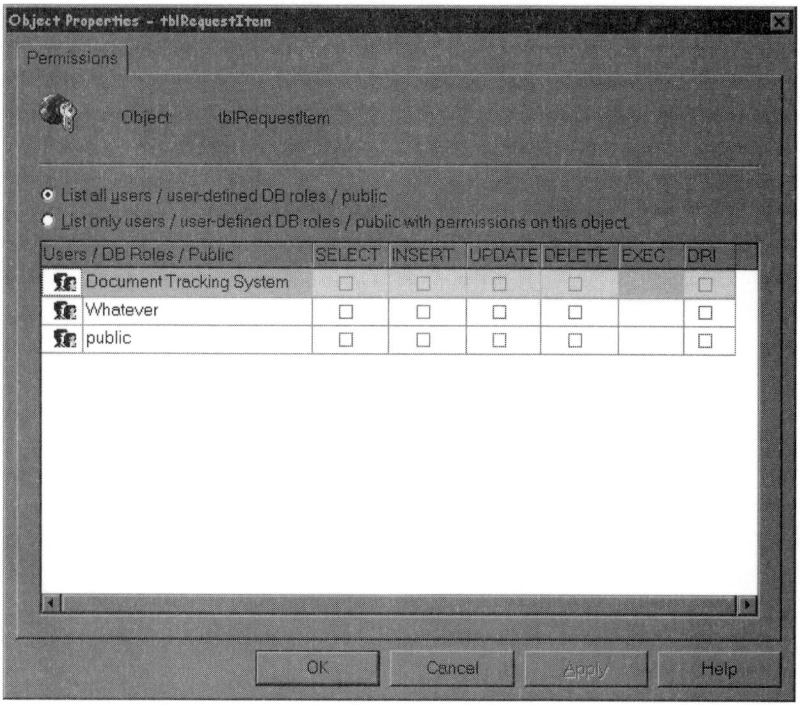

Figure 7-8. Permissions tab of Object Properties

DRI column. Each of the checkboxes has three possible states. You can grant access to a user or role by selecting the checkbox once, and a checkmark will appear. To explicitly deny a user or role access to a certain function, click the checkbox until a red X appears in the column. To reset the rights for the user or role (so that the user can inherit rights from any other roles he or she may belong to), click the checkbox until it is cleared.

You can also determine the dependencies of an object by selecting All Tasks ➧ Display Dependencies. This lists all of the objects that the object depends on and all objects that depend on the object. This can be very useful for determining what objects affect other objects in the database and how changes in one object can influence others. For example, Figure 7-9 shows the dependencies for a table named tlbRequestItem.

On the left, SQL Server shows the objects that depend on this table. These include foreign tables based on the primary key of this table and triggers that reference this table. In the right pane, the objects that this table depends on are shown. In this case, these are lookup tables that tblRequestItem is the child table in a one-to-many relationship.

One final piece of shared functionality is the ability to generate the SQL code that can be used to re-create an object. When you select All TasksGenerate Scripts, you are given the opportunity to create these scripts for one or all of the objects in your database (see Figure 7-10).

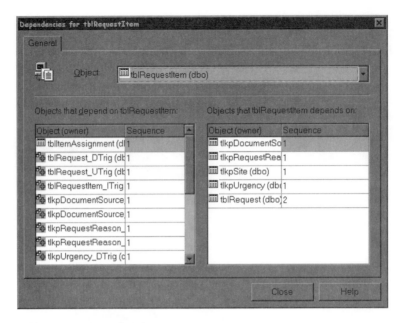

Figure 7-9. Dependencies

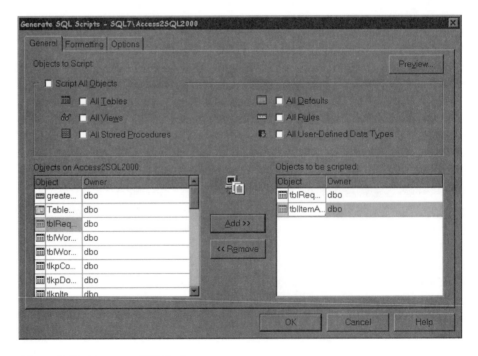

Figure 7-10. Generate SQL Scripts

You can choose what objects you want to create the scripts for, select formatting and other options, and save these scripts to a file, so that you can run them against another database later on. This can be used as a very effective method of duplicating the structure of a database on another server or in a different database on the same server.

Once you click OK, you are prompted to save the script to a file. Select the file to create on disk. Once the file has been saved, you can run the script it contains by opening the file in SQL Query Analyzer and executing it. The object changes defined in the script will be implemented.

Managing Diagrams

Database diagrams provide a great deal of functionality in SQL Server. Database diagrams can be used to define and illustrate relationships, manage tables, and even to add or delete tables from the database. To create or access them, use the toolbar and right-click commands available in the Diagrams section for your database in MMC. Because there are other utilities for managing tables and the functionality in diagrams can be quite complex, we will only concentrate on using diagrams to administer relationships. However, you can look at the functionality that is available from this tool by using the right-click menu to determine what you can do with the tables and what you can do within the diagram itself. When you create or edit a diagram, you do so with the Diagram Designer shown in Figure 7-11.

When you create a new diagram, a quick wizard steps you through adding your tables to the diagram. You can use this wizard or go straight to the designer by canceling the wizard. Add tables to the diagram by clicking on the Add table button on the toolbar and selecting the tables from the list, adding them, and then closing the dialog.

To create a relationship between tables, click and drag the field (using the gray field selector to the left of the field name) that you want to include in the relationship from one table, and drop it on the related field in another table, just as you would do in Access. You are prompted to enter the information that defines this relationship, as shown in Figure 7-12.

Enter a meaningful name for the relationship in the Relationship name box. If the fields that you selected were incorrect, or if you want the relationship to be based on multiple fields, make the appropriate changes in the field names in the primary and foreign tables field selections.

The first option, Check existing data on creation, tells SQL Server to check that existing data does not violate the relationship. Select this option if you want to check the data as soon as you save the relationship. If this option is not selected, existing data in the table that does not conform to the rules of this relationship will not raise an error. It is best to use this option to ensure that your data does not violate the referential integrity.

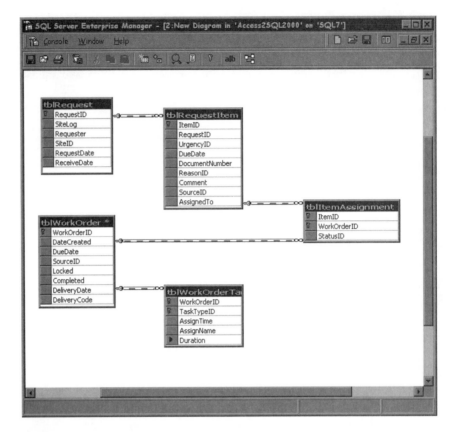

Figure 7-11. Diagram Designer

Figure 7-12. Create Relationship

The second option, Enable relationship for INSERT and UPDATE, tells SQL Server that this relationship should be enforced, and that data should be validated as it is entered. If you don't want your relationship to be enforced when updates are made, do not select this option. Using this option is equivalent to setting the Enforce Referential Integrity option when creating relationships in Access.

The final option, Enable relationship for replication, replicates this constraint whenever the table is replicated to another database.

If you want to create a table that has fields that are related to other fields in the same table in a Microsoft Access database, you have to add that table to the diagram twice and define the relationship between the first copy of this table and the second. In SQL Server databases, you can relate a field in a table to another field in the same table by simply dragging the field off the table, and then dropping it onto the related field. The Diagram Designer does not allow you to add the table twice, so you must use this method for self-referencing relationships.

To edit a relationship, simply right-click it, choose Properties from the drop-down menu, and switch to the Relationship tab. This tab contains the same information as the Create Relationship dialog. To remove a relationship, right-click the relationship line, and choose Remove Relationship from Database from the right-click menu.

If you want to remove a table from the diagram, right-click the table, and choose Remove Table from Diagram from the menu. Be careful not to select the item above it, Delete Table from Database, as this will permanently remove your table from the database.

SQL Server databases can become quite large and relationships can become extremely complex. Because showing all relationships on all tables can make a diagram almost impossible to read, SQL Server has the capability to create as many diagrams as necessary. Use this feature to compartmentalize the relationships in your database to make them easier to read and understand. The relationships in a database are actually made up of the sum of all of the relationships defined in all diagrams in the database, but each diagram only needs to show some of the relationships for the database.

Managing Tables

Tables are considerably easier to manage in SQL Server 7 than they were in version 6.5. The graphical utilities for creating them are much easier to understand. When you create a table, or choose to modify it by selecting Design Table from its context menu, you will be able to modify the table in much the same way that you design a table in Microsoft Access. Figure 7-13 shows an example of the SQL Server Design Table dialog.

All of the characteristics of the columns in the table can be edited from this screen. Simply modify, add, or delete fields as necessary in exactly the same way

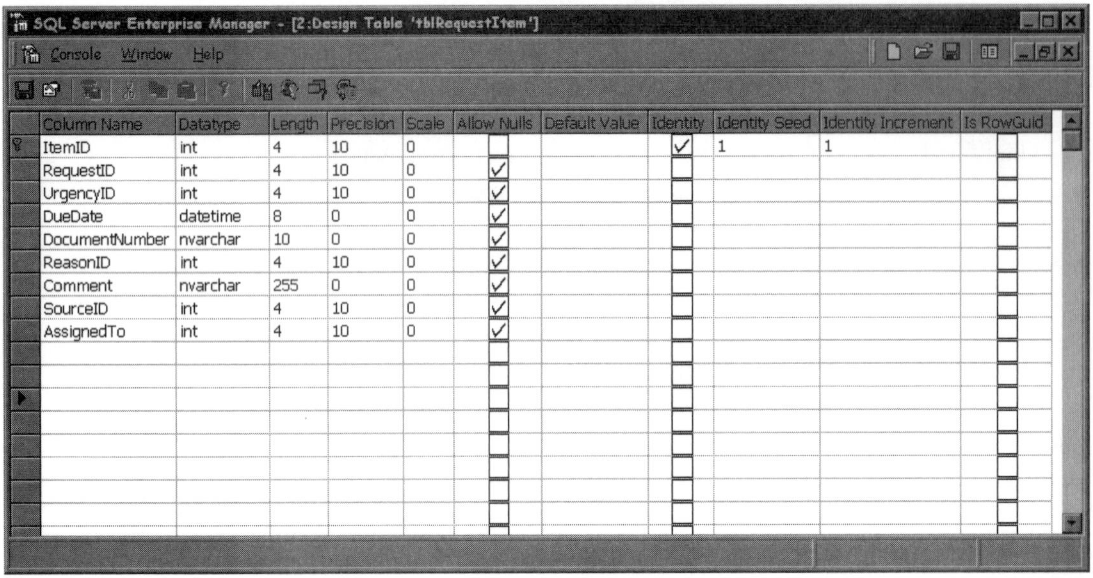

Figure 7-13. Design Table

you would in Access. The primary key can be set in this screen by selecting the columns you want to use in the key, and then selecting the Set Primary Key button from the toolbar.

If you have used the graphical tools included with Visual Studio for database administration, this tool will look very familiar to you. In fact, the design tools are identical between the two products.

Although you can manage triggers, indexes, and relationships from this screen, it is best to do so using other the tools that are discussed in the "Managing Indexes", "Managing Triggers", and "Managing Diagrams" sections. . However, familiarize yourself with the items on the toolbar. If you are already in the process of designing a table, it is often faster to access these functions at that time than to jump back and forth between the various functions in Enterprise Manager. You can also view the data in the table by right-clicking anywhere in the design of the table, and selecting Open Table from the Task submenu, provided you haven't made any changes to the table design.

Managing Indexes

Indexes in SQL Server can be managed by right-clicking any table and selecting All Task ➡ Manage Indexes. This opens the Manage Indexes dialog, shown in Figure 7-14.

This dialog allows you to manage all of the indexes in all of the tables in all of the databases on the server; no matter which table was selected when the dialog opened. Select the database and table from the drop-down lists at the top. The

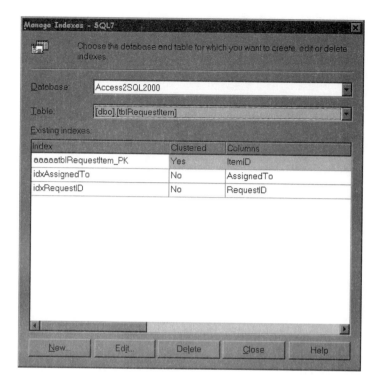

Figure 7-14. Manage Indexes

selected table and database will be the ones displayed when you open the form. Any existing indexes are shown in the list at the bottom. You can create a new index, edit an existing one, or delete an index using the appropriate command buttons at the bottom of the screen.

When you choose to create an index or edit an existing one, you are taken to the Index creation/edit screen shown in Figure 7-15.

This screen is the same whether you are editing an index or creating a new one. The only exception is that if you are creating a new index, the index name is blank and must be filled in. You cannot rename an index. If you want to rename an index, you must delete the original, and create a new one under the new name.

The grid on this screen shows you the major characteristics of the fields in the table. Choose the fields that you want to include in the index by selecting the checkbox beside each field. To change the order of the fields in the index, select the field you want to reorder, and use the Move Up or Move Down buttons to place it correctly within the index. You must then select the appropriate index options at the bottom.

You can specify that the values in your index are unique by selecting the Unique values option. If duplicate values exist in the table, the index creation will fail, and you will have to modify your data as necessary to allow the index to be created. If you want to cluster your index, select the Clustered index option. If there already is a clustered index in the table, this option will be disabled.

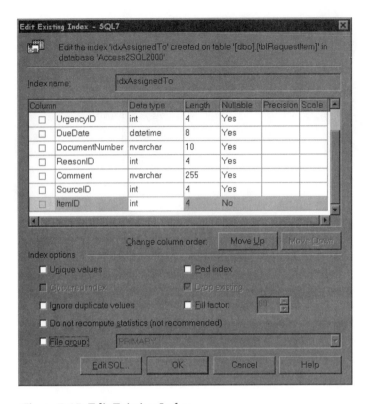

Figure 7-15. Edit Existing Index

The Ignore duplicate values option affects what happens when data is inserted into a unique index that duplicates the values in that index. If you do not select this option, all records inserted in a multiple record insert or update will be rolled back if any one of those records duplicates the unique index. If you select this option, only the record that violates the unique key will be ignored, all other records will be successfully inserted into the table. An error message will still be generated. Although it may be tempting to use this option, you should carefully consider how it will affect the performance of your application. It is often better to back out of the whole operation than just ignore a few records. You may not know exactly what was successfully added to the table and what was not.

The Do not recompute statistics option for the index is not recommended. Selecting this option tells SQL Server not to adjust its method of data retrieval when data changes in the table. This can severely affect performance and should only be used by advanced users who are familiar with how to use this option effectively.

If you have multiple file groups for your database, you can select one on this screen to improve performance by moving the index to a specific file group.

Padding an index tells SQL Server to leave empty space between records to speed insertion of data after the index has been created. This can improve the performance of tables that have new records being inserted on a regular basis. The amount of empty space between the records is specified in the fill factor. The fill factor determines the amount of space that is taken up by records in an index as a percentage of the total records in the index. The lower the fill factor, the more space is left between records. The fill factor alone determines how much space is left when the index is created and can change over time.

If you are creating a new index, the Drop existing option is not selected. If you are editing an existing one, it is automatically selected. You cannot change this option from this screen—it is only included for informational purposes.

The Edit SQL button at the bottom of the screen allows you to view and edit the Transact-SQL string that is used to create your index. If you want to learn how to create indexes using the standard data definition language for SQL Server, create your index graphically, and then view it on this screen. This output can often answer more of your questions than the online help can.

When you are ready to create your index or to commit your modifications, click OK, and your changes are saved. The saving process may take some time depending on how much data exists in the table. If your database is online and in use by an application, do not make index changes because they will lock the table, and other users will not be able to access the table in which they reside. Always make these changes when the database is not in use.

Managing Triggers

Triggers in SQL Server can be managed using the Trigger Properties screen, shown in Figure 7-16.

This screen opens when you select All Tasks ➧ Manage Triggers for a table. Select the trigger you want to modify from the drop-down list or create a new one by selecting the <new> item. Triggers must be created using Transact-SQL code. Enter the appropriate code into the window. You can verify the validity of the code using the Check Syntax button at the bottom of the screen, or delete the entire trigger using the Delete button.

Depending on how the triggers were originally defined, you may run into problems modifying triggers from this screen. The trigger illustrated in Figure 7-16 was created by the Upsizing Wizard and contains an improper definition. When the trigger was opened for editing, the name of the trigger in the definition was already in quotes. This should not be so unless your database has the Enable quoted identifiers option set. If you encounter an error (specifically error 21037) applying your changes, check the trigger name. Remove the quotes from the name, and you should be able to apply your changes (assuming the rest of the syntax is correct).

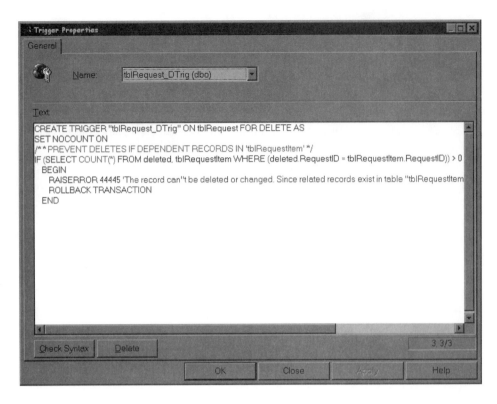

Figure 7-16. Trigger Properties

Managing Views

One of the innovative features in SQL Server 7 is the new graphical utility for designing views. In the past, views had to be created using hand typed SQL statements. Views can now be designed using a graphical utility, shown in Figure 7-17, similar to the Microsoft Access QBE grid.

This screen is the same as the screen that is opened when you choose to open a table and return all rows, which was described in Chapter 1. You can select tables from the database by choosing the Add table button on the toolbar. Relationships that are already defined in the database are automatically shown in the view, and the necessary SQL join code is created. You can view the different panes by selecting the appropriate button, and you can choose to include, filter, sort, or output fields by selecting them from the tables or in the grid pane. You can also directly modify the SQL that the designer creates and preview the results of the view. Advanced properties are available by selecting Properties on the toolbar or from the context-menu.

When you have finished creating or modifying your view, save your changes if appropriate.

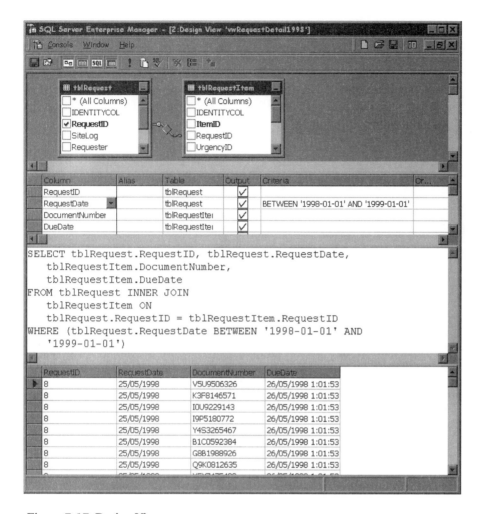

Figure 7-17. Design View

You can also view the Transact-SQL definition of a view by double-clicking it in Enterprise Manager. This displays the full definition of the view, so that you can see what language you should use to define a view without the designer.

Managing Stored Procedures

Stored procedures cannot be created graphically because they can contain multiple Transact-SQL statements and can become quite complex. Instead, they must be created and managed using a simple SQL editor, such as the one included in SQL Server. This editor, shown in Figure 7-18, contains a few useful formatting properties.

Figure 7-18. Edit Stored Procedure

If you choose to create a new stored procedure, the editor starts you with a simple stored procedure template. If you choose to edit an existing stored procedure, the editor opens with the T-SQL for that stored procedure displayed. Either way, the text in the stored procedure is colored using the standard SQL Server colors for identifiers in code. Change or create your stored procedure as necessary. You should always check the syntax of your stored procedure before you apply the changes using the Check Syntax button at the bottom of the screen. However, this only checks to ensure that there are no syntax errors in the code. It does not check object names. In order to ensure that your code is correct, test it using Query Analyzer by calling your stored procedure with the syntax:

```
EXEC ProcedureName [arg1, arg2, …, argN]
```

This will better help you to diagnose errors in the procedure.

Managing Users

You can manage the database users from the Users section within each database. This is an alternate method of giving users access to a particular database, outside of using the Logins administration. Database users are managed using the screen shown in Figure 7-19.

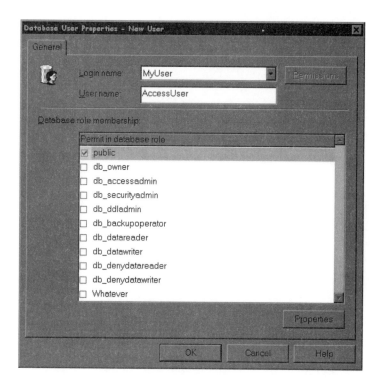

Figure 7-19. Database User Properties

When you create a database user, you must select an existing login in the Login name drop-down list that does not already have access to the database. If the login is already configured to access the database, you will not be able to select it. Enter a user name that the login will have for this particular database or accept the default. You can then add the user to different roles within the database, so that the user has the necessary permissions to perform the functions that are required of the user. Once a user has been saved, you can manage his or her permissions to all objects by selecting the Permissions button.

Managing Roles

Database roles are an extremely powerful new feature of SQL Server 7 and can make the job of administering security considerably easier. When you choose to create or edit a role, you do so using the Database Role Properties screen shown in Figure 7-20. This screen can be accessed using the toolbar or right-click menu options available in the Roles section for your database.

Figure 7-20. Database Role Properties

You must first give your role a name. Make this name meaningful, so that you know what the role is for and what rights it must have. If you are editing a role, you can only modify the permissions of the role or the members. Select the appropriate role type for this role. Consult the SQL Server documentation for a full explanation of the differences in role types. If you are creating a standard role, you must also create the member list. Select members by selecting the Add button or remove them using the Remove button. You can add users or even other roles to this role. If you are creating an application role, assign a password for that roll.

Before you delete a role, you must remove all existing members. Do so by opening the Properties, removing the members, and saving your changes.

Managing Rules

As mentioned in Chapter 1, rules are provided mainly for backwards compatibility, but can be used to limit values in user defined data types. When you create or edit your rule, you do so using the Rule Properties screen shown in Figure 7-21. This screen can be accessed from the Rule section for your database in MMC.

If you are creating a new rule, enter an appropriate name for it. You must then enter the text for the rule. In order to bind a new rule, save it, and then reedit it. You will then have access to the Bind UDDTs and Bind Columns buttons.

Using SQL Server 7

Figure 7-21. Rule Properties

The Bind UDDTs command allows you to bind the rule to any of the user defined data types in your database. The screen that this command opens is shown in Figure 7-22.

Figure 7-22. Bind Rule to User-Defined Data Types

You can bind your rule to the UDDT by checking the bind column. If you do not want existing data checked against this rule, select the checkbox in the Future Only column and existing data will be ignored.

To bind a rule directly to a field, click the Bind Columns button on the Rule Properties dialog. This opens the screen shown in Figure 7-23.

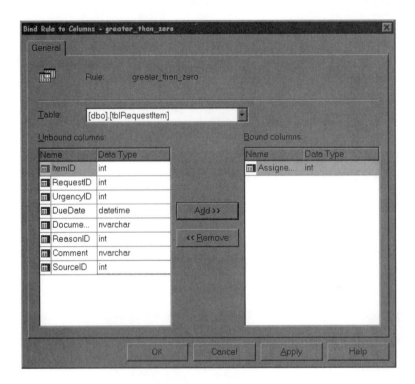

Figure 7-23. Bind Rule to Columns

Select the table you want to bind the rule to (or remove it from), and use the Add >> and << Remove buttons to bind or unbind the column. Exercise caution when binding your rules. If the rule you created is invalid for the data type of the column you bind it to, SQL Server will not generate an error message when you bind it. A message will only be displayed when you attempt to enter data into the column. Check your rules carefully before you bind them to a field.

You can rename a rule using the shortcut menu for a rule in Enterprise Manager. When you do so, all implementations of the rule are updated to reflect your name change. If you need to delete a rule, you must unbind it from all columns and UDDTs before doing so.

Managing Defaults

Defaults, like rules, are provided mainly for backwards compatibility, and you normally want to simply set the default value in the field itself. However, you may want to use them in user defined data types and, as such, defaults must be created. The Default Properties screen, shown in Figure 7-24, allows you to define and bind your default.

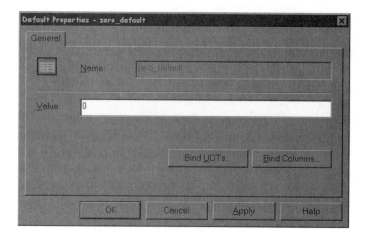

Figure 7-24. Default Properties

Enter a name for your default if you are creating a new one, and enter a value. This value can be a literal value or any Transact-SQL system function that returns a value. If you are creating a new default, you must save it and reedit it before you can bind it. When you are ready to bind your default, you do so using screens identical to the binding of a rule.

Managing User-Defined Data Type

User defined data types can be a very useful feature of SQL Server. They allow you to implement a single set of rules, defaults, and data types against multiple columns in many tables. This occurs most often due to a business need. Figure 7-25 shows the properties you must enter when creating a UDDT.

A name must be provided for your UDDT and can only be changed from within the Enterprise Manager main screen once it is committed. Because all UDDTs are based on regular data types, you must select the data type it is based on. You can then select a rule and a default, if either item applies. Once your UDDT is saved, you can determine what columns use it by selecting the Where Used button from this screen. Because you cannot delete a UDDT while it is in use, this function can be quite useful.

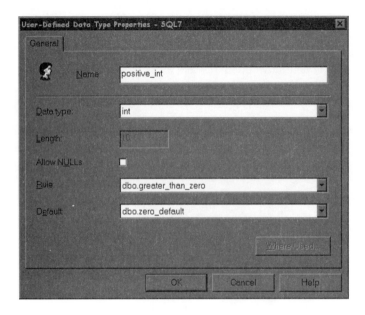

Figure 7-25. User-Defined Data Type Properties

Other Tools

Although you can administer SQL Server using Enterprise Manager, there are a few other ways of administering a database. If you have downloaded the Upsizing Wizard for Access 97, the installation of this wizard adds a menu item to the Tools⟶Add-Ins called SQL-Server Browser. This tool, shown in Figure 7-26, can be used to administer most of the objects in a SQL Server database and is designed to look like the regular Access 97 database window.

This tool will ask you if you want to link a table to the current database as soon as you create it. It also provides quick access to a SQL Server database without having to start Enterprise Manager.

If you do plan to use this tool, keep in mind that it does not provide the full functionality of what can be done in Enterprise Manager. You cannot bind rules directly when you create them. You must open the table that they are based on before you can do so. You also cannot bind defaults when you create them, and you cannot create user defined data types. Additionally, you cannot configure security from this utility.

The browser does not properly format items that are not created within it. If you create views or rules in Enterprise Manager, they might not show up properly in the browser. You may also find that you cannot design tables in this browser that were not created in it to begin with.

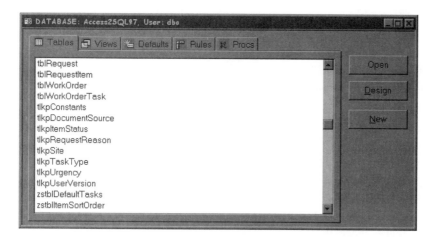

Figure 7-26. SQL Server Browser

Access 2000 has completely changed the way that databases are administered by introducing the concept of Access Data Projects (ADP). By creating your application as an ADP, you can directly manage SQL Server tables, diagrams, stored procedures, and views. However, you cannot manage security, rules, defaults, or UDDTs from an ADP. You must use Enterprise Manager to do this.

For these reasons, your best bet is to use Enterprise Manager to manage your database.

A Special Note on Security

One property of SQL Server that hasn't been discussed much is how the security you design on your server affects the names of objects. I have left this subject to the end of the chapter because I think it deserves special attention, especially for people who are used to creating database objects in Microsoft Access.

When a user creates an object in SQL Server, the name of that object is actually made up of two pieces of information. The first piece of information that is used to define the object is the owner name. If the login is aliased in the current database, this owner name is the alias for the login. If the login does not have an alias for the database, the login name is used to create this piece of information. The second piece of information that goes into the object name is the name of the object as supplied. For example, if a user connecting to a database under the alias of "application_user" creates a new table name "tblMyOrders", the fully qualified SQL Server name of this object becomes "application_user.tblMyOrders"—the owner of the table followed by the table name. This naming may lead to some confusion when you attempt to access objects in your database. SQL code that references a table named "tblMyOrders" may not reference the table you expect. The convention of adding the owner name before the object name means that there can actually be many tables with the same name, but created by different users. A user named "admin_user" might have a table named "tblMyOrders" as well, and this could be the table that you actually reference.

So how does SQL Server decide what table you are referencing if there are multiple tables with the same name but with different owners. The first table that SQL Server returns is the table owned by the person who is requesting the information. So if "application_user" logs in to the database and requests data from "tblMyOrders", SQL Server first looks for a table with the fully qualified name of "application_user.tblMyOrders". If this table is not found, SQL Server then searches for a table that is owned by the dbo user—"dbo.tblMyOrders". If no matching table name is found under the user's name or under dbo, the table will not be found.

The affect that security has on object names means that you must be careful when you create objects that other users need to access. Unless you fully qualify the name when you call the object, it must belong to the current login or dbo.

Moving On

I hope that the information provided in this chapter helps you to understand how to use SQL Server a little better. I have tried to cover as much information as a single chapter allows. There is much more information available if you want a more in-depth understanding of how to use SQL Server. The SQL Server Books Online in your SQL Server program group on the Start menu is a good place to begin. The information contained in these books is complete and can tell you just about anything you need to know about SQL Server.

However, the Books Online probably have far too much information for most users, and the information may not be organized in a fashion that you find easy to read and understand. If you really want to find out more about SQL Server there are plenty of good books on the subject that can help you find your way in SQL Server. My personal favorite is *Microsoft SQL Server 7 DBA Survival Guide* by Spenic, Sledge, and Herb (Sams Publishing, June 1999). It contains a great deal of information that is not covered by some of the more basic books.

CHAPTER 8
Enabling Data Access

ONE OF THE KEYS TO THE SUCCESS of a SQL Server database application is how efficient the data access methods are. Your application will use SQL Server tables and views as the main interfaces for accessing data. Designing tables and views so that they make data available efficiently is one of the most important parts of a migration. It is not sufficient to just copy the design of a table from Access to SQL Server. The rules that affect the performance of data requests on tables are very different between these two systems, and you should be aware of these rules, so that you can get the most out of SQL Server in your new application.

Tables

Tables in SQL Server, as in Access, are the objects that hold all of the data that is used in your application. They are the most important objects in any database. Let's begin by discussing how SQL Server tables can be designed, so that they are as efficient as possible for your application. When designing your tables there are a number of considerations you should take into account:

- What are the best data types for the information you want to store?

- Are the indexes in your tables necessary and efficient?

- What actions are regularly performed against your tables?

In this chapter, each of these items will be explored further.

Choosing the Appropriate Data Type

You may be thinking, "I used the Wizard to upsize my tables, didn't it already translate my data types for me?" The answer to this question is yes. However, the Wizard is a generalized migration tool. It is not the be-all and end-all of database translators. The Wizard is designed to fulfill a very general need for migrating data from Access to SQL Server. The Wizard does not have the capability to look at how your data is used. For this reason, you need to do your own evaluation of the data types that you use in SQL Server. The data type that you choose for a field depends strongly on what data you will be storing in that field.

You should first consider the size of each field in your tables. It is almost always best to reduce the size of your fields as much as possible, even though memory and hard drive space is relatively cheap. The more data you have in your database, the harder SQL Server and the operating system must work to manage and manipulate your data. By reducing the size of the columns that store your data, you make the database more efficient. In order to get a better understanding of this concept, let's look at each of the various data types and what you should consider when setting your field sizes.

Character Data Types

The choices you can make for your character data types differ considerably between SQL Server 6.5 and 7. Version 7 includes Unicode versions of all of the character data types that exist in version 6.5 (a single character in Unicode takes up twice as much space as the same standard ANSI character), and the maximum size of each of these data types has dramatically increased. In version 6.5, *char* and *varchar* data types are limited to 255 characters, just like an Access Text field. In version 7, these data types can hold up to 8000 characters (the Unicode data types *nchar* and *nvarchar* can hold half of the characters held by their non-Unicode counterparts). The *text* data type can hold a maximum of 2,147,483,647 characters (the Unicode version included in SQL 7—*ntext*—can hold half that many). When a field of type text is created in SQL Server, it is not created with a predefined size, much like Memo fields in Access. The only limitation on the size of fields of type text and ntext is the two billion character system limit.

The first step in selecting data types for character data is to select the smallest possible data type and size possible. If it is possible to limit the size of your field to a number less than the maximum size of the data type, do so. Access developers often overcompensate in text fields by making them larger than is really necessary. Although this can prevent some problems in the short term, it makes your application less efficient in the long term. By the time your application has reached the point that it needs to be migrated from Access to SQL Server, you should be very confident about your data requirements. If your text fields are bigger than they need to be, reduce their sizes. Often, the choice of field sizes in Access is a result of the default settings provided by Access itself. Text fields that default to 50 or 255 characters, for example, are often larger than they need to be. Memo fields are often used where a large text field would suffice. You should address these types of problems as a part of planning your migration.

You can also reduce the size of your fields by using the non-Unicode character data types. The Unicode data types nchar, nvarchar, and ntext require twice as much space per character than their non-Unicode equivalents (char, varchar, and text). If your application is designed for use only with standard western characters, do not use the Unicode characters because they will only add to the amount of space your database requires. However, if you are developing an application that might be used in a country that does not use the standard western alphabet, you should use the Unicode types. Choosing the Unicode data types for international applications helps to ensure that your application can work in all languages.

The second step in choosing data types is to avoid using, if at all possible, the text data type in SQL Server, especially in versions prior to version 7. The text data type is extremely inefficient in older versions of SQL Server and is prone to numerous problems. The Access equivalent data type—Memo—is often overused in Access applications. Access developers, myself included, tend to err on the side of caution and leave as much room for data entry as possible. However, this type of practice should be avoided in SQL Server. Larger database systems perform better, but more consideration needs to be given to choosing data types for performance. If the 255 character limit of the SQL 6.5 character data types really is too small for what you want to include, you will have to live with the performance limitations of the text data type.

Variable length fields, such as varchar and varbinary, have a certain amount of overhead associated with them that fixed length fields, such as char, do not. However, variable length fields do not require the same amount of space as fixed length fields for storage because they only store the data that is entered and do not pad the field with blank spaces. The char data type pads all entries with spaces, so that they fill the entire field. This means that there is a tradeoff between the overhead imposed by the variable length fields and the padding done by the fixed length data types. The best rule to use for these fields is to use char for fields that contain eight or less characters and use varchar for larger fields. This will help you balance the performance differences between the two types of character fields. The only exception to this rule is if your field can contain Null values. SQL Server treats nullable char fields exactly the same as it treats varchar fields of the same length. In this case, use varchar.

Integer Data Types

SQL Server includes four integer data types: int, smallint, tinyint, and bit. Using integer data types is probably the only place where you might want to break the rule of always using the smallest data type possible. Most computers that are capable of running SQL Server use Intel chips, which currently deal with 4 bytes of data at a time. The int data type takes up exactly 4 bytes. The smallint takes up 2 bytes, whereas tinyint and bit take 1. Because of the architecture of the processor on the computers in use today, you may find that using an int data type for integer fields increases the response time of your application. The processor can deal with int fields more effectively and your application could perform better.

Precision Numeric Data Types

Precision numeric data types are those numeric data types that contain a decimal component. The type of precision number you should use in SQL Server depends on what you are going to be using the data for and how you want your data to be rounded. Two floating-point (variable precision) number types are available: float and real. Float is a configurable data type. You can set the number of bits used to store the digits to the right of the decimal (in scientific notation) for the float number and therefore determine the storage size required. This value must be between 1 and 53. Using a value of 24 or less requires 4 bytes of data to store a value and a value of 25 or more requires 8 bytes. Real is equivalent to float(24) and is a quick way of selecting this data type. Because you set the number of bits that are stored to the right of the decimal for scientific notation, the actual number stored in these types of fields may vary considerably in the data it contains. This means that the field will be rounded differently if you have 10 digits to the left of the decimal in standard notation than if you have one digit to the right of the decimal. If you are storing numbers that are very large, but you are not too concerned with how they are rounded, you can select one of these types.

If you want to control the precision of your data, you should use the decimal data type. (The numeric data type is synonymous with the decimal data types and is provided mainly for backwards compatibility with older versions of SQL Server, which didn't have decimal). This data type is the best one to use if you are working with statistical or financial data where you require exact rounding of your data. With the decimal data type, you can specify the exact precision (total number of digits in the field – left and right of the decimal place) and scale (number of digits to the right of the decimal place that are stored in your field) of your data. This allows you greater control over the behavior of your data. SQL Server always rounds your data up to the next value when necessary. The more precision you choose, the more space is required to store your data.

If your application is dealing with monetary values, you may want to use one of the currency data types provided with SQL Server. As with other data types, it is best to choose the smaller (smallmoney) data type over the larger (money) if you can because it reduces the amount of space necessary to store your data and improves server response time. If you are going to be dealing with monetary data over $200,000, you should choose the larger data type because smallmoney is limited to values between $214,748.3647 and -$214,748.3648.

Date Data Types

There are only two date data types in SQL Server: datetime and smalldatetime. Although the datetime data type requires twice as much storage space (8 bytes) as the smalldatetime data type does, you will almost always want to use it as the type for your date fields. The reasoning behind this is twofold. First of all, the smalldatetime data type is only accurate to the minute. If your data requires accuracy to the second, smalldatetime cannot fulfill your needs. The datetime data type is able to store times accurate to $1/300^{\text{th}}$ of a second. This means that your data will be more accurate and comparison will be more discriminating.

The second reason is that smalldatetime can only store dates before June 6, 2079. This may not sound like a problem for your application, but anyone involved in the preparation that was necessary for Y2K will understand how this may become a problem. If you are doing any kind of forecasting of data, this problem is compounded. Financial and insurance applications often deal with data up to 40 years in advance. If you use the smalldatetime data type, you may be leaving your successors with an issue similar to Y2K. For this reason also, you should use the datetime data type in your date fields.

Binary Data Types

Binary data types can be used to store binary data as hexadecimal values. These types can store either numeric values or files, but they are usually used to store the content of files or other binary information. For most of us, their use is quite limited. However, if your application needs to store files in database tables, you should use one of these types. Choose the type depending on the maximum size you expect a file to be. In SQL 6.5, you will almost always want to use the image data type. However, this data type is difficult to use and error prone in version 6.5. You may want to rethink your data storage and use a character field to store the full pathname to the file, rather than storing the file itself.

Indexing

One of the biggest challenges faced by Access programmers in creating SQL Server tables is figuring out how to manage indexing. Indexing is a very important subject because how you index your tables in SQL Server can dramatically affect the performance of your database. Bad indexing can cause a database to bog down on user requests or make Access unable to update the SQL Server data.

Indexes have two effects on a database. The first effect is that they provide a faster method for the RDBMS to search data in the indexed column(s). This speeds up your data retrieval when indexed columns are filtered in a query. The second effect that indexes have is that they increase the amount of work the RDBMS must do when the data in tables is modified. Indexes must be maintained by the RDBMS when updates, deletes, or inserts occur. Not only does the RDBMS have to handle the actual data changes, it must maintain each index on the table. This adds overhead to the data manipulation process.

When it comes to SQL Server and Access, the two RDBMSs handle the choices you have for indexing very differently. Depending on how Access is configured, it will set some characteristics of indexes and even create indexes that are not explicitly added by the database designer. This does not happen in SQL Server. As a database developer, you have complete control over what indexes are created and what characteristics those indexes have. For this reason, you should understand what needs to be indexed and what characteristics those indexes require.

Deciding What to Index

There are a number of factors that determine what to index in a table. When you are deciding what indexes to create for a table, you must consider how the data in the potential index will be used, what type and range of data will go into the indexed columns, and how the table itself is used in daily functions. Indexes always involve tradeoffs. Indexing generally makes querying data faster. SQL Server (and all RDBMSs) retrieves, summarizes, and groups data much faster when an index is used. However, indexes increase the amount of time it takes to insert or update a record in a table. Each time you insert a record or modify an indexed value, the RDBMS must maintain the index, moving records or pointers around to accommodate your changes.

When looking at how data in the indexed columns will be used, you should consider what types of queries might be run against that data. Indexes can dramatically improve performance in queries run against the indexed columns. If columns are often used in aggregations, search ranges, ordering, or table joins, they can be good candidates for indexing. For example, if your users often want to summarize sales figures in reports or for display, you may want to create an index on the column that contains the summarized data. Likewise, if you have an Orders table and you often use information from a related Order Details child table by joining the tables in a query, you almost always want to index the foreign key field in the Order Details table. When you join an Order table record to its matching record in the Order Detail table, SQL Server must search the Order Detail table for the matching foreign key value. If the column is indexed, searches on that field will run faster. Similar to using the index in a book to find all the pages where a specific word appears, using an index is significantly faster than sequentially reading every page in the book.

The next factor you should look at is what type and ranges of data will be used in the columns in the index. Indexes tend to degrade performance when they are used against columns that contain a wide variety of values. This would be true for a Comments field in a table. Because the text in this type of field is almost never the same, you should avoid indexing it. You should also avoid indexing large fields. Generally, you do not want to index fields that are greater than 24 bytes in size. Indexes on these fields take a great deal of overhead to manage and your application will suffer. Although you may get a performance gain when searching these columns if they are indexed, the gain will most likely be outweighed by the over-head that goes into maintaining the index if the table is updated frequently.

How the table is used greatly affects the indexing that you consider. This is especially true in SQL Server tables that are linked into Access. One of the problems with external data sources (even in an ADP) is that if you do not provide a unique index for the table, you will not be able to update it. This can cause confusion when you go to update a table that does not have a primary key or other unique index. You cannot edit these tables from the interfaces within Access. Only after you have created a unique index for the table are you able to edit the table or a view based on the table in Access. However, these types of tables can be updated using SQL statements passed directly to SQL Server.

If the data in your table is constantly being updated, you should minimize the indexes on it. Each update to the table requires SQL Server to have to maintain all of the indexes, adding extra processing. This should be avoided if at all possible. Index as few fields as possible in this situation.

Finally, if your table will only ever contain a few rows, you should limit the indexes used in it. When dealing with small tables in SQL Server, it is often faster to allow SQL Server to search the raw data without an index than to use an index and have SQL Server maintain it. The overhead involved in maintaining the index negates any performance gain when searching the data. Index only those fields that define a unique index for the table, so that you can maintain the table in the Access user interface.

Clustering

The concept of clustered indexes is usually new to Access programmers. Cluster-ing an index tells the RDBMS to physically sort the data on disk by the clustered index. Access does not give you the ability to specify what index is clustered, if any of them really is. In SQL Server, you are able to tell the server what index should be clustered. Clustering improves the response time for data selection that is based on the selected index. When you run queries that use the field(s) contained in the clustered index, your queries run faster. With this in mind, you should select an appropriate index to cluster. This should be the unique key that is most often used to return or search for records.

The most commonly clustered index is the primary key because data is usu-ally retrieved from the table based on the values in this field. If this is the case in your application, cluster the primary key. If you usually select data from the table filtering on data in fields other than the primary key, you should consider creating a clustered index on those fields. This will improve data retrieval for your table and increase response time from the server. For example, a table—the Order Detail table—that is frequently joined to another table—the Order table—might be use-fully clustered on the foreign key from the Order table.

Indexes and ODBC

When connecting to SQL Server data in Access through ODBC, there is a special consideration you should take into account that affects the indexes you should create on SQL Server. Access requires a unique index for a table in order to update it. When you link a table or a view into Access, Access selects a primary key to use for that table based on the indexes the table contains. The index Access selects may not always be the one you expect. Access either selects a unique index from the table definition or, if it cannot determine an index to use, it prompts you to specify an index to use based on the fields the table contains. When you are prompted to select an index, Access has no way of knowing that the index you selected is actually unique. It assumes that you selected a unique index and uses that index to update data in the table. If you choose a nonunique index, Access may update more than one record in a SQL Server table when you make changes to a single record. When Access prompts you to select a unique index, ensure that you make the appropriate selection.

The index that Access selects is determined by the characteristics of the indexes in the table. With ODBC, the first choice for a unique index is a clustered index. If you want to force Access to select a particular index as the primary key, the best way to do this is to cluster the index. If there are no clustered indexes, the first unique index (in a list of available indexes that is sorted alphabetically) is elected as the primary key. This is the reason that the Upsizing Wizard names upsized primary keys with the prefix "aaaaa". This index naming forces the "aaaaa" index to be sorted first and therefore causes Access to select it before all others. You can use this same trick when naming your indexes to force the index selection. If your primary key is not clustered, you should name it, so that it is sorted alphabetically before all others.

Timestamps

One other consideration when designing your tables is deciding whether or not you should use timestamps. Timestamps are a system data type that SQL Server updates automatically for each record whenever a record is changed or added. Each timestamp value is unique within a table and is never reused. Timestamps should be used on tables that contain many records and that are updated on a regular basis. This is mainly true for ODBC connections to SQL Server, but can also be true for Data Projects. In order to understand why this is necessary, you need to understand what is going on in the background when you update a table.

When you update a value in your table, Access does not directly update the table. Instead, the ODBC driver creates SQL code that it sends to the database server to have the data updated. The SQL code that the ODBC driver creates to update the row will try to compare all values in all fields (with the exception of text, image, and precision numeric fields) when committing the data to the server. The reason that the ODBC driver does this is to ensure that no changes have occurred to the record since it was retrieved. If a matching record is not found in the table, then another user has modified the record and the update fails. For example, if you updated the customer in an Orders table that contained the fields OrderID, Order-Date, CustomerID, EmployeeID, and PurchaseOrder, the SQL to update the row in the database would look something like this:

```
UPDATE Order
SET CustomerID = 5
WHERE OrderID = ? AND OrderDate = ? AND CustomerID = ?
    AND EmployeeID = ? AND PurchaseOrder = ?
```

where the question marks represent the values in the fields before the update takes place. The update forces SQL Server to compare the values in all fields before updating the row. Unless all of the fields are indexed, this can result in very slow performance because SQL Server has to compare the values in each of the columns to the values in the table. This means that the information for each field must be sent across the network and each field must be compared on SQL Server. This adds to the load on the network and SQL Server. Using a timestamp column prevents the ODBC driver from trying to compare every field in the table to the original values.

With a timestamp field in the table, the ODBC driver would generate the SQL code:

```
UPDATE Order
SET CustomerID = 5
WHERE OrderID = ? AND timestamp = ?
```

This type of change greatly improves updates, especially for tables with a high volume of transactions. This change also affects how SQL Server deals with requests to update data. It allows SQL Server to better manage concurrency issues, where multiple users attempt to update the same record. Once a user updates a record, the timestamp automatically changes. If another user already has a copy of the same record and attempts to update it, the update will fail because the code used to update the row will not find a matching source row on the server because the timestamp value in the table will have changed.

Views

SQL Server views are very similar to saved SELECT queries in Microsoft Access. Views are basically SQL statements that are used to return records to your applica-tion. Views are designed so that you can selectively return columns from one or more tables using a single SQL Server object call. Views can be used "as-is" in an ADP, or they can be attached as a table into a regular database using ODBC. When using data with Access, you should attempt to use views to return data whenever possible, rather than directly connecting to the tables that contain the data they are based on.

Using views to return your data, rather than directly accessing the tables, has two benefits. First, it improves the security of your database. When someone creates a view, the rights to access the tables that make up the view are based on the view creator's rights in the database. Anyone who is granted the rights to be able to open the view does not need to have rights to access the tables on which the view is based. This allows you to control exactly what columns from a table that users have access to, and it prevents users from being able to directly edit the tables, which could jeopardize the integrity of your data.

Second, it makes your SQL Server database and Access application easier to maintain. By defining a view as the source for a form or report, you can customize what data is returned to the form, and you will not have to worry about maintaining SQL statements in your Access user interface.

Creating Views

Views are very versatile and can be used to filter and summarize data. Views support most of the regular expressions that you would normally use in SQL for creating queries. The official syntax for creating a view is:

```
CREATE VIEW [owner.]view_name
[(column_name [, column_name]...)]
[WITH ENCRYPTION]
AS select_statement [WITH CHECK OPTION]
```

In SQL Server 6.5, you must create views using these SQL text definitions. SQL Server 7 provides a graphical interface for creating views (described in Chapter 7), but the tool doesn't support all the features available using the SQL CREATE VIEW command. Because this is the case, let's look at the syntax necessary to create a view, and then look at a few examples of how the statements might be used.

In order to create a view in SQL Server, you must use the CREATE VIEW statement. This, like other object definition statements, tells SQL Server what you want to create. This name can be qualified with a user name if you have the necessary security rights and want to create a view under a different user's login. In order to create a view under the dbo login named vwMyView, the syntax would be:

```
CREATE VIEW dbo.vwMyView
```

The next step in creating a view is optional. If you want the columns in your view to be aliased (be returned with names that are different than they are in the tables), you must enter each of the column names after the views name. These aliases must appear in brackets and be separated by commas. If you use this technique to alias any columns, you must include all column names to use in the output. For example:

```
CREATE VIEW dbo.vwMyView (CustomerID, ContactFullName, PhoneNumber)
```

This statement creates a view that returns three fields. These fields appear to the client as if they are named CustomerID, ContactFullName, and PhoneNumber. However, they may have different names in the database or may be based on calculated values.

The next option in a view's definition, WITH ENCRYPTION, must be placed immediately after the column list, or after the view name if no column list is supplied. This option is a special SQL Server command designed to make the view more secure. SQL Server stores the definition of your view in such a way that other users may be able to view that definition. Usually, this is not a problem because you are only concerned with users accessing the data that your view returns. If, however, you do not want anyone to be able to see the definition of the view, you must use the WITH ENCRYPTION option.

The next section of the view definition is where you define what the SQL statement is that returns the records. This statement can be any single SQL SELECT statement including GROUP BY queries and queries that contain multiple tables. This statement must be preceded with the keyword AS, which tells SQL Server that the SQL statement to return data will follow. However, there are a few limitations surrounding how data can be returned and how you can edit that data.

You cannot use the ORDER BY, COMPUTE, COMPUTE BY, or SELECT INTO keywords within the definition of a view. SQL Server generates an error if you try to create a view that contains any of these keywords. This means that you cannot sort data in a view that is not part of a grouping. You also cannot directly transfer data from one table to another using views.

When editing data based on a view, you should keep in mind that only one source table can be edited at a time. When you return data from multiple tables using a view, the updateable table will either be the "many" table in any one-to-many relationships, or it will be one of the tables in a one-to-one relationship. In cases of a one-to-one relationship, it is possible to edit the data from both tables, but you cannot edit columns from each table in the same action. You must update the fields from one table and commit those changes before you are allowed to update fields from the other table. The other restriction to editing data from views is that, as in Access, you cannot edit summarized, grouped, or calculated data. If your view contains a GROUP BY clause, it is, by definition, read-only.

Continuing with our example, the view we would create might look like this:

```
CREATE VIEW dbo.vwMyView (CustomerID, ContactFullName, PhoneNumber)
WITH ENCRYPTION
AS
  SELECT CustomerID, ContactFirstName + ' ' + ContactLastName,
  ContactPhoneNumber
  FROM tblCustomers
```

This view returns the CustomerID, a full name of the contact made up of the contact's first and last name concatenated together with a space in the middle, and the contact's phone number.

The final optional parameter, WITH CHECK OPTION, is used in special cases where your view has criteria included in a WHERE clause. This setting is used when you create a view that is updateable. The setting causes SQL Server to check data when new records are added to the database through the view, so that the data conforms to the criteria in the WHERE clause. This can be very useful if you not only want to limit the data that is returned to your application to certain values, but also want to prevent values that do not meet that criteria from being entered into the system. Without this setting, any values that are permitted for the table columns can be updated or added using the view. A view that uses this option might be:

```
CREATE VIEW vwOrders1999
AS
  SELECT tblOrders.*
  FROM tblOrders
  WHERE tblOrders.OrderDate BETWEEN '1999-01-01' AND '1999-12-31'
WITH CHECK OPTION
```

If a user attempts to enter an order in this view, which is dated before or after 1999, SQL Server returns an error. This can be a useful way of limiting the data that the user can see and also limiting the data that a user can enter.

Why Use Views

Although you may see a use for views in certain situations, you may not understand why you should use them whenever you work with data within Access. There are a few very good reasons for doing this.

The first reason for using views as the source for most data in an Access database is security. Although SQL Server has the capability to set user permissions on columns in a table, this type of security can be difficult to implement and to maintain.

You must set column level permissions for each column to which you want your users to have access. If you design your database around the concept that all updateable data will be provided by views, you can remove all access to the tables from different users. You can then create views that only return the columns the users need to access and give them the necessary permissions to the view only. This makes security administration easier and is the preferred method of most database administrators.

A second reason for using views is that they can improve the response time from the server. When you save a view, SQL Server saves it in a compiled state. This means that SQL Server includes information with the saved view that it uses to optimize the methods used to retrieve data from tables and returns that data to the client. If you use a simple SQL statement, SQL Server has to compile this statement and plan the most efficient method to return the data to your application each time you use that statement. This adds overhead, but if you use a view, this information is already available to the server. Also, when you use a view, you generally do not include all fields from all of the tables it uses, or you may filter the data that is returned from the tables. This means that less data must travel over the network than if you used the tables directly, which improves the performance of your application.

Another good reason for using views is that they give you the ability to return data from multiple tables. If your application needs to display data from multiple tables and provide the capability to update one of those tables, views are a very good choice. You can create a view that includes multiple joined tables and returns all of the necessary information. Although you can only edit the contents of one table at a time, you are able to view the necessary information from all tables at once.

Finally, views connected by ODBC allow you to define a unique index for updates, rather than depending on Access to choose one. Because of the methods that Access uses to select the index that will be used for updates, the choices Access makes are not always the best. You as a developer often know better than Access which index would be best. With a view that is linked via ODBC, you must define what the primary key is. This gives you a bit more flexibility when it comes to performance enhancements.

An Ounce of Prevention

Designing tables and views in SQL Server for use in an Access application is much more complex than designing tables and queries in a regular Access database. There are many considerations that you must examine in order to ensure that your application performs well. SQL Server allows you to build a database that can store a great deal of information. However, as the amount of information in the database grows, the small problems that seemed inconsequential in an Access database can seriously hamper the performance of your application. Design your tables and views well at the outset, and you may never have to modify them again.

CHAPTER 9

Stored Procedures

As described in previous chapters, stored procedures are sets of instructions for SQL Server that are compiled into a single plan. Stored procedures are a new concept to most Access programmers because there is no equivalent in Access. For this reason, stored procedures are often misused or implemented poorly. Also, Access developers tend not to use stored procedures to their full potential or as much as stored procedures should be used in SQL Server. Stored Procedures can be very powerful and can be used to replace much of the VBA code and macros that most programmers use in an Access application. Because they are so important in SQL Server, I will provide you with information on how to create them, how to use them effectively, and how to determine what portions of an Access application can be migrated to stored procedures.

Using Stored Procedures

Stored procedures are exactly what their name implies: They are procedures that are saved or "stored" in a SQL Server database. Stored procedures are written in the SQL Server programming language Transact-SQL (T-SQL) and are very similar to subroutines and functions in VBA code. Although stored procedures aren't necessarily capable of the same functions that a VBA procedure is capable of, they are very powerful tools.

What Stored Procedures Can Do

Stored procedures can be used to accomplish a number of tasks. One of their most important tasks is the capability to work with data from SQL Server. A single stored procedure can contain any number of SQL data manipulation statements. In Access, in order to execute multiple SELECT, INSERT, UPDATE or DELETE SQL statements, you must run each statement individually. A stored procedure can contain any number of SQL statements in one single, easy to manage script.

Stored procedures can also be used to perform functions that do not interface with data in any way. They can calculate values and compare complex data relations.

And, they can even be used to perform complex functions that manipulate values of the data you pass in. For example, with stored procedures you can:

- Write a function that calculates the difference between two dates and returns the result to another stored procedure or to a client.

- Determine the amortization period for a loan.

- Determine the next position to play in a game of tic-tac-toe (although I have yet to really need this from SQL Server).

Stored procedures can also be used to manage SQL Server objects. You can use T-SQL code to add, delete, modify, and update objects on the server. For example, you can use a stored procedure to add a new table to a database, to manage the logins and security for your server, and to create or delete entire databases if necessary.

Finally, the greatest power of stored procedures is their capability to return recordsets to a client. As with SQL Server views, stored procedures can be used to return data from a table to an application. However, stored procedures are much more flexible than views because they support all of the keywords in T-SQL. Stored procedures also have the capability to return more than one recordset at a time.

Stored Procedure Types

SQL Server actually includes three different types of stored procedures: system stored procedures, user defined stored procedures, and extended stored procedures.

System stored procedures are procedures that are already created for you and are a part of SQL Server itself. They provide textual commands for managing the database or the server.

User defined stored procedures are the stored procedures that a database developer creates in the database to provide some required functionality. This is the type of stored procedure that you will create in your database.

Extended stored procedures are a special kind of stored procedure that is actually created in a low-level programming language, such as C. This type of procedure is actually saved in a DLL and registered with SQL Server. Extended stored procedures can then be called in SQL Server as if they were a normal procedure in the system.

Components

A SQL Server stored procedure consists of a number of components:

- Procedure name

- Parameters

- T-SQL code

- A return value

A stored procedure's name is the name that is used when the stored procedure is invoked. Like all other objects in SQL Server, the name must be unique to the database, and it must conform to the SQL Server naming convention for objects.

Parameters in a stored procedure are optional. You can create a stored procedure that does not require arguments just as you would create a VBA function that does not require parameters. However, when parameters are used, they can be used to input values to the stored procedure or return values to the calling application. Depending on whether they accept or return data, arguments must be identified as INPUT or OUTPUT arguments.

When you define a stored procedure, you must include some T-SQL code to do the work that you want the stored procedure to accomplish. T-SQL statements can include any number of data manipulation statements, calculations, calls to other stored procedures, function calls to external applications, and so on. This is where the work that your stored procedure needs to do is defined.

Finally, a return value can be assigned to your stored procedure. This value is separate from the OUTPUT parameters of your stored procedure, and it must be an integer value.

Stored Procedure Syntax

Stored procedures are created using the CREATE PROCEDURE T-SQL statement. The syntax for the CREATE PROCEDURE statement is

```
CREATE PROCedure [owner.]procedure_name[;number]
    [(parameter1 [, parameter2]...[parameterN])]
[{FOR REPLICATION} | {WITH RECOMPILE}
    [{[WITH] | [,]} ENCRYPTION]]
AS sql_statements
```

The first part of a stored procedure declaration is the CREATE PROCEDURE statement. This can be abbreviated to CREATE PROC, which tells SQL Server that you want to create a new stored procedure in your database. The CREATE PROCEDURE statement is followed by the user name of the owner of the procedure, if desired, and the procedure's name. The name must conform to the SQL Server rules for object naming and must be unique for the database. The last part of the procedure header, the number, allows you to create multiple stored procedures with the same name, but qualified by a number. This feature is intended to group procedures, so that they can be deleted from the database using a single DROP PROCEDURE call. This allows DBAs to group a set of related procedures, such as the procedures that must run for an order to be added to the database. However, this function is of little practical use in an Access application and can lead to confusion. I recommend that you do not use the *number* feature.

To better understand how to use the CREATE PROCEDURE statement, let's walk through a sample CREATE PROCEDURE statement. Explanations will be included as we step through each part. A simple declaration might look this:

```
CREATE PROCEDURE dbo.usp_UpdateOrderDiscount
```

This statement creates a procedure called usp_UpdateOrderDiscount in the current database.

The declaration of the procedure can be followed by parameters. These define the requirements for the arguments that are used when the procedure is called. Parameters are optional and must be constructed using the following syntax:

```
@parameter_name datatype [= default] [OUTPUT]
```

In T-SQL, all user defined variables, like parameters, must be preceded with the "at" symbol (@) and must conform to the SQL Server rules for naming identifiers, as outlined in Chapter 4. All of the parameters for a stored procedure must be enclosed in brackets and separated by commas. After you provide a name for your parameter, you must specify its data type. The parameter's data type can be any of the SQL Server native data types or any user defined data type (UDDT). Beware of using UDDTs, however, because you cannot be sure that they will exist when you call your stored procedure. If you delete a UDDT from SQL Server, you will not receive a warning that it is being used by a stored procedure. Instead, the procedure will simply fail the next time it is called.

You can optionally supply a default value for a parameter by adding an equal sign (=) after the parameter name and entering the default value. This value will be used if no value for the parameter is assigned when the procedure is called. You can also specify that the parameter's value is an output of the procedure using the OUTPUT keyword. The OUTPUT keyword is similar to the VBA ByRef keyword. OUTPUT means that the value of the parameter may be modified by the stored procedure, and the client can check its value when the procedure is complete. Using this syntax for optional parameters, if you want to declare a parameter for a CustomerID that would assume a default value of 0 and was of type integer, you could use this code:

```
@intCustomerID int = 0
```

If you want to create an output parameter that returned the discount as a decimal value with 4 digits of precision, a scale of 3 (e.g., 0.015), and a default value of 5.5, you could use this code:

```
@decDiscount decimal(4, 3) = 5.5 OUTPUT
```

If the stored procedure does not modify the value of @decDecimal, the value 5.5 is automatically returned to the caller. Note that if you do not provide a default value for a parameter when you create the stored procedure, your application must supply a value for that parameter when the stored procedure is called. For this reason, you should always provide a default value for output parameters. It makes your stored procedures easier to use and maintain.

Combining all of this information to create a single declaration for the stored procedure, you could begin to define the stored procedure as

```
CREATE PROCEDURE dbo.usp_UpdateOrderDiscount
(@intCustomerID int = 0, @decDiscount decimal(4, 3) = 0.0 OUTPUT)
```

In SQL Server 6.5, you are limited to 255 parameters in a single stored procedure. This is sufficient for most developers' needs. However, due to the increasing demand for larger and more complex databases, SQL Server 7 now supports up to 1024 parameters in a single stored procedure.

Once the main declaration is done for your stored procedure, you can use any or all of three optional statements for the stored procedure: RECOMPILE, ENCRYPTION, or FOR REPLICATION. Two of these options, RECOMPILE and ENCRYPTION must be preceded by the WITH keyword. However, if both are used, only one WITH should be used, and a comma must separate the two options (for example, "WITH RECOMPILE, ENCRYPTION"). The RECOMPILE option forces SQL Server to recompile the stored procedure each time it is run. It is intended for use in abnormal situations and is probably not of much use for the average programmer. DBAs may add this option to a stored procedure that is linked to a table that changes dramatically between each call to the table, such as having two million records added between each call. The ENCRYPTION option, however, is of some use. As with views, the WITH ENCRYPTION statement tells SQL Server to encrypt the definition of your stored procedure so that no other users can edit it. This prevents users who have access to the syscomments table in your database from being able to directly read the stored procedure definition from that table. The FOR REPLICATION option is intended to be used for stored procedures that are used as part of replicating a database (and are not, themselves, to be replicated). If you are not using replication, you do not need to use this setting.

Before you can start to create the code for your stored procedure, you must add one more word: AS. This keyword tells SQL Server that you are about to provide the SQL statements that your stored procedure will execute. Once this is done, you can begin to define the actions of your stored procedure.

Coding Stored Procedures

Stored procedures are created using Microsoft's SQL Server programming language, T-SQL. T-SQL is much like other programming languages in that it allows you to define a sequence of commands to be run against a database. Although it does not have as much functionality built in as VBA does, it is still a very powerful language. Before you can create your stored procedures, you must understand how to write T-SQL code. So, let's take a look at some of the basics of T-SQL including how to create and use variables, how to create logical constructs, and what operators you can use to compare data.

Transact-SQL Basics

T-SQL is designed with the idea that the majority of work you will be doing will be with SQL Server data. For this reason, it supports all of the SQL Server data manipulation and definition statements that you would normally use in a query, and a lot more.

One major difference between T-SQL and VBA coding is that T-SQL code does not work with white space in the same way that VBA does. When you press the Enter key to end a line in VBA code, the line itself is considered to be a single, complete statement. In T-SQL, this is not always the case. Although you generally end a single statement by adding a line break, T-SQL is smart enough to allow you to have a single statement that spans multiple lines. It will keep reading the code until it reaches an end-of-line character that satisfactorily completes the syntax for the call being made. For example, you can use a SELECT statement that spans multiple lines, adding line breaks where it is convenient to ensure that the code is formatted to be readable to a developer. If the stored procedure parser cannot determine a satisfactory end for the statement, an error is raised. In such a case, check your procedure syntax for errors, watching for lines that may continue when you think they shouldn't.

Another difference between T-SQL and VBA is that in T-SQL your code runs directly against a database without having an intermediate object model to manage the database calls. This means that when you use a SELECT statement in T-SQL, you do not need to assign it to a recordset object in the code, and you don't need to qualify the statement in quotes. Instead, you write the SELECT statement exactly as you would in an Access query.

An additional difference between the two languages is that the utility functions that are available in T-SQL are all functions designed for use in SQL statements. These functions are similar to the Jet functions that you can use in Access queries. They can be used to manipulate strings, convert data types, perform mathematical functions, and aggregate data. This means that there are many things that you can do in VBA that you cannot duplicate in T-SQL. However, because the purpose of stored procedures is to manipulate data and the calling program performs the other necessary functions, in general, you won't find yourself missing the functions provided in VBA.

Using Variables

As with any other programming language, you can use variables in T-SQL. You must explicitly declare variables in order to use them, and they must follow the SQL Server rules for naming identifiers. You can declare a variable to be of any SQL Server standard data types (except image) or any UDDT. However, I recommend that you do not use UDDTs in stored procedures because the procedure will fail if you ever delete the UDDT or change parts of the UDDT that the stored procedure depends upon, which could result in the code not working. If a UDDT that is used in a stored procedure is deleted, you will not receive any errors from SQL Server until that stored procedure is executed. The syntax for declaring local variables in T-SQL is

```
DECLARE @variable_name datatype [, @variable_name datatype...]
```

As with parameters in stored procedures, variable names must be preceded by the "at" (@) symbol. When you declare your variable, you must start by using the DECLARE keyword followed by the variable name and data type. Multiple variables can be declared with a single DECLARE statement as long as they are separated by commas, and the data type is specified for each parameter. For example, to define two local variables in a stored procedure that would hold the annual purchases for a customer and the discount rate, you would declare them in your stored procedure as

```
DECLARE @mnyAnnualPurchases money, @decDiscountRate decimal(4, 3)
```

You now have two variables that you can use in your code. However, because they do not yet have values, you will want to assign values to them. This must be done in a separate statement from the declaration. When you want to assign a value to a variable in T-SQL, you must use the SELECT keyword (in SQL 7, you can also use the SET keyword) to set the variable's value. For example, you could initialize both of the variables to zero using the following T-SQL code:

```
SELECT @mnyAnnualPurchases = 0.00
SELECT @decDiscountRate = 0.0
```

SQL Server variables are very versatile. You can set their values to literal values, as in the previous example, or you can set their values to the data returned from a SQL statement. When a recordset is used to set a variable's value, the recordset that is used must be one-dimensional. In other words, the SQL statement must only return a single field with a single record. So, if you want to determine the discount rate based on a customer's annual purchases and assign it to the variable @decDiscountRate (assuming you have a Discounts table that contains a MinPurchases field—minimum purchases to get a certain discount—and a DiscountRate field) you could use this code:

```
SELECT @decDiscountRate = (SELECT MAX(Rate) FROM Discounts
                           WHERE (MinPurchases <= @mnyAnnualPurchases))
```

This code assigns the value returned from the statement to the variable, so that you can use the value at a later time.

The SELECT statement can also be used with variables to return a recordset to the client that contains only the value of the variable. So, if you want to retrieve a recordset that contains the value for the variable @decDiscountRate, you could use the following syntax:

```
SELECT @decDiscountRate
```

This would achieve the same result as selecting values from a table. This value would be returned to the calling program as a recordset containing only one field and one record.

One final note on variables: In VBA, variables that have not been assigned a value have a default value. For numeric variables, it is zero; for strings, it is an empty string and so on. In T-SQL, the default value for a variable is always Null. Because the data types that you use in T-SQL are all based on SQL Server data types, they all have the potential to be Null. For this reason, you may need to rethink some of your strategies for using variables. You may need to add extra error handling or checking to ensure that you are using the right values. In the previous example, a purchase total of $0.00 could potentially return a discount rate that is Null because the recordset might have no records in it. If this were the case, you would have to add code to ensure the value is not Null before attempting to use it in a calculation. Null values can cause you a great deal of grief if not handled correctly.

However, the fact that all T-SQL variables can hold Null values can be very useful if you are assigning variables to field contents. If you want to set a field to Null to indicate that the actual value for the field is unknown, you can simply use the Null value from any variable. You do not need to add code that converts empty values to Null in your code explicitly, as you would in VBA.

Flow Control

T-SQL supports four of the control of flow constructs that are available in many other programming languages:

- IF…ELSE

- WHILE

- CASE

- GOTO

Each of these constructs differs from their VBA equivalents, so I will describe each one separately.

Before you begin to use the control of flow constructs, you should understand how blocks of code are executed in T-SQL. When you use the constructs to control the flow of your code, SQL Server only executes a single unit of code in association with the construct. This means that unless you qualify multiple actions as a single block, SQL Server will only associate the first command following your flow control construct with the control itself. Let's use the following pseudocode as an example.

```
IF @myValue = 1
    Do Action 1
    Do Action 2
    Do Action 3
```

This code is intended to execute actions 1 through 3 if @myValue is equal to 1. However, that is not what happens. The T-SQL compiler only links the first statement "Do Action 1" with the IF statement and treats the other actions as separate entities. If @myValue is 2, actions 2 and 3 are still executed, and only action 1 is skipped. In order for this code to work as desired, a BEGIN…END block must be used. These keywords, used in conjunction with the control of flow constructs, define a block of code as one unit. To have the previous example behave as desired, you would have to change it to

```
IF @myValue = 1
    BEGIN
        Do Action 1
        Do Action 2
        Do Action 3
    END
```

Now, none of the actions will be run unless @myValue is equal to 1. Let's look at using these constructs.

IF...ELSE

IF statements in T-SQL do not have a corresponding THEN as they do in VBA, instead, an IF...ELSE statement is defined as

```
IF boolean_expression
    statement_block
ELSE
    statement_block
```

The ELSE portion is optional, as in VBA, but there is a small difference in the syntax. In VBA, you can create a single, multiple step IF statement using the ElseIf keyword. You can use as many ElseIfs as you like, and they will still be considered part of the same logical construct. The ElseIf keyword does not exist in SQL Server. However, you can nest IF statements by simply including IF constructs in the ELSE statement block. The syntax to do this is

```
IF boolean_expression
    statement_block
ELSE
    IF boolean_expression
        statement_block
    ELSE
        statement_block
```

because the IF statement is a single block itself. However, this can become difficult to read if you are entering a large number of nested IF statements. Standard practice is to format them as

```
IF boolean_expression
    statement_block
ELSE IF boolean_expression
    statement_block
ELSE
    statement_block
```

This code is easier to read and accomplishes exactly the same task.

The Boolean expression that is tested in an IF statement can be any statement that evaluates to True or False, just as in VBA. These expressions can be comparisons, functions, or even complete SQL statements that return a Boolean value.

WHILE

The WHILE control of flow construct is very similar to the Do While...Loop construct in VBA. The main difference is that there is no terminating keyword (the "Loop" keyword in VBA). This means that if you want to execute multiple statements, you must enclose them in a BEGIN...END block. The basic syntax used for a WHILE loop is

```
WHILE boolean_expression
    statement_block
```

You can also control the flow of a WHILE loop within the statement block by using the BREAK or CONTINUE keywords. The BREAK keyword forces the WHILE loop to be exited immediately without executing any other parts of the block. The CONTINUE keyword forces the WHILE loop to restart, bypassing the lines in the statement block following the CONTINUE statement.

GOTO

The GOTO statement in T-SQL probably sounds familiar to anyone who has programmed in VBA or any relative of the BASIC programming language. The GOTO statement allows you to pass the control of the code to another location in the procedure. As with other languages, you must first define the labels to which control will transfer. A label must conform to the standards for identifiers in SQL Server and must, as in VBA, be followed by a colon, as in the following example:

```
ThisIsALabel:
```

As with VBA, if a line of code preceding a label is executed and it does not explicitly change the flow to bypass the label or exit the procedure, execution will continue at the line following the label.

Whenever you want control the flow so that execution continues at a label, you use the GOTO keyword followed by the label you want execution to continue after. For example, to move code execution to the label just created, you would use the code:

```
GOTO ThisIsALabel
```

Overusing the GOTO breaks the rules of structured programming and should be avoided. As I will discuss in the "Handling Errors" section, you must use the GOTO keyword in T-SQL error handling, and its use should be restricted to error handling only. For a detailed example of how to use the GOTO statement, see the "Examples" section later in this chapter.

Operators

T-SQL supports many of the comparison, mathematical, and logical operators that you are used to using in VBA or Jet SQL, but a few of them have different notation. Table 8-1 lists the T-SQL operators, their purposes, and their VBA equivalents. If you find your stored procedure generates an error when it is saved, you should check to ensure that you are using the T-SQL operators, not the VBA operators.

Table 9-1. Transact-SQL Operators

OPERATOR	PURPOSE	VBA EQUIVALENT
=	Equal to	=
>	Greater than	>
<	Less than	<
>=	Greater than or equal to	>=
<=	Less than or equal to	<=
<>	Not equal to	<>
!=	Not equal to	<>
!>	Not greater than	
!<	Not less than	
&	Bitwise AND	And
|	Bitwise OR	Or
^	Bitwise exclusive OR	Xor
AND	TRUE if all expressions are TRUE	And
OR	TRUE if any expression is TRUE	Or
NOT	Reverses Boolean value of expression	Not
BETWEEN	Value is within a range	Between (Jet SQL)
IN	TRUE if value is in a comma-delimited list	In (Jet SQL)
LIKE	TRUE if pattern is found in value	Like
+	String concatenation character	&

In conjunction with these standard operators, T-SQL includes a CASE opera-tor. This operator does not have the same purpose as the Select Case statement in VBA, so I will take the opportunity to explain it fully.

CASE

The CASE expression in T-SQL is not designed for conditional execution of blocks of code. Instead, it is designed to return a value based on a comparison. In VBA, a Select Case expression is intended to control the flow of code execution based on a value. The CASE construct in T-SQL is more like a function in that it has a return value, and that value must be assigned to a field or variable. There are two ways that this construct can be used. The syntax for the first method, called a simple case expression, is

```
CASE expression
    WHEN expression1 THEN result_expression1
    WHEN expression2 THEN result_expression2
    ...
    WHEN expressionN THEN result_expressionN
    ELSE result_expressionX
END
```

When used in a simple case expression, a CASE construct returns a value based on the comparison of a single expression to other expressions. For example, if you want to assign the textual name for a weekday based on an integer value to a variable, you could use this code:

```
SELECT @vchWeekday =
  CASE @intWeekday
    WHEN 1 THEN 'Sunday'
    WHEN 2 THEN 'Monday'
    ...
    WHEN 7 THEN 'Saturday'
    ELSE 'Invalid Weekday'
  END
```

This piece of code uses the CASE statement to check the numerical value of the int variable @intWeekday. When a matching value is found in a WHEN clause, the textual name of the data is returned to the varchar variable @vchWeekday. If @intWeekday is not between 1 and 7, @vchWeekday is set to "Invalid Weekday".

The next type of CASE expression is called a searched case expression. It allows you to compare completely different values in each WHEN statement. The syntax for this type of expression is

```
CASE
    WHEN boolean_expression1 THEN result_expression1
    WHEN boolean_expression2 THEN result_expression2
    ...
    WHEN boolean_expressionN THEN result_expressionN
    ELSE expressionX
END
```

This type of CASE statement evaluates the Boolean expression in each WHEN statement independently. The Boolean expressions do not have to be related in any way. You can use this type of expression in more complex situations to return a value to a variable or field. For example, you might want to answer the age-old question—Which came first, the chicken or the egg?

```
SELECT @vchFirst = CASE
    WHEN @dtHatchDate > @dtEggLayDate THEN 'Chicken'
    WHEN @dtEggLayDate > @dtHatchDate THEN 'Egg'
    ELSE 'Lobster'
END
```

Of course, this comparison cannot really answer the question, but it does show how to use a searched case expression.

You must include at least one WHEN clause to use either of the CASE constructs (although you can use as many as you like); the ELSE is optional. The ELSE statement is necessary when none of the WHEN clauses are matched. If none of the WHEN clauses are matched and there is no ELSE clause, the CASE statement returns Null.

One more detail you should know about the CASE construct is that its use is not limited to just returning a value to a variable. You can use the CASE statement in any SELECT, INSERT, UPDATE, or DELETE statement as well. This allows you to use a CASE statement to return a calculated value for a field. To assign the return value to a field name, use the AS keyword after the CASE statement followed by a name for the calculated field. If you wanted to base the chicken or egg example on a value in a table, and return the value in a stored procedure, you would use the following statement:

```
SELECT tblChicken.HatchDate, tblChicken.EggLayDate,
  tblChicken.ChickenName
CASE
    WHEN tblChicken.HatchDate > tblChicken.EggLayDate THEN 'Chicken'
    WHEN tblChicken.EggLayDate > tblChicken.HatchDate THEN 'Egg'
    ELSE 'Lobster'
END
  AS WhoCameFirst
FROM tblChicken
```

This query uses a CASE statement to evaluate the values in the HatchDate and EggLayDate fields in the table tblChicken and returns a result as a calculated field WhoCameFirst. This is done for every record in the SELECT statement, so the value that is returned can change for each record.

Creating Temporary Tables

Quite often when you are working with data in stored procedures, you will find that some processing requires temporary tables. When you do this in Access, you often create tables especially for this need. These can be permanent tables that are stored in a local database, or they can be tables that are created, used to hold data, and destroyed when the processing is done. The ability to create temporary tables that you do not have to explicitly destroy is a feature built-in to SQL Server. SQL Server provides temporary tables as a simple way to create and destroy tables on an "as-needed" basis.

Temporary tables must be built using the SQL Server Data Definition Language (DDL). This language, a subset of T-SQL, is used to create or manage any object in SQL Server. Temporary tables are always stored in the tempdb database, which is automatically created as part of any SQL Server installation. This database is designed as a temporary storage area for processing of data. SQL Server automatically uses tempdb to process data when you call functions that interface with data. You can use tempdb explicitly to hold temporary tables that you need to handle some of your own processing. To create temporary tables in tempdb, you use T-SQL's DDL keywords with special qualifiers.

To create a temporary table, you define the table name with a hash sign in front of it (#). For example, you could create a temporary customer table with the following code:

```
CREATE TABLE #Customers(
    CustomerID int,
    CustomerName varchar(100))
```

You can then use this table in your stored procedure as you would any other. You can add indexes to the table, insert data, update fields, and use the data in it. You just have to ensure that anytime you reference the table, you include the hash sign in the name.

When you are done with your table, it is not necessary to delete it explicitly. SQL Server does this for you. Temporary tables created with a single hash sign are only visible to the connection that is using them, and they are destroyed whenever that connection falls out of context. This means that the temporary table is generally deleted when your stored procedure completes. If you want your temporary table to be visible to other users or connections, you can create it with a double hash sign (##, e.g., ##Customers). This type of table is visible to all connections and is deleted as soon as the last connection that references it falls out of context. This type of table can be very useful if you have a series of stored procedures calling each other that need to have access to the same table. For more information on how to use DDL to create tables, look up the CREATE TABLE statement in the Books Online. You can also generate the scripts for some of your own tables to determine which language to use to define different characteristics.

Handling Errors

Errors in SQL Server can be caused in a number of different ways, but they are usually attributable to an action on data. This means that updating, deleting, or inserting data in a table or tables can potentially raise an error. There are many types of errors that can occur, from referential integrity violations to resource problems to deadlock issues. When you build your stored procedure, you cannot always be sure if and when an error will occur. For this reason, you should implement error handling in your stored procedures.

> **NOTE** *SQL Server includes a number of system variables that can be used in code from any procedure that you create. All of these variables are differentiated from variables that you create by having two "at" (@) signs in front of their names. For example, the variable @@VERSION contains the internal version number of SQL Server that indicates the version, revision, and build number of the server. There is also a more useful variable called @@IDENTITY that retains the last used identity (autonumber) value for an insert into a table.*

When you want to find out if an error has occurred, you must check the system variable @@ERROR. This variable contains an integer, which is zero if no error has occurred or some other value if an error has occurred. However, unlike VBA, an error does not stop execution of your code. There is no equivalent to the VBA statement *On Error Goto*. If an error occurs in T-SQL code, the value in @@ERROR will change, but your code will continue to execute. This means that you must explicitly check the value of @@ERROR whenever you think an error might possibly have occurred in your T-SQL code. When you check this value, you can include code that redirects the code execution to a cleanup portion of the stored procedure, just as you would define your error handler in VBA. The code to do this would look something like this:

```
IF @@ERROR != 0
    GOTO Cleanup
```

That's all that's required to redirect processing to your error handling code. You can then define the cleanup that must take place in your Cleanup section. This might include functions to reset tables, clean up disk space, or rollback transactions.

If you want to be able to raise your own errors, you can use the RAISERROR function in T-SQL. This function allows you to set an error number, severity, and a description for your error, much like the VBA Err.Raise method. These errors are passed by SQL Server to your calling application, allowing you to raise errors in stored procedures that inform the user of what went wrong. See the SQL Server documentation for complete details on how to call this function.

Transactions

Once you know how to handle errors, one of the most important places you might want to do this is in transactions. In case you have not used transactions before, a brief introduction follows. Transactions allow you to define a group of SQL statements or commands that will be executed and committed as a batch. It is a single unit of work. In a transaction either all of these statements will be executed successfully or none of them will. Transactions are commonly used when inserting data into or deleting data from multiple, related tables. Essentially, a transaction allows you to attempt to execute a series of data manipulation statements and ensures that they will all complete before you commit all of the changes they entail. All of the rules and constraints that have been defined in the tables that these changes affect are tested as the transaction is run, so if any conflicts occur during the transaction, your code can react by backing out of the whole operation, rather than just the failing portion.

For example, you might want to delete all of the orders that were placed in 1994 because you have determined that this data is no longer necessary. A constraint in the database requires that you delete all of the records in the OrderDetails table before the orders themselves are deleted. If you are unsure as to what other data these deletions may affect, you could implement a transaction to delete the details and then the orders. If either command fails to complete successfully, both sets of deletions on both tables will be backed out, and the data will revert to the state it was at before the procedure was run.

There are two main parts to a transaction. The first part defines where the transaction will begin. This is done in SQL Server by using the BEGIN TRANSACTION statement (the keyword TRANSACTION can always be abbreviated to the word TRAN). This tells SQL Server to start a new transaction that will encompass the data manipulation or definition statements that will follow. Once you are finished doing the work with all of your data, you must then define the second part of the transaction: The part that tells SQL Server what to do with the tentative changes. This is done with one of the two transaction ending statements: COMMIT TRANSACTION or ROLLBACK TRANSACTION. The COMMIT TRANSACTION statement tells SQL Server that everything is okay and that SQL Server can commit all of the changes that you made. However, if an error occurs, or you are not satisfied with the results of the statements, you can cancel all of the changes in the transaction by using the ROLLBACK TRANSACTION statement. This statement cancels all changes that were made and returns the data to the state it was in before the transaction began.

There is one other statement that can come in useful in transactions: the SAVE TRANSACTION statement. This statement defines a save-point in the transaction to which the transaction can be rolled back without affecting portions of the transaction that occurred before it. A save-point must be given a name, so the syntax is:

```
SAVE TRANSACTION MyTransactionSavePointName
```

This name can then be used later with a ROLLBACK TRANSACTION statement. If you want to rollback the transaction to the save-point and not rollback the entire transaction to the beginning, you must use the save-point name, as in:

```
ROLLBACK TRANSACTION MyTransactionSavePointName
```

Whenever you use a SAVE TRANSACTION statement, the main transaction itself must still be dealt with as normal. You must commit or rollback the main transaction by calling the COMMIT or ROLLBACK TRANSACTION statements, as appropriate. Failing to do so will generate an error from SQL Server when the stored procedure is run.

The following pseudocode example illustrates using transactions in T-SQL code.

```
BEGIN TRANSACTION
    UPDATE Table1
    DELETE FROM Table2
SAVE TRANSACTION ToTable2
    UPDATE Table3
    DELETE FROM Table4
ROLLBACK TRANSACTION ToTable2
COMMIT TRANSACTION
```

This code would only commit the changes for tables 1 and 2, but not tables 3 and 4.

Transactions may also be nested. However, committing or rolling back inner transactions will have no effect on the final outcome. Only the outermost transaction will affect what happens with the data. If an inner transaction is rolled back and the outer one is committed, the entire operation will be committed, including the changes made in the inner transaction. Nesting transactions only add extra headaches because you must still remember to pair a BEGIN TRANSACTION with either a COMMIT TRANSACTION or ROLLBACK TRANSACTION. It is best not to use nested transactions in T-SQL for just this reason. If you do not know what a nested transaction is, don't worry. There is no point in using them in the first place.

You may be wondering how you should handle errors in a transaction. After all, you will probably want to roll them back using a standard error-handling routine. This is where another system variable—@@TRANCOUNT—can come to the rescue. This variable returns the number of active transactions in the current context. This means that if you check the value of this variable and it is greater than zero, a transaction is in effect. If you have nested transactions, it will return the number of transactions that are in the nesting. So, you can easily write error-handling code to rollback your transactions by checking this value, as in the following code sample:

```
BEGIN TRANSACTION
    /*...Update data here...*/
    IF @@ERROR != 0
        GOTO ErrorCleanup
COMMIT TRANSACTION
/*...Do something here then exit, skipping error cleanup...*/
ErrorCleanup:
    WHILE @@TRANCOUNT > 0
        ROLLBACK TRANSACTION
/*...Other error handling...*/
```

This sample shows how you can use the @@ERROR variable to determine if an error occurred, and then pass the control to a cleanup section. If an error occurs, the lines after the GOTO are completely skipped. The error-handler then checks @@TRANCOUNT and rolls back every active transaction, saving you from having to remember how many transactions are in place.

Returning from a Procedure

One piece of information that is still missing is how you exit a procedure and return control to the client. In VBA, this is done using the Exit Sub or Exit Function command. T-SQL has a similar command—RETURN. This command exits unconditionally from a stored procedure. You can optionally add an integer value that will be returned to the client. The returned value can be used to specify the execution result of the stored procedure. The convention with this value is that it should be zero if all operations in the stored procedure succeeded and any other value if any function failed. It is recommended that if you want to use your own values, you use values over 100 because the first 99 positive and negative integers are reserved for specific errors in SQL Server.

The RETURN statement immediately exits the procedure. No other lines after the statement are processed. To use it, simply enter the word RETURN on a new line and optionally add any return status, as in the following example:

```
RETURN 201
```

If you call RETURN without specifying a value, zero is assumed by SQL Server. A common practice when using this function is to return the value of the @@ERROR variable. This can help to ensure that a useful number is returned and signal to the calling program what went wrong in the stored procedure.

Migrating to Stored Procedures

One of the most beneficial tasks you undertake when migrating an Access database to SQL Server is, if possible, to migrate your code, queries, and macros to SQL Server stored procedures. This can be a very onerous task, but you should ensure that you thoroughly review your Access objects to see if you can convert them to SQL Server stored procedures. Moving complex DAO, ADO code, or VBA to stored procedures can dramatically improve the performance of your application. When you analyze your objects, there are a number of criteria that you should use to evaluate their potential for migration.

Migrating Queries

Queries tend to be one of the places where Access migrations fail to take advantage of the power of SQL Server. These objects are often overlooked because developers don't fully understand how the Jet engine deals with Access queries using linked SQL Server tables. Also, developers working in an ADP often do not realize the true potential of stored procedures as replacements for queries because they are unfamiliar with stored procedures. The first general rule to keep in mind when migrating queries to SQL Server is that stored procedures are not limited to single SQL statements. You can include as many SQL statements as you can fit into a single stored procedure (SQL 6.5 stored procedures can be up to 65025 bytes and SQL 7 procedures up to 128MB in length).

Before you review your queries, you need to understand how the Jet engine deals with queries against linked tables in a normal Access database. When you run a normal query against linked tables, Jet attempts to determine what portion of the query the server can perform. If Jet decides that the server can execute the entire query, Jet simply passes the command to SQL Server. The server must then parse this query, determine an execution plan, execute the query, and then return the results to the client. If Jet decides that any part of the query is not compatible with SQL Server, Jet passes the SQL Server executable portion to the server in order to return the data. Jet then works with this data locally to implement the Jet-only functionality. Usually, the portions of a query that are executed locally are those portions that use Jet-specific or user defined functions in the SQL string. However, Jet has been known to evaluate queries poorly in this process. If the Jet engine cannot determine whether SQL Server supports certain functions, it defaults to local processing. This increases network traffic and the amount of processing that must be done on the client. Add to this the overhead of having SQL Server parse the commands and determine an execution plan each time, and you will find that local Access queries are very inefficient.

When analyzing your application to determine what types of queries should be migrated to stored procedures, remember to review any objects that use SQL strings as the source of their data (SQL strings not saved as full queries). The types of queries that should be migrated to stored procedures are those that update data or those that return read-only data to the application. The best places to find these types of queries are:

- Access action queries defined in the Query tab in the database window and in code

- Report and form data sources

- List and combo box data sources

There's very little that you have to do to migrate a query from Access to a stored procedure. In fact, the SQL for most queries (in cases where table and field names have not been changed) can simply be cut and pasted from the Access query to a SQL Server stored procedure.

When you cut and paste SQL statements from Access to SQL Server, you should make a few modifications to the statements to ensure that the code will work. Most notably, you should:

- Delete any parentheses used in JOIN clauses. SQL Server does not require them.

- Change Access-SQL specific functions to SQL Server equivalents where equivalents exist.

- Remove all references to user defined functions or functions not supported by SQL Server. Instead, use a stored procedure to return the bulk of the data, filtered if necessary, and then create a local query to filter the stored procedure data.

- Remove all square brackets used for parameters, and change parameters to use SQL Server syntax as described previously.

- Delete any references to the TOP keyword if migrating to SQL Server 6.5, and replace it with code on the client to use only the first X rows or a stored procedure to better filter the data.

- Modify DISTINCTROW SQL statements to work without the DISTINCTROW keyword because SQL Server does not support it. This keyword can often simply be deleted to accomplish this task.

- Change string concatenation characters from "&" to "+".

- Remove the "*" from DELETE statements (for example, Access's "DELETE * FROM tblOrders" is equivalent to SQL Server's "DELETE FROM tblOrders" and will generate a syntax error if it isn't changed).

- Do not directly migrate cross-tab queries. SQL Server does not support the PIVOT function found in Jet SQL. Instead, create a stored procedure that returns the base data for the cross-tab query to Access, and then create a simple cross-tab locally in Access to do the work. If you are using an ADP, cross-tab queries are completely unsupported, so you will have to do without them.

- Change implicit data type conversions to use the CONVERT T-SQL function (see the SQL Server documentation for syntax). SQL Server does not allow certain implicit conversions, and these statements will generate an error.

Finally, ensure that you group related queries in a single stored procedure if possible. Access developers often develop solutions that use three or four different queries in a particular order. In SQL Server, you can include all of these actions in a single stored procedure. This helps to make your objects easier to maintain and enhances the performance of your application.

Migrating Macros

You can use stored procedures to replace many of the macros in your database. Doing so can help to make your application run much faster and help to centralize all database code. The two best macro actions to migrate are OpenQuery and RunSQL These macro actions are designed to call SQL commands either as text strings or in queries. RunSQL commands are usually designed to run updates or deletes on data. These items should be moved to stored procedures, so that SQL Server runs the update, not Access. OpenQuery commands should be replaced by other functions that allow the user to access the data and filter that data on SQL Server. By moving macros to stored procedures, you improve the response time and performance of your application.

You should also check some of the other actions that are executed in your macros. If your macro is working with data in any way, it may be possible to migrate the entire macro, or at least large parts of it, to SQL Server. Of course, any portions of the macros that directly interact with the user cannot be migrated because stored procedures cannot be used for user interface activities. But you can combine the stored procedure with your macros to achieve better results in your application.

Migrating Code

Migrating code from VBA to stored procedures is another good area to gain performance improvements in your application. The key is to look for any code that uses recordsets to accomplish some task. One of the best rules to follow when developing a database application is that all SQL statements that are used by the application should reside on the server. This means that anywhere in your code that you have a SQL statement, whether it is used to retrieve or update data, you should start using stored procedures or views. The reasoning behind this is that using stored procedures allows you to store all your SQL code in the database, making your application easier to maintain. It is a better practice to call views or stored procedures, rather than building SQL strings when you need to retrieve data. It becomes much easier to make changes to the table structure on the server if all SQL statements are stored in the database because you can also use the utilities built into SQL Server to determine what other objects will be affected by your changes. If your SQL strings are built into the client application, you could make changes to the database on SQL Server that detriment the client. There would be no warning that the changes you made could be a problem until the application itself generates an error. With SQL strings built-in to the client, there is no telling what objects may be affected by a table change.

Along these same lines, you don't necessarily want to spend a lot of time migrating functions that do not access data. Functions, such as custom calculations, string manipulations, or network calls, should remain in VBA and should not be moved to SQL Server. The overhead introduced in calling them over the network makes them much slower as stored procedures. This is because VBA code functions that do not access data tend to execute faster than equivalent nondata-interfacing T-SQL code. However, if your code interfaces with data in any way, you should consider moving it to SQL Server. Doing so reduces network traffic and allows you to take advantage of the power of SQL Server.

When you are analyzing the code that should be migrated to SQL Server, do not forget to examine the forms in your application. The most common places to find code that can be converted to stored procedures in form events are in the Update, Delete, and Insert data events. It is very common for Access applications to use these events to perform data-related functions. This might include code that updates product quantities, changes sales totals, or deletes related records. In such cases, it is often better to use stored procedures to accomplish the task. For example, if your form contains code that deletes the subrecords when a parent record is deleted, it is a good idea to transfer this logic to SQL Server. You could create a stored procedure that deleted all of the records in the related table, and then call it in the form's Delete event. This would allow you to implement a controlled cascading delete without having to code it into a trigger. When you implement a cascading delete in a trigger, your database automatically deletes child records when the parent is deleted, and the user is not warned that this is about to happen. If you use a stored procedure instead of using a trigger, you can control when that procedure is called. This allows you to warn the user as appropriate or prevent unauthorized users from running the delete, which makes your database more secure and enhances your control over the user experience.

Examples

Let's take a look at some real examples that may help you to better understand how to implement stored procedures.

In the first example, let's suppose that you want to delete a customer from the database. This not only requires that you delete their information, but all of their orders and the details of those orders. You might not do something so drastic in the real world, but it does help to illustrate the process. For this stored procedure to work, it must delete the information in the order that is required by the referential integrity rules in the database. In this case, that means deleting the order details, then the orders, and then the customer. To make the stored procedure easy to use, it only requires that the calling program provide the CustomerID. This is how the stored procedure would look (T-SQL comments can be entered by starting with a "/*" and ending with a "*/"):

```
CREATE PROCEDURE uspDeleteCustomer (@intCustomerID int)
AS
    BEGIN TRANSACTION
        /*Delete the order details for customer's orders*/
        DELETE FROM OrderDetails
        WHERE OrderID IN (SELECT OrderID FROM Orders
                    WHERE CustomerID = @intCustomerID)

        /*Delete the orders the customer has placed*/
        DELETE FROM Orders
        WHERE CustomerID = @intCustomerID
```

```
        /*Delete the customer*/
        DELETE FROM Customers
        WHERE CustomerID = @intCustomerID

        /*Check for errors and direct flow if any*/
        IF @@ERROR != 0
            GOTO ErrCleanup


ExitSuccess:
    WHILE @@TRANCOUNT > 0
        COMMIT TRANSACTION
    RETURN 0

ErrCleanup:
    WHILE @@TRANCOUNT > 0
        ROLLBACK TRANSACTION
    RETURN @@ERROR
```

This stored procedure uses a number of the syntactical functions that have been talked about so far. When the stored procedure starts, it begins a new transaction using the BEGIN TRANSACTION statement. Then, the data is deleted from all three tables in the necessary order. After the deletion, the @@ERROR system variable is checked to ensure that no errors occurred. If @@ERROR is not zero, then an error has occurred and the control of the procedure is passed to the ErrCleanup label. In either the success cleanup code or error cleanup code, all open transactions are either committed or rolled-back (as appropriate) by looping until the number of open transactions equals zero. This stored procedure handles the full data delete for you and recovers from any unexpected errors. Unless all functions complete successfully, no changes will be committed.

The next stored procedure is a simple stored procedure that returns the contents of a table as a recordset. This particular stored procedure is designed to return all of the states in the USA ordered by name. This type of stored procedure could be used to return the contents of a list box or combo box for your application.

```
CREATE PROCEDURE uspGetStatesUSA
AS
SELECT StateName FROM States
WHERE Country = 'USA'
ORDER BY StateName
```

This may look simple, but it can be expanded to return much more complex data. You can even use this type of stored procedure to return information on the different objects in your database. Stored procedures, such as this one, are probably the ones that you will most commonly use.

Let's look at one more example. This one is a bit more complex. Suppose you want to determine from the quantities of a product on hand what you need to order, so that you can maintain an optimum stock level. This optimum stock would be determined by analyzing the orders that were placed for these products in the past two years and averaging that information over a certain timeframe—let's say one month. There are many ways to implement this, but in order to illustrate some of the functionality you have learned, let's use the following method:

- Retrieve a list of all products, determine how many of each product has been ordered in the past two years, and store it in a temporary table.

- Calculate the average number of products ordered per month, and store it in a temporary table.

- Return a recordset containing the difference between the quantity on hand and the optimum quantity.

The following example stored procedure will do just what you want:

```
CREATE PROCEDURE uspProductsToOrder AS
/*Get the totals ordered for all products*/
SELECT Products.ProductID, SUM(OrderDetails.Quantity) AS TotalOrdered
INTO #TotalOrdered
FROM OrderDetails INNER JOIN
    Orders ON OrderDetails.OrderID = Orders.OrderID RIGHT OUTER JOIN
    Products ON OrderDetails.ProductID = Products.ProductID
WHERE (Orders.OrderDate >= DATEADD(yyyy, - 2, GETDATE()))
GROUP BY Products.ProductID

/*Get the average products ordered per month as an optimum*/
SELECT ProductID, (TotalOrdered/24) AS Optimum
INTO #OptimumProducts
FROM #TotalOrdered

/*Return the quantity to order to the client,
  using zero if more on hand than needed*/
SELECT Products.ProductID, Products.ProductName,
    CASE
    WHEN Products.OnHand >= #OptimumProducts.Optimum THEN 0
        ELSE (#OptimumProducts.Optimum - Products.OnHand)
    END
    AS NeedToOrder
FROM Products INNER JOIN
    #OptimumProducts
        ON Products.ProductID = #OptimumProducts.ProductID
ORDER BY ProductName
```

This procedure uses temporary tables to save the data; it then joins one of these tables to an existing table in the database and returns all of the necessary data to the client. This is just a small illustration of what is possible when you use SQL Server stored procedures. Explore the capabilities of stored procedures using the Books Online and through testing to see how you can improve your application by using them.

Testing

Before you begin to use your stored procedures in Access, there is one final process to do—test them. You can do this directly in Access if you use the SQL Server browser or an ADP by selecting the stored procedure and executing it. Or you can do this in SQL Server Query Analyzer (SQL 7) or ISQL/w (SQL 6.5). These applications are available in the SQL Server menu on the Start menu, and they provide a text interface for executing commands. To test your stored procedure, connect to the appropriate server, and select the database you want to test against in the drop-down list at the top of the ISQL or Query Analyzer screen. To test your stored procedure, use the syntax:

```
EXEC procedure_name [parameter [, parameter2 [..., parameterN ]]]
```

You supply the values for your parameters implicitly by entering them in the order that they appear in the stored procedure, or you can explicitly set each parameter by using the syntax:

```
@parameter_name = value
```

For example, you could call the first example stored procedure using either of the following two statements:

```
EXEC uspDeleteCustomer 2
EXEC uspDeleteCustomer @intCustomerID = 2
```

If your stored procedure contains output parameters and you want to check their values, you must create temporary variables that will take the values returned, and then view those values using the SELECT statement. For example, if you have a stored procedure that has a header that is defined as

```
CREATE PROCEDURE uspMyProc (@intValue int, @vchText varchar(25) = NULL OUTPUT)
```

you would use the code:

```
DECLARE @vchTextResult varchar(25)
EXEC uspMyProc 2, @vchTextResult
SELECT @vchTextResult
```

You can check the return value of the stored procedure by assigning it to a temporary variable. This is done by including the variable name after the EXEC statement and following it by the equal (=) sign, as in

```
DECLARE @intReturn int
EXEC @intReturn = uspDeleteCustomer 2
SELECT @intReturn
```

You will then be able to see if your procedure will work and what results you swill receive.

SQL Power Tools

SQL Server stored procedures are very powerful tools. They can take much of the need for VBA code and local queries away from an Access application. In many cases, they can be used to replace large parts of an Access application. They make your database easier to maintain, faster, and more efficient and can save you a great deal of extra work. When you begin your migration, take the time to fully understand how they can be used and what benefits they can offer. Using stored procedures can turn your database into a true powerhouse.

CHAPTER 10

Getting Connected

NOW THAT YOU KNOW what needs to be done to create your database in SQL Server, you need to know how to connect that database into Access. As we have discussed, there are two ways to do this. The first is to use Open Database Connectivity (ODBC) to link the SQL Server tables and views into a standard Access database. The second method, unique to Access 2000, is to create an Access Database Project (ADP) and connect that project to a SQL Server database.

Choosing a Connection Method

The method you use to connect your SQL Server database to the Access interface depends on a number of factors. Most important of which is what version of Microsoft Access you are using. If you are using a version that is older than Access 2000, you must connect using ODBC, at least when linking objects into Access. Access 2000 is the only version that currently has database projects. Database projects allow you to completely bypass the Jet engine and connect directly to SQL Server. The method you choose is also dependent on what engine you want to use. If you want a faster database engine that is more tailored towards SQL Server, you should create a database project. ODBC connections are slower because they must be by managed by the Jet engine and the ODBC driver. This adds two extra layers to your connection schema. In addition, the connection method you use is dependent on what features you want to have available in your database. If you need to create and use local Access tables, you cannot use an ADP. ADPs can only be connected to a single SQL Server database. Before you can start attaching tables and views and using stored procedures in your database, you need to understand how to build the connections that you need.

ODBC

Let's first discuss using ODBC to connect to SQL Server. You can use ODBC to connect to SQL Server in all versions of Microsoft Access, back to version 1.0. However, the real power of this type of connection was not truly realized until Access 95, when new functionality was added to the Jet engine. ODBC connections in Access are quite powerful in Access 95, 97, and 2000.

ODBC Data Source Names

When you connect to an ODBC data source from Access, be it SQL Server, Oracle, Sybase, or any other relational engine, you need to create what is called a Data Source Name (DSN). DSNs define the type of RDBMS you are connecting to, where that RDBMS resides on the network (or your own computer), and what specific database should be used, among other characteristics. DSNs are created using the ODBC Data Source Administrator. This administrative module can be found in your Windows Control Panel. The specific name of this module may change depending on the version of Windows that you are running, but it is usually called *ODBC Data Sources (32Bit)* or some variation of those words. To start it, open the Control Panel from your Start menu, and then double-click the ODBC Data Sources (32Bit) item. This opens the ODBC Data Source Administrator, shown in Figure 10-1.

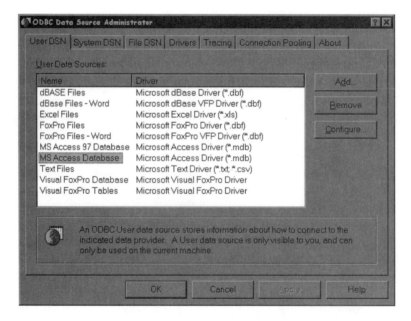

Figure 10-1. ODBC Data Source Administrator

The Administrator allows you to create, edit, and delete DSNs, check driver information, trace ODBC calls, and configure connection pooling. We are mainly concerned with DSNs, so let's look into these features.

In Windows, there are three types of DSNs that you can create: User DSNs, System DSNs, and File DSNs. They all accomplish the same task of allowing you to define the characteristics of an ODBC connection, and the interface they use for configuration is exactly the same. The main difference lays in where the information you configure is stored and who can see it.

User DSNs, the first tab in the Administrator, are only visible to the user who is currently logged into the computer and are only available on the local computer. If you are logged into a computer and you log out then log in as another user, the DSNs that are configured in the User DSN area will change. This feature can be useful if you want to ensure that only authorized people can connect to your database. Essentially, DSNs created in this area will not be visible to any other users. These types of DSNs are stored in the Registry under the HKEY_CURRENT_USER key.

System DSNs are shared by all users of a particular computer. These connections can be configured, and anyone who logs into the computer can use them to connect to a data source. Also, given the correct security permissions for the computer, anyone can change these data sources. This can be a positive and a negative aspect of System DSNs. If a user purposely or inadvertently changes a setting, the DSN may stop working. However, you can also "walk" users through changing DSNs as necessary if your system changes. These types of DSNs are stored in the Registry under the HKEY_LOCAL_MACHINE key.

A File DSN is considered a "portable" DSN. The settings for a DSN are stored in a file on your computer that can be copied to other computers. Assuming that the destination computer is on the same network and that the user and computer have the same network rights as the source computer, the target computer can instantly use the DSN. These types of DSNs are saved as a file. Before we go too far into the technical aspects of DSNs, lets take a look at how to create them for SQL Server.

Creating SQL Server DSNs

In order to create a DSN, you must open the ODBC Data Source Administrator, select the appropriate tab for the DSN type you want to create, and then click the Add button. The steps involved in creating the different DSN types are essentially the same. The first step in creating a DSN is to select the driver and file information for your DSN. Once you select the Add button, you are prompted to select the ODBC driver to use for this DSN, as in Figure 10-2.

Scroll down and select the driver called *SQL Server* (on some systems it might be called *Microsoft SQL Server* or *MS SQL Server*). If you want to view the full details of the driver DLL including the version, company, file name, and date, scroll across to see all of the columns in the list. Once you have found and selected the SQL Server driver, click the Finish button.

If you are creating a File DSN, you will have a Next > button instead of a Finish button at this point. Select this button, and you will be taken to a dialog that asks you where to store the file. Enter a meaningful name in the dialog and, if you do not relocate it by using the Browse button and selecting a directory, it will be saved in the default location set for File DSNs. Click Next > again and a screen appears asking you to confirm your selections. Click Finish, and you will then be on the same path as if you were creating a User or System DSN.

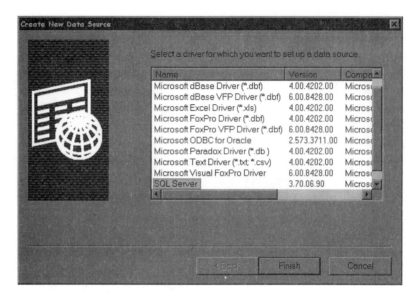

Figure 10-2. Create New Data Source

The second step in the process is to provide some basic information needed by the ODBC Data Source. The screen shown in Figure 10-3 allows you to define a name, description, and server for your DSN. If at any point in the setup of your DSN you are not sure what an option does, you can click on the Help button for detailed information on what information needs to be entered and what the option will do.

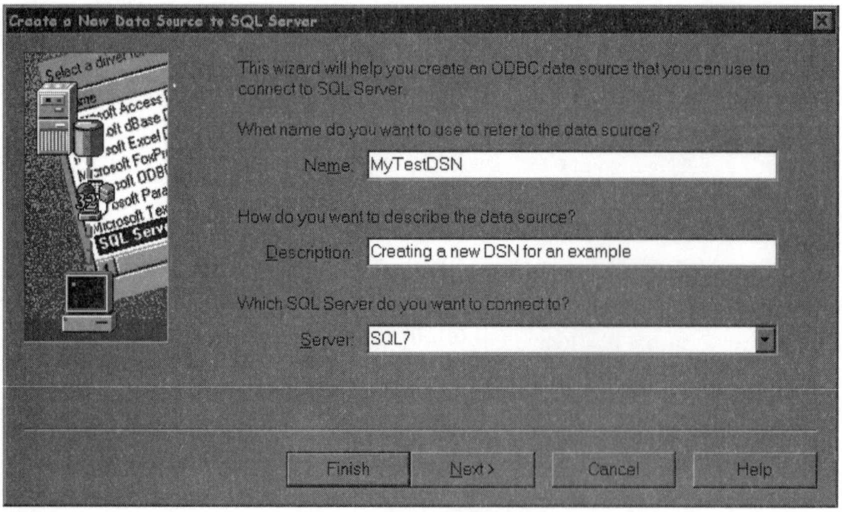

Figure 10-3. Create a New Data Source to SQL Server

If you are creating a File DSN, the name will be disabled. Otherwise, enter a meaningful name for your DSN. This name will be the name you use to refer to this DSN in Access when you are attaching objects from SQL Server or using SQL Server data in ODBC-connected code. If you want to, you can enter a description in the appropriate box. This description appears when you select a DSN in Access. Finally, you must select a server. You can select a server from the drop-down list, or type in the name of any server you like. In fact, you can use any name that you like because you will have the opportunity to define the connection information in the next dialog. However, it is best to use the real server name or the name that it is configured to use under the Client Network Utility. Enter a server name, and click Next > to move to the next screen.

The screen shown in Figure 10-4 allows you to specify how to connect to the server.

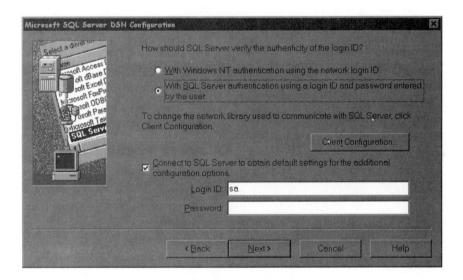

Figure 10-4. DSN Connection information

This connection information includes the security and network information necessary to connect to the server. The first option allows you to define the authentication method that will be used. If your server is configured to use NT authentication, you can select that option. If you want to connect to your server using SQL Server authentication, select that option. The Client Configuration button allows you to define the name, network IP address, and port necessary to connect to SQL Server. If the server you want to connect to is not included in your Client Network Utility or you are using an alias for the server, select this button to open the dialog where this information can be set. This dialog is identical to the dialog for adding a server in the Client Network Utility (see Figures 1-1 or 1-4). Next, you can select whether or not to connect to the server to obtain the necessary defaults for other configuration options. In most cases, you should select this item. It will set most of the necessary information for your connection and save you some time. If your server is not running for some reason or you know that you will not be able to connect to it, you can clear this checkbox. Finally, if you chose to use SQL Server authentication and to connect to obtain default settings, you must enter a Login ID and password. This should be valid login information for the SQL Server database. Once all necessary information is entered, select Next > to move to the next screen.

The screen shown in Figure 10-5 allows you to define the database you want to connect to and how the server should interact with your connection.

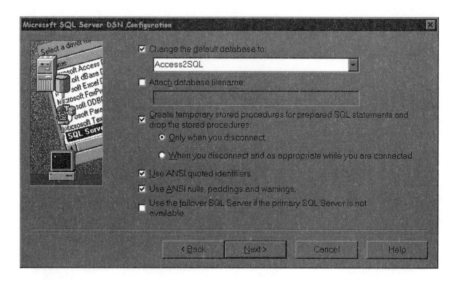

Figure 10-5. DSN Server and Database Options

Depending on the version of SQL Server you are using and if you chose to connect to the server to obtain default connection information, some of the options on this screen may be disabled. The first option allows you to define which database you want to connect to. Usually, you will want to select this option. It will ensure that you are always connecting to the correct database. If, however, you want to define different databases for different users, set their default database in SQL Server and leave this option clear. SQL Server will provide this information to the DSN when your users connect to the server. This option could be useful in cases where different users need to connect to different databases from the same application. Once the item is selected, you must select a database from the list to connect to or manually enter a database name.

You can also select to attach to a database by file name. This allows you to connect to a SQL Server 7 database file directly without having to specify the database name. This can be useful if you are using Microsoft Data Engine (MSDE) or you just want to ensure that the database remains constant, even if the name changes. Usually, you would not select this option for a standard SQL Server database.

The next option allows you to create temporary stored procedures for actions that you run against data in the database. If you are using SQL Server 7, this item will not be available (or should be left unchecked). If you select this option, you have another choice: You can delete these temporary stored procedures only when the connection is closed or when the connection is closed and occasionally while still connected. If you are using the same commands over and over and you don't do any major data manipulation outside of these major tasks, you may choose to select the first item because it will result in faster processing for common functions. However, it is recommended that you select the second function because it will clear out unnecessary objects from the database more often and reduce the overhead associated with managing these objects.

The Use ANSI quoted identifiers option tells the DSN to interpret all text enclosed in double quotes (") as SQL Server identifiers, and not as string literals. With this setting turned on, all string literals must be enclosed in single quotes ('). It is best to leave this setting enabled. The Use ANSI nulls, paddings, and warnings option is provided so that you can use ANSI standard SQL behavior if you desire. This particular setting disables some of the extensions provided in Transact-SQL so you may not want to leave it enabled. Consult the ODBC Administrator help and the SQL Server Books Online for more information on how these settings will affect your connection.

If your server has a failover SQL Server, you can use the last option to allow your connection to immediately change servers in case the main server fails. A failover server is a second copy of SQL Server running on a separate machine that mirrors the data and actions on the main server. If you don't have a failover server, this option will not be available. When you have completed setting your options, click the Next > button to move on to the next screen.

This screen, shown in Figure 10-6, is the final configuration screen for creating your DSN. It allows you to define the behavior of your client when accessing SQL Server data.

The first option on this screen allows you to change the default language that will be used for SQL Server system messages to the client. If you are working in a multilingual environment and you have configured your server to handle this, you can select this option and choose a language from the list. Otherwise, leave it unchecked and accept the default setting.

The Perform translation for character data option allows you to specify that translation between ANSI and Unicode character types should take place where necessary. This option may change depending on the version of SQL Server to which you are connecting. When using SQL Server with Microsoft Access, accept the default value provided by the server.

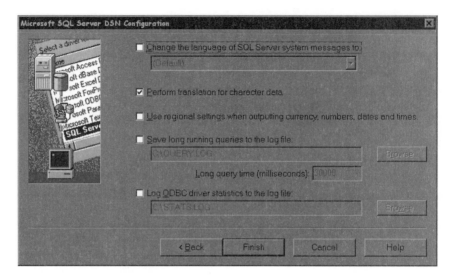

Figure 10-6. DSN Client Options

The Use regional settings when outputting currency, numbers, dates, and times option should always be left unchecked when using Microsoft Access to connect to SQL Server. It is intended only for applications that display, but do not process data. Selecting this option could cause problems when you attempt to update data from Access.

The last two options allow you to define what logging should take place in your connection. You can log long-running queries to a file (you can also specify what long is in milliseconds). This option could be used to diagnose problematic queries if necessary. This kind of information is usually analyzed using the tools included with SQL Server, not from the client. However, you can set it if you desire. You can also log ODBC statistics if you want. This information can be used to diagnose network transmission and response information.

Click Finish to complete your changes. A dialog, shown in Figure 10-7, appears that allows you to preview the full configuration of your DSN.

You can click OK to save your DSN or Cancel to return to the DSN setup if any item is incorrect. Before you save your DSN, you should always test it by clicking on the Test Data Source button, which displays a second dialog that attempts to connect to the database and reports any errors. If the connection fails, read the error information that is generated and take appropriate action. When your connection completes successfully, click OK to save your DSN.

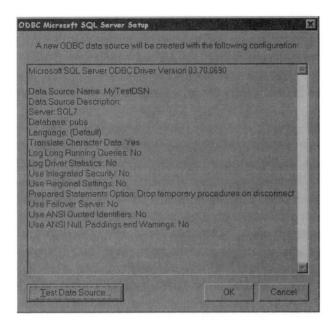

Figure 10-7. DSN Summary

Managing DSNs

Once you have created DSNs, they are very easy to manage. You can edit them by opening the ODBC Administrator, selecting the DSN you want to manage, and clicking on the Configure button. Or you can delete them by selecting them, and then clicking Delete. However, you may be interested to learn how Windows manages DSNs.

As mentioned previously, User and System DSNs are stored in the Registry, and File DSNs are stored in individual files. The location for the User and System DSNs under the keys mentioned earlier is under the Software\ODBC\ODBC.INI subkey. Each DSN you create will create a new section under this key that contains the name of your DSN and the details it uses. This information can be very useful if you want to see just how your DSN is created. Also, an entry is added under the ODBC Data Sources key in this same section that contains the name of your DSN. This forces your DSN to appear in the list of DSNs on the computer. This can be a useful feature in that, in certain circumstances, you can delete the name in the ODBC Data Sources key in the Registry and still use the DSN. This makes the DSN invisible to your users. However, exercise caution when working with the Registry. Some simple changes can have unexpected side effects. You should also ensure that you only delete this value once you are sure that you won't need to use it again in your application. You can only use visible DSNs from Access, so you may be forced to re-create the Registry value as it existed before. Always document it before you delete it.

File DSNs are just text files that you can edit using any text editor. The default location for these files is in C:\Program Files\Common Files\ODBC\Data Sources (the drive may be different if you installed Windows on a different drive). File DSNs can often be more useful to read than User or System DSNs. This is because the information they contain can be used to manually create a DSN-less connection in Access using code. We will talk about this more in Chapter 11. In the meantime, know that you can create a File DSN anywhere on your computer. These files do not have to be located in the default directory. When you create them, all you have to do is change the directory you are working in by selecting the Look in drop-down menu and browsing to a different location, even to other computers on your network. You also have the ability to change the default location for these files by changing the folder in the ODBC Administrator and selecting the Set Directory button. This will permanently change the default directory for storing DSNs for your current login. You can still select other DSNs by browsing to the appropriate location.

Linking Objects

We now come to the part that all of you who are planning to use ODBC have been waiting for: actually connecting SQL Server to Access. In order to use ODBC tables in Access, you need to link those tables into the database. This is done by selecting File➠Get External Data➠Link Tables when you have your Access database open. You can also access this command by right-clicking anywhere in the database window with the Tables tab active. This function opens a standard Office File Open dialog that allows you to select the type of table (and for file-based tables, the location) to link into your database. In order to connect to an ODBC Data Source, you first need to change the type of file to use. In the Files of Type drop-down list in the dialog, select the item called ODBC Databases (). The File dialog closes and you are taken to the Select Data Source dialog, shown in Figure 10-8.

This dialog contains two tabs. The File Data Source tab allows you to select a File DSN from the list or browse for its location. The Machine Data Source tab contains a list of all of the System and User DSNs configured on your machine and the type and description of each DSN. You can also create a new DSN of any type by selecting the New button on either tab. This takes you through the exact same steps as if you created the DSN using ODBC Administrator. Select the DSN you created earlier, or create one as necessary. Once you have done so, you are asked to login to the server using the dialog shown in Figure 10-9 (unless you are using integrated security and your NT login has access to the database).

Not all of this form is displayed when you first open it. You can click the Options >> button to display the extended options at the bottom of the form. These options allow you to bypass some of the settings in your DSN, namely the database you will connect to, the language to use, and the name of the application and Workstation ID that SQL Server will see as being connected to the database.

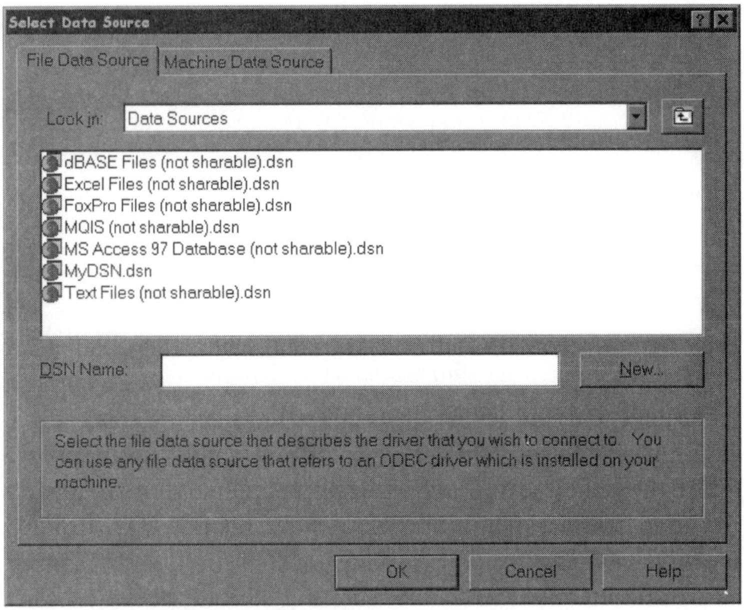

Figure 10-8. Select Data Source

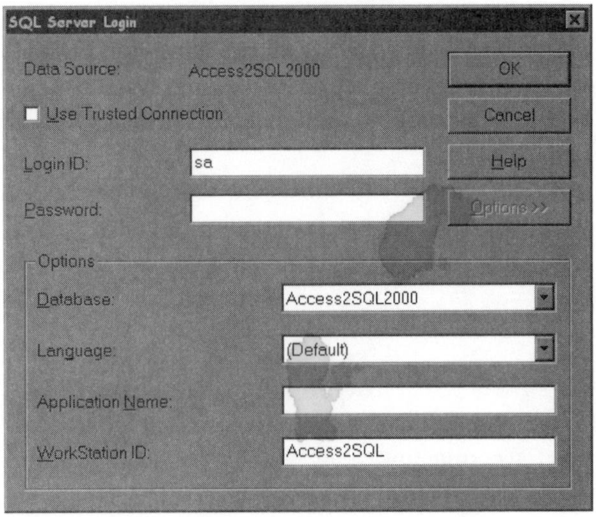

Figure 10-9. SQL Server Login

To login to the server, enter a valid SQL Server user name and password, or select the Use Trusted Connection if you want to connect using integrated security. Click OK when you are done to move to the next screen—the Link Tables dialog.

The Link Tables dialog allows you to select the tables and views that you want to connect into your Access database. Access treats SQL Server views as if they were just normal tables. This allows you to attach them without having to access them using queries. If you are using SQL Server 7, you may also notice that there are a number of views listed that you did not create. The names of these views all start with *INFORMATION_SCHEMA*. These views can be used to return information on the various objects in SQL Server. They are designed to allow a developer to determine what objects exist on the server and what characteristics they have. For example, the view INFORMATION_SCHEMA.TABLES contains a list of all of the tables and views in the database and some of their characteristics. These tables can come in useful if you want to find out how the database is designed.

The Link Tables dialog, shown in Figure 10-10, allows you to scroll through the list of tables in the database and select those tables that you want to link into your Access database.

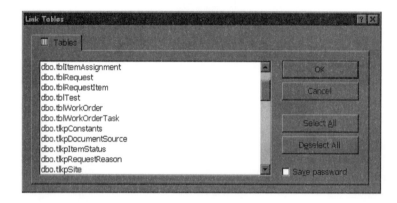

Figure 10-10. Link Tables

The names of the tables and views will be fully qualified with the owner name (in this case dbo), so they may not be sorted as you would expect. Select the tables you want to link into Access by selecting them one at a time in the list or clicking the Select All button.

There is one option on this form that requires you to understand a bit more about security in linked tables. The option Save password saves the login information you entered earlier to open the connection along with the table definition. This does not mean that anyone can read it from the table definition. However, it does mean that no one will be required to login when they use this database to connect to your SQL Server database. This is a security risk, and you really should not select this checkbox. With this option turned off, each time you open this database with a new instance of Access and attempt to open a table, you will be prompted to login. However, the login information will not have to be entered for each table. Access caches the password until you completely exit Access itself. This preserves your security while being as unobtrusive as possible. For this reason, I recommend that you do not select the Save password option.

Once you have selected your tables and views, click OK to link them into Access. As has been discussed in previous chapters, Access requires that any linked table have a unique index defined so that it can be updated. However, views do not have their own indexes, and some tables do not have indexes that Access can determine is a unique key. For this reason, Access must prompt you to specify a unique index to use for each of these objects. The Select Unique Record Identifier dialog, shown in Figure 10-11, contains a list of all of the fields in the table or view.

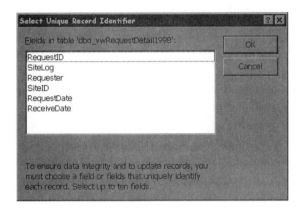

Figure 10-11. Select Unique Record Identifier

If you want the view or table to be updateable, you must select the fields that make up a unique index (preferably the primary key on the main table you want to update using the view) for Access to use. Select all of the fields that make up *one* unique index. If the unique index only contains one field, select only that field. Click OK to commit the changes or Cancel to cancel the link. You should keep in mind that Access does not verify that the key you select is a viable unique index. If you select an index that is not unique, you may cause Access to update information incorrectly. Be very careful when selecting your indexes to ensure that they define unique records in the SQL Server tables.

One factor that you should be aware of when linking tables and views is that the definition of these objects is not automatically updated in Access. This means that if you make changes to a table or view in SQL Server, that change will not be propagated to Access. New fields will not show up and changes to fields, such as removing them from a view or table, will cause an error in Access when you attempt to open the object. For this reason, you need to reattach each table and view that changes. You can do this manually by deleting the linked table or view and relinking it back into the database. Needless to say, this is an issue if you are planning on deploying your application. You don't want your users to have to do this. The best solution would be to use a VBA function to do this for you. However, one other issue arises. When you link a table or view using code, you are not prompted to select a unique index to use for the object. This means that it will not be update-able if a unique index is not found. So what can you do?

Fortunately, there is a solution to this issue using code. Essentially, you want to loop through each table, grab a copy of the unique index on the table, refresh the table link, and then rebuild the index if it does not already exist. The following DAO code accomplishes just this:

```
Public Sub RebuildODBCAttachments()
On Error GoTo Err_RebuildODBCAttachments
    Dim db As Database, tdf As TableDef, idx As Index, fld As Field
    Dim strIndexSQL As String, strFieldList As String
    Dim strPKName As String, boolPKExists As Boolean
    Dim boolHasPK As Boolean
    Set db = CurrentDb
    'Loop through all of the tables checking for ODBC attachments
    For Each tdf In db.TableDefs
        If (tdf.Attributes And dbAttachedODBC) > 0 Then
            'Loop through indexes looking for the primary index
            boolHasPK = False
            For Each idx In tdf.Indexes
                If idx.Primary Then
                    boolHasPK = True
                    'Build the SQL DDL to recreate the index
                    strPKName = idx.Name
                    strIndexSQL = "CREATE UNIQUE INDEX " & idx.Name _
                        & " ON " & tdf.Name & " ("
                    strFieldList = ""
                    For Each fld In idx.Fields
                        If Len(strFieldList) > 0 Then
                            strFieldList = strFieldList & ", "
                        End If
                        strFieldList = strFieldList & fld.Name
                    Next
                    strIndexSQL = strIndexSQL & strFieldList & ")"
                    Exit For
                End If
            Next
            'Refresh the link so that the definition is updated
            tdf.RefreshLink
            boolPKExists = False
            'Check to make sure that the index was not auto-recreated
```

```
            For Each idx In tdf.Indexes
                If idx.Name = strPKName Then
                    boolPKExists = True
                    Exit For
                End If
            Next
            'Recreate the index if it no longer exists
            If boolHasPK And Not boolPKExists Then
                db.Execute strIndexSQL, dbFailOnError
            End If
        End If
    Next
Exit_RebuildODBCAttachments:
    Exit Sub
Err_RebuildODBCAttachments:
    MsgBox Err.Description
    Resume Exit_RebuildODBCAttachments
End Sub
```

This function checks each table in the database to see if it is an ODBC attached table. If it is, it determines if a primary key exists. If it does, a SQL data definition string is built that, when executed, can re-create the index in Access. The link is then refreshed and the table is checked to see if the primary key exists. If it does not and the table had a primary key before, then the SQL DDL string is executed to add the index on the table locally. This SQL has no effect on the backend database; it will only update the index locally so that Access can use it to optimize requests to the server. Also, this code will not rebuild indexes for any tables that did not have a unique index in SQL Server or Access before the reattachment occurred.

Managing Connections

One of the real challenges when connecting to SQL Server through access is managing how connections are established. This means managing how DSNs are distributed and how people login to the system. Fortunately, Access provides some very good solutions to these problems.

Access VBA contains a method, the RegisterDatabase method, which can be used to create DSNs on the fly. This function allows you to specify all of the information necessary to create a DSN and use it in Access. Often, when you distribute your application, you need to re-create this information. If this is the case, use the RegisterDatabase method. This method is a method of the DBEngine object, so it requires that you have a reference to Microsoft DAO in your code. If you are using Access 97 or earlier, this will already be present. If you are using Access 2000, you will have to add that library by adding it in the references of the project from the VBA coding environment. The syntax for this command is:

```
DBEngine.RegisterDatabase dbname, driver, silent, attributes
```

This function creates a User DSN on the local machine. The first parameter, *dbname*, is the name to use for the DSN. The second parameter specifies what ODBC driver to use. This is a string value that is identical to the value in the Name column when you first create a DSN, as shown in Figure 10-2. In the case of SQL Server, the value is "SQL Server". The next parameter, *silent*, is a Boolean value that specifies whether or not to show the ODBC configuration dialogs. In most cases, you don't want this dialog to appear, so set the value to True. Finally, you must set the extended attributes of the driver. This is the configuration you set when you configured your own DSN. The string is a list of all of the properties and their values using the syntax property=value separated by carriage returns (VBA constant *vbCR*). To find out what values to use, create a DSN that has the configuration you want, and then check the values for it in the Registry. For example, Figure 10-12 shows the Registry values for a System DSN that was already created.

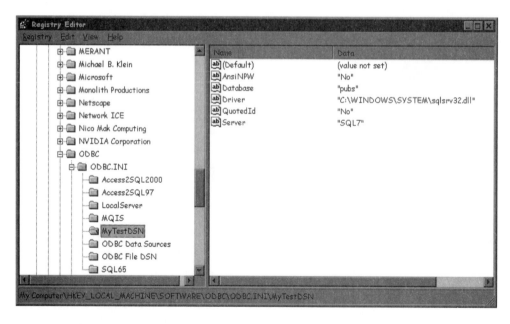

Figure 10-12. ODBC Registry Settings

All of the data in the values in this list need to be added to the DSN as extended attributes with the exception of the Driver value, which is automatically created for you. The code to create a User DSN called *MyNewDSN* with the same characteristics is

```
Dim strAttributes As String
strAttributes = "AnsiNPW=No" & vbCr
strAttributes = strAttributes & "Database=pubs" & vbCr
strAttributes = strAttributes & "QuotedId=No" & vbCr
strAttributes = strAttributes & "Server=SQL7" & vbCr
DBEngine.RegisterDatabase "MyNewDSN", "SQL Server", True, _
  strAttributes
```

This code creates a DSN for the pubs database on a server called "SQL7". When you use this method of creating a DSN, you may find that some properties cause errors when you attempt to use them. For example, if you have a LastUser property, setting it in the RegisterDatabase method will generate an error. The best method to handle this type of problem is to only include the information that you remember configuring when you set up the DSN. You can often also make educated guesses as to what can be omitted.

The next problem with using ODBC tables in Access is ensuring that people can login at an appropriate time and that they do not have the ability to change too much of the configuration in the login. The best method to handle this issue is to make the first form that your users see a customized login form. This form should be opened before any data is accessed, so that the default login dialog is not displayed. The only information you require to show on this form is a user name and password. Once you have this information, you only need to attempt to connect to the database to set the login information that will be used for the rest of the session. The easiest way to do this is to create a temporary query using code, connect it to the SQL Server database, and then attempt to run any SQL command. The following procedure accomplishes this in only a few short commands:

```
Public Function ValidLogin(ByVal strUserName As String, _
                           ByVal strPassword As String) As Boolean
On Error GoTo Err_ValidLogin
    Dim db As Database, qdf As QueryDef
    Set db = CurrentDb
    Set qdf = db.CreateQueryDef("")
    'Set the connection information
    qdf.Connect = "ODBC;DSN=Access2SQL;UID=" & strUserName & _
      ";PWD=" & strPassword & ";DATABASE=Access2SQL"
    'Specify that the command does not return records for simplicity
    qdf.ReturnsRecords = False
    qdf.SQL = "SELECT GETDATE()"
    qdf.Execute
    ValidLogin = True
```

```
Exit_ValidLogin:
    Exit Function
Err_ValidLogin:
    ValidLogin = False
    Resume Exit_ValidLogin
End Function
```

This particular function is specific to a particular database, but you can change it to accommodate your situation. You can call this function to test the login details, and it will return a value, True or False, depending on whether the login was valid. It does this by simply assuming that an error is a login problem. This is a bit simplified because there may be other types of errors, but the ODBC driver often does not return enough useful information to allow you to tell the difference. The advantage to using this function to validate login information is that if the login is successful, Access will cache the login information for use with any attached tables in the database. This prevents the default login dialog from being displayed to the user and thereby limits the possibility of them viewing and modifying the advanced options.

Using SQL Server Objects

Now that you have access to your tables and views, how should you use them? Should you use them in the exact same way as you used Access tables? Well, the answer is yes and no. Generally, you should be able to use linked tables and views just like you would normal Access tables. However, there are a few details you should be aware of, which will allow you to make your application more efficient.

As mentioned previously, one of the major changes that should be made when using SQL Server data in Access is that all SQL statements should be moved to the server. In other words, all access to data should take place through the use of views and stored procedures. In fact, it is best to not even link in any base tables if it can be avoided. All of your forms, reports, and controls should be based on views or stored procedures. This does bring up a few issues.

The first question that some of you may have relates to the functionality available from views. If you think back to Chapter 8, you may remember that view definitions cannot contain an ORDER BY clause. This means that views are always sorted by the indexes in the source tables. You cannot define your own sorting for the view. So what can you do about this? This is one of the few instances where you actually have to use full SQL queries in your Access database. Although SQL Server cannot sort a view, there is no reason you cannot sort it locally in Access. Simply create a local query based on the view and sort the fields in that query. You can then use that query as your data source for forms and reports. One caveat, however, is that you may want to limit the amount of data returned by the view if this has not been done already. You can do this by changing the definition of the view or by filtering data in your query. The reasoning behind this is that Access will occasionally pull down the entire result set of the view before any sorting takes place. This means that extra processing is done locally that should be done on the server. It is best to test the query for performance as you develop it to see how fast it will run. You can also use ODBC tracing (described in Table A-2 in Appendix A) to determine how the request is sent to the server.

The next problem you may have is figuring out how to use stored procedures. There does not appear to be any way to link these objects into the Access database. One of the real shortfalls in ODBC connections in Access is the failure to include full support for stored procedures. Don't worry, however, because you can get at them and use them, you just can't update the data they contain or use "dynamic" parameter values easily.

In order to use a SQL Server stored procedure within Access, you must use a special kind of Access query called a *pass-through* query. Pass-through queries are designed to allow you to send commands directly to SQL Server via the ODBC driver without letting Jet parse or analyze the command. Basically what this means is that when you create a pass-through query, you use SQL Server language to create the SQL statement. This also means that you can do in a pass-though query just about anything you can do in SQL Server itself. This type of query is not analyzed by Access at all. For this reason, you must set some of the extended properties of this type of query so that Access knows how to handle the query.

To create a pass-through query, you must first create a query without any tables selected. In the design view for the query, select Query➠SQL Specific➠Pass-Through. This takes you to a blank SQL editor where you can define your query. You need to enter a few of the properties for your query. You can open the Properties dialog, shown in Figure 10-13, by selecting View➠Properties or by selecting the Properties item on the toolbar.

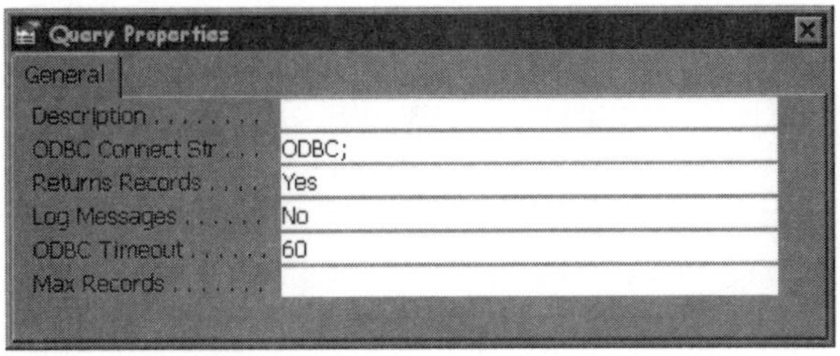

Figure 10-13. Pass-Through Query Properties

If you are using Access 2000, you will have a few extra properties not shown in this figure that allow you to define the subdatasheet information for this query.

This information is entered in exactly the same way that you would enter information for a standard Access query. There are six properties that can be defined for any pass-through query. The Description property is an optional textual description of the query. You can enter any description you like for the query. The ODBC Connect Str property is the connection information used to link to the ODBC data source. You can manually type in the connection information, or you can have Access enter the information for you by using a builder. When the property is active, a builder button (…) appears to the right of the field. Click on this button to select an ODBC data source, and set the login information for the query. This is done using the same dialogs you would use to attach an ODBC table into Access. When you have selected a DSN and entered the necessary login information, Access will ask you if you want to save the password in the connection string. As with tables, it is best not to do this because it could cause some security concerns. And, as with tables, it is not necessary to save the password in the connection string because Access uses the cached user name and password if you have already connected to the server once using any table or the login function described earlier. In fact, the login test function uses a dummy pass-through query to accomplish the password caching by building this query in code. Once your connection information is set, you can then set the other properties of the query.

The Returns Records property allows you to tell Access how to deal with the command. If the SQL statement that you put in the pass-through will return records (or if the stored procedure you are calling does so) set this property to *Yes*. If you are running actions against SQL Server data and no data is being returned, set this property to *No*. You can even set this property to No if you don't want Access to use the recordset returned by the query (once again, a trick used in the login function).

Next, the Log Messages property allows you to specify whether informational messages returned by the stored procedure should be saved in a table in the Access database. This does not mean that error messages from the server will be logged into a table. It means that messages that you purposely raise in your stored procedure that are not critical errors will be logged. However, the logging of these messages is not dependable in Access, so there is little point in using this feature.

The next property that should be set is the ODBC Timeout. This setting defines how many seconds Access waits for a connection to be established to SQL Server. This allows you to ensure that a connection is successfully established to the server. Network traffic and ODBC server load can occasionally cause long delays in response time from the server when a request is sent. Setting the timeout value allows you to automatically cancel the call if it is delayed for too long. This allows your users to move on to other tasks if the server is not accessible.

Finally, the Max Records property allows you to limit the number of records returned by any command. This setting prevents queries or commands from returning excessively large recordsets. Marshalling large amounts of data across the network can be very draining on network resources. Set this property to the maximum number of records you want a user to see at any one time. The number you should choose is entirely dependent on the type of data being returned. If you have a table with any image fields in it, the data it returns per record could be large. In this case, you may want to limit the records in tens or hundreds. In the case of tables with few small fields, you might want to limit the results to thousands or tens of thousands of records.

Once all of your properties have been set, you should then enter the command you want to run. Any command you run should be called using standard SQL Server syntax. So, if you want to run a stored procedure, you should use the EXECUTE statement, as described in the "Testing" section in Chapter 9. You can also run any standard SQL SELECT, UPDATE, INSERT, or DELETE clauses within this type of query, but this type of command should be saved as a stored procedure to begin with.

One of the challenges when using pass-through queries is that you cannot dynamically set the parameters for any stored procedures that you call. This means that you must hard-code the parameter values into the pass-through query. So what can you do if you want to call a stored procedure with different parameters each time? This is where you must use VBA code to handle your database calls for you. One of the best ways to handle this type of situation is to create a simple function that you can call to set the SQL statement in the pass-through query. You can easily set the full SQL statement for any query, but you don't usually want to do this. What would be best is to use a function to set only the parameters of the stored procedure each time you need to call it. The following procedure can help you to do this. All you have to pass in is the name of the local Access pass-through query and the arguments for the stored procedure in the form of a string. The function will read the preexisting SQL for the stored procedure, as long as you use the syntax `EXEC procedurename [arguments]` (or `EXECUTE procedurename [arguments]`).

```
Public Sub SetSPArguments(ByVal strQueryName As String, _
                          ByVal strArguments As String)
On Error GoTo Err_SetSPArguments
    Dim db As DAO.Database, qdf As DAO.QueryDef
    Dim strSPCall As String
    Set db = CurrentDb
    Set qdf = db.QueryDefs(strQueryName)
    strSPCall = qdf.SQL
    'Get the string before the second space character as the SP call
    strSPCall = Left(strSPCall, InStr(InStr(strSPCall, " ") + 1, _
      strSPCall, " "))
    'Use the SP call with the argument string passed in
    qdf.SQL = strSPCall & strArguments
    qdf.Close
```

```
Exit_SetSPArguments:
    Set db = Nothing
    Set qdf = Nothing
    Exit Sub
Err_SetSPArguments:
    MsgBox Err.Description
    Resume Exit_SetSPArguments
End Sub
```

Admittedly, this may not be the most convenient solution, but it does give you the functionality you need. If you want to requery a drop-down list from a stored procedure based on other values on the form, you can call this function in the ComboBox GotFocus event supplying the necessary information to change the pass-through query. Then, call the Requery function on your ComboBox immediately afterwards. For example:

```
Private Sub cboMyCombo_GotFocus()
    SetSPArguments "qrySPCall", Me!txtOne & ", " & Me!txtTwo
    cboMyCombo.Requery
End Sub
```

If the text in the pass-through query was initially "EXEC uspUpdateMyData 3, 20" and the control txtOne contained the value 1 and txtTwo contained the value 50, this code would change the SQL string in the query qrySPCall to "EXEC uspUpdateMyData 1, 50". This allows you to dynamically change the parameter values as necessary.

One type of stored procedure that hasn't yet been discussed is a stored procedure that returns multiple recordsets. As discussed earlier, you can use multiple SQL commands in a stored procedure. This includes multiple SELECT statements. If you open a stored procedure via a pass-through query in Access, you will only be able to view the first recordset retrieved by the stored procedure. So how can you get at the rest of them? Unfortunately, the solution that was originally built into Access is not a good one. It involves using a second query to create tables based on the returned data.

First, create a pass-through query that calls the stored procedure as required. Second, create a standard Make Table query (SELECT...INTO) in Access with the source query as the pass-through you just created. Do not specify individual fields to copy. Instead, make sure that all fields are selected by using the * item, as in Figure 10-14.

When you run this query, a table will be created for each recordset returned by the stored procedure. They will be named starting with the name that you selected to create the table as and a number will be appended onto the names of any other tables that are created. So, if you specified that you wanted to create a table named

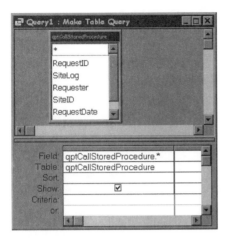

Figure 10-14. Make Table Query for a stored procedure

tblSPResults and the stored procedure returned three recordsets, you would end up with three tables: tblSPResults, tblSPResults1, and tblSPResults2.

The big disadvantages to this solution are that the tables are not indexed, they can clutter your local database, and the data is not always current. If you need multiple sets of data to be returned in Access, you are much better off using code to manage this functionality for you (which is discussed in Chapter 11), or you can simply design your stored procedures around this limitation.

Access Database Projects

With the release of Access 2000, client/server developers have a whole new development environment in which to build integrated SQL Server applications: the ADP. ADPs are a truly innovative new tool. Microsoft took the best features of Microsoft Access—ease of design, integrated database binding, and the powerful reporting engine—and combined them with the raw power of SQL Server. When you create an ADP and connect to SQL Server, you completely bypass the Jet engine. All connections are made through OLE DB. This means that the extra layer of management that is present when using ODBC attached tables is gone. This makes your linked application much faster because the commands only need to go through the OLE DB library to get to SQL Server.

Creating a Project

ADPs are created from the New Database dialog in Microsoft Access 2000. You can access this screen, shown in Figure 10-15, by selecting the Access database wizards, pages, and projects option from the Access startup screen, and then selecting the

General tab. Or you can access this screen by choosing File➡New (Ctrl+N) at any time when working in Access.

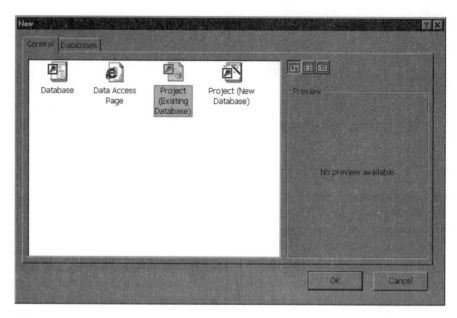

Figure 10-15. New Database

Two items on this screen allow you to create an ADP: Project (Existing Database) and Project (New Database). These options pertain to the SQL Server backend database. If your SQL Server database already exists, select the option to use an existing database. If you want to create a new SQL Server database, select the other option. Click OK to proceed when you have made your choice. You are then prompted to save the Project as a file with the extension ADP. This file contains the main interface that your users will interact with.

If you chose to create a new database, you will be prompted with the Microsoft SQL Server Database Wizard, shown in Figure 10-16, to enter the details for the new SQL Server database you want to create.

The options for creating a new database for your ADP are identical to the options you have when creating a database through the Upsizing Wizard. For complete details on what settings to use and what options may be shown, see "Create New Database" in the Access 2000 Wizard section of Chapter 4. When you have entered all necessary information, click Finish to complete your connection. Your database then opens with the database window showing, and you are connected your new SQL Server database.

If you selected the option to use an existing database, you are prompted to enter the connection information for this database in the Data Link Properties dialog, shown in Figure 10-17.

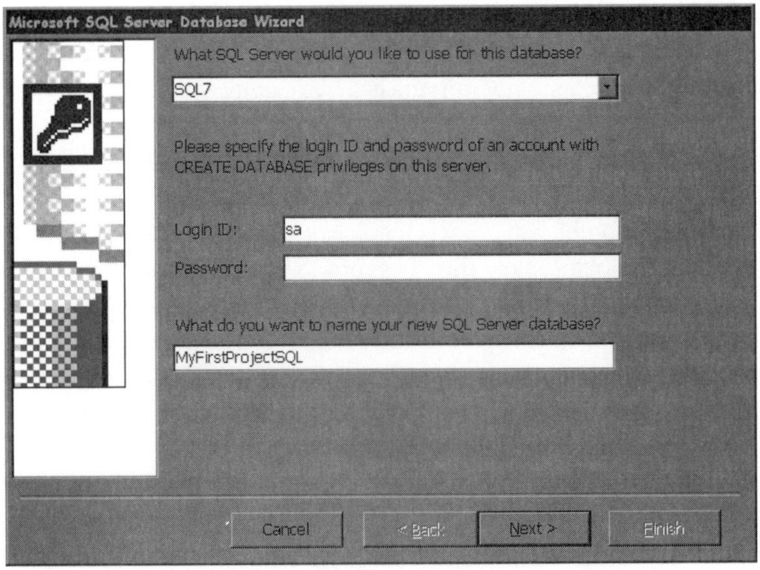

Figure 10-16. Microsoft SQL Server Database Wizard

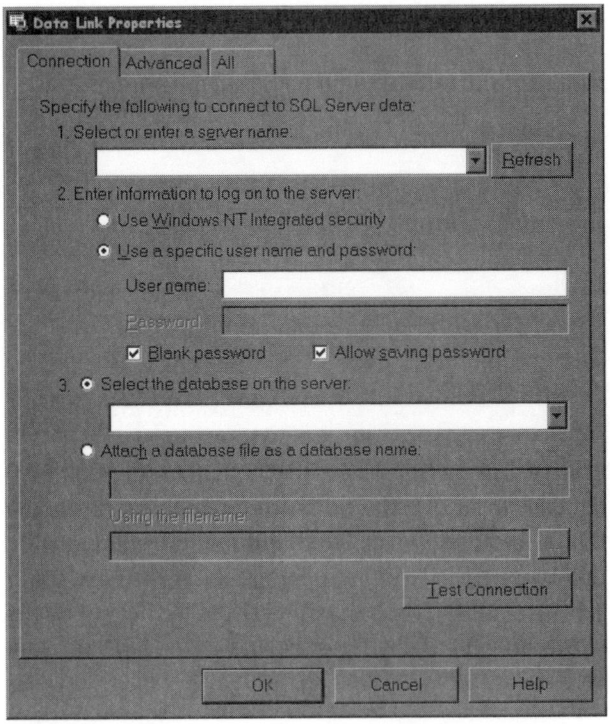

Figure 10-17. Connection tab of Data Link Properties

This Connection screen is the standard dialog for any SQL Server OLE DB connection. Enter the name of the server you want to connect to. You can manually type the server name in or select one from the list. Next, enter the security information necessary to connect to the database. If you are using integrated security on the server, select that item. If you want to use standard SQL Server security, select that item, and enter a user name and password in the appropriate boxes. If the password for the user name you enter is blank, you must select the Blank password checkbox. If it is not blank, clear this checkbox to enter a password for the user. You also have the option of saving the password with the connection information by selecting the Allow saving password option. If you are handling security on SQL Server (which you should be doing), clear this option. It will force users to login each time they open the database. This login information is passed to SQL Server and their security is managed by the server.

The Advanced and All tabs allow you to set some advanced properties of the connection. Just accept the defaults for now. Test your connection to ensure that you have entered everything correctly by clicking the Test Connection button. A message will pop up telling you if the test succeeded. Correct any errors if necessary, and retest the connection. Click OK when your test succeeds to move to the ADP database window.

The main database window in a database project looks much the same as the window in a standard Access database except that the types of objects that can be managed are different (see Figure 10-18).

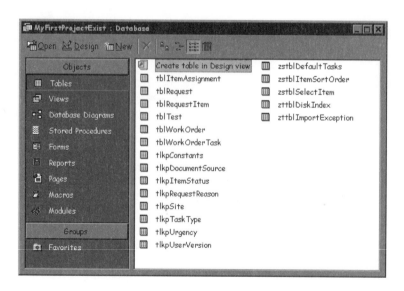

Figure 10-18. ADP database window

In a normal Access database, the only available data objects are Tables and Queries, whereas in this database, you now have four object types: Tables, Views, Database Diagrams, and Stored Procedures. These are direct links to the SQL Server objects. When you want to create a new object in one of these groups, you do so using the same technique as you would in a normal Access database. You can create an object, edit it, open it, or delete it by selecting the appropriate button from the database window toolbar or by right-clicking within the object list. The designers that are opened when editing an object are identical to the designers you would use with SQL Server 7 or the Microsoft Visual Studio Database Designer (if you have it installed). For using SQL Server 6.5, you have the same design tools as are available for SQL Server 7. For information on how to work with the objects, consult Chapter 7.

Connection Information

There may be any number of reasons you cannot connect to the SQL Server database at any one time. Because this is a very common occurrence, Microsoft built a valuable feature into database projects—the ability to work without being connected to the backend database. When your connection to your backend database fails, there is no need to panic. You can still work with your project, you just cannot access any data. This means that development can continue, within limitations. If this occurs, cancel any dialogs prompting you to enter login or connection information. Once this is done, you will be taken into the database in a disconnected mode. You can purposely work in disconnected mode by canceling the login if you are using standard SQL Server security. You can tell that you are in this mode by the fact that the caption *(disconnected)* appears beside your project name in the title bar of the database window (or Access if the window is maximized).

When working in disconnected mode, you cannot access any data or SQL Server objects. The list of tables, views, diagrams, and stored procedures will be blank and any forms, report, or data access pages you create will not be able to access any data. However, you can continue to develop your application to the extent that you can design and code your objects as necessary. You will not be able to select objects and fields to bind them, but there is no reason that you cannot create your user interface with the knowledge that you can connect it to the data later.

Occasionally, you may need to change the connection information for your project. This could be because you are deploying your solution and you need to switch from a test database to a production database, or your server might have moved and had its name changed. Regardless of the reason, this is a very simple problem to resolve. Select File ➡ Connection to open the standard Data Link Properties dialog described earlier. Make changes as necessary, test your changes, and then click OK to save your changes. Note, however, that you must be able to connect using the new information at least once before the changes are saved.

Using SQL Server Objects

Once you have a connected project, you will want to use the objects in the SQL Server database. You can use SQL Server objects in an ADP in exactly the same way that you would use standard Access objects, with a few differences. The first difference you will encounter is that there are two new record navigation buttons when you open a table, view, stored procedure that returns records, or a form. The new record navigation toolbar, shown in Figure 10-19, places these two buttons to the right of the New Record button.

Figure 10-19 ADP record navigation toolbar

The first button is only enabled when Access is loading the data from SQL Server. You can watch the record count increase as the data is loaded; this button appears in red. This button, called the Cancel Query button, allows you to cancel the query or command that is being used to load the data into the Access object. This can be very useful if the command is taking too long. The next button, called the Maximum Record Limit button, allows you to set the maximum number of records that can be returned at any one time by the underlying command. When you click the button, a dialog appears, shown in Figure 10-20, to allow you to change this threshold.

Figure 10-20. Maximum records

You can change the maximum number of records by entering a number in the text box, or you can use the slider to change the setting. If you want to see all of the records returned by the command, move the slider to the far right to the No Limit selection, or delete the value in the text box. In addition, you can change the default record limit for all objects by opening the Access Options dialog from the Tools menu, selecting the Advanced tab and entering a new number in the Default max records setting.

When you are working with forms in a project, there are also a few new properties that you can set. Examine the form data properties in Figure 10-21.

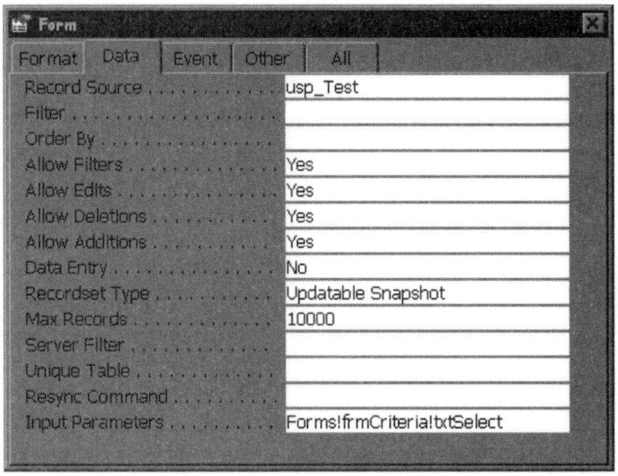

Figure 10-21. Form Data properties

The first change is that the values in Recordset Type property have changed. The two options are now Snapshot and Updatable Snapshot (no one ever said that good spelling was a requirement in programming). With a plain snapshot, none of the data in your form is updateable. With an updateable snapshot, all data is updateable.

The next new property is the Max Records property, which allows you to configure the default settings for the maximum records that will be retrieved for your form at any one time. Enter a setting, or clear this box to show all records.

The new property, Server Filter, allows you to define a filter for the data, much as you would in the Filter property in a regular Access database. The main difference is that your filter is applied to the data on the server before it is presented to Access. With a regular filter, which you can still set, the data is filtered after it is fetched from the server. This increases the amount of data that is being sent across the network. If you use a server filter, you can reduce the traffic and allow SQL Server to handle as much of the data manipulation as possible. This property is ignored if the data source for the object is a stored procedure.

The next property, Unique Table, applies when the data that your form uses comes from multiple tables. This might be the result of a situation where the SQL statement used in the record source contains multiple tables, or your form may be based on a view that contains multiple tables. This property can be set by selecting a table from the drop-down list. Setting a unique table allows Access to better understand what data you want to update and therefore optimizes updates for that table alone. Access generally only allows you to modify one table at a time. Setting this property allows you to update the data and forces updates to be logged against the selected table. You should ensure that you set this property to the table that is the many side of any one-to-many relationship.

The next property, Resync Command, is designed to be used for forms and reports based on stored procedures or for data access pages. The concept is this: When you update a row of data returned in a stored procedure, Access has no way of knowing how to retrieve that information from the server once it is committed. The stored procedure you use may contain multiple tables, and Access often cannot determine how to retrieve the underlying data. In this case, you must supply a parameterized SQL statement that can be used to retrieve a row of data. This statement must include exactly the same rows as are returned by the stored procedure and must have a where clause that contains the primary key field(s) necessary to update that data. For example, if you are working with data that includes the CustomerName field from a Customers table, and the OrderID, TotalCost, and OrderDate from an Orders table, which has a primary key of OrderID, you would set this to the SQL statement:

```
SELECT Customers.CustomerName, Orders.OrderID, Orders.TotalCost, Orders.OrderDate
FROM Customers INNER JOIN Orders ON Customer.CustomerID = Orders.CustomerID WHERE
OrderID = ?
```

The WHERE clause includes the primary key for updating OrderID, parameterized with a question mark. Access understands that this question mark means that a value must be supplied. In this case, you would set the Unique Table property to Orders, and Access would know which index to use. If the primary key for the Unique Table is made up of multiple fields, you must create a parameterized WHERE clause that includes these fields in the order in which they appear in the key.

Finally, the new property Input Parameters allows you to define parameters passed to a stored procedure or parameterized SQL statement that is used as the record source for the object. In a standard database, you can include values and object references directly in the Record Source property. This is not allowed in a database project, so you need to have some other method to specify this information. This new property can include literal values or object references (Figure 10-21 contains a reference to a field on another form). These values should be entered in the order in which they are listed as parameters of the stored procedure or SQL statement.

There are also two new properties in a project that are listed on the Other tab. The first property—Max Rec Button—allows you to set whether or not the Maximum Record Limit button is available in the record navigation toolbar. If you don't want your users to be able to change the value in the Maximum Records, you can disable the button. The next property is called Server Filter by Form. This property allows you to specify that you want the form to open in Filter-by-Form mode to set the Server Filter property. However, the choices it returns are considerably less than a standard Filter-by-Form.

Once you are familiar with the new functionality, you should understand a few details about SQL Server objects used in ADPs. A major item of note is that if you make design changes to your objects using SQL Enterprise Manager while your project is loaded, you may not see those changes in your project right away. For example, if you make a change to a view by adding or deleting fields while a project is open, you may get errors when you try to open that view in Access. To resolve these problems, exit the project, and reopen it. Your connection will be reset, and your objects will be updated. If you make changes to your SQL Server objects in the ADP, the changes will be viewable immediately.

Another item of note is that when you use SQL statements in your project, you must use ADO or SQL Server-compatible syntax. This means that you may have to relearn some SQL language. If in doubt, use SQL Query Analyzer or ISQL/w to check your syntax (in the SQL Server group on your Start menu).

Finally, remember that you want SQL Server to do as much of the work for you as possible. This means that you should be using views and stored procedures to return your data as much as possible. It also means that you should attempt not to include functionality that forces data to be sorted or filtered locally. Instead, design your application in such a way that SQL Server does the work on the server, and Access is used only to present the data to the user and to submit changes to the data to the server.

Other than these stipulations, you can use SQL Server objects in exactly the same way that you are used to using standard Access objects. ADPs were designed to allow you to leverage your knowledge with Access to create robust SQL Server applications. A valuable tool that makes us all happy.

CHAPTER 11

Coding with
SQL Server Data

WE AS DEVELOPERS REGULARLY NEED to extend the behavior of Access by writing code that does some work for us. This code repeatedly needs to access data to include in a report, to update as part of a transaction, or for many other reasons. This means that you must find ways to access and work with the data that your application uses.

Data Coding Choices

When working with Access data in any version of Access before 2000, you had to use Data Access Objects (DAO) as the data access technology to modify Jet data. If you have done any programming against Jet data, chances are that you have used DAO. In Access 2000, DAO is still available but the default data access technology is ActiveX Data Objects (ADO). ADO is Microsoft's newest data access technology and is designed to make any data source accessible using a single object model. ADO is supported natively in Access 2000, but you can use it in Access 97 and 95 as well by adding a reference to the ADO library in your code. The last choice for accessing external data in Access is ODBCDirect. This data access technology is intended to be used to access remote data sources directly using the ODBC API, without involving the Jet engine. Let's take a more in-depth look at each technology.

Data Access Objects (DAO)

DAO is the native standard for programming against Jet databases. It is designed to work with Access databases. It also allows you to work against connected data sources using the objects that you can normally create within Access, such as tables based on connected tables or views and pass-through queries to run commands on a specified data source. However, this is not the intended purpose of DAO. It is designed to perform best when working with Microsoft Jet databases. When DAO is used to access remote data sources, such as SQL Server, the Jet engine sits in between the user or programming interface and the ODBC API that connects to the external data. This adds an extra level of overhead that is incurred between the server and the client.

ODBCDirect

Due to the poor performance and compatibility issues that arose from code being developed using DAO to access external data sources, Microsoft added a feature to Access when Access 97 was released, which was the capability to connect to ODBC data sources directly, completely bypassing the Jet engine. This feature was called ODBCDirect and provided Jet programmers with an object model that was very similar to DAO, but did not involve the unnecessary overhead of running the data through the Jet engine.

ODBCDirect provides similar functionality to Jet, but it also allows you to connect to any ODBC data source directly. This means that you can work in the language of the data source, send customized commands, and work with and edit data from that data source using code that looks almost identical to DAO. In fact, you probably won't even notice that DAO and ODBCDirect are separate libraries when you are working with ODBCDirect. You don't need to make any changes to your module references; you just change the type of workspace you are working in to an ODBCDirect workspace.

ActiveX Data Objects (ADO)

The latest data access library to arrive on the scene is ADO. ADO is a COM programming interface to OLE DB, which basically means that ADO is an accessible interface that is used as a wrapper around OLE DB. It insulates programmers from having to understand the intricacies of OLE DB and provides a standard object model that can be used to access a wide variety of often dissimilar data sources. The object model in ADO was designed with DAO programmers in mind. Much of the functionality, and even some of the methods and properties, is very similar to DAO. This means that it is easy to understand for most DAO programmers. However, unlike DAO, ADO is not limited to a single type of data provider. ADO can be used to access virtually any data source that can be described using recordsets. This includes relational databases, directory services, text files, and even hierarchical products, such as Distributed Transaction Coordinator.

Choosing a Data Access Technology

The particular technology you use in your code is dependent on a number of factors. The most important factor is the version of Access you are using. This restriction applies to Access 95 and 2000. If you are using an Access database project (ADP) (available only in 2000) to connect to SQL Server, you must use ADO. This is the native data technology of ADPs. All connections made through a database project actually use OLE DB to connect to SQL Server. This includes all of the tables, views, diagrams, and stored procedures that are contained in your project. Because all objects are accessed using this technology, it is best not to try to introduce another layer of functionality on top of what is provided. As for Access 95, you cannot use ODBCDirect; it is only available in Access 97 and 2000.

Another factor that should affect your technology choice is the type of code you will be writing. If you are connected to SQL Server using ODBC attached tables and you need to modify native Access objects, such as pass-through queries and linked tables, you must use DAO to make these modifications. In a standard Access database, you cannot make design changes to tables and queries using ODBCDirect. This applies if the tables are local tables or if they are linked from an ODBC data source. This means that you must make these types of changes using DAO.

A final factor that should influence your choice is the versatility of each technology. You are probably well aware of the capabilities of DAO, so we won't discuss that technology here. Table 11-1 shows a comparison between ODBCDirect and ADO. Consider this table when making a choice between these two technologies.

Table 11-1. Comparison of ODBCDirect and ADO

FUNCTIONALITY	ODBCDIRECT SUPPORT	ADO SUPPORT
Ability to return output parameters from stored procedures	Yes	Yes
Asynchronous queries	Yes	Yes
Batch updating	Yes	Yes
Can be bound to Access forms	Not supported	Supported with SQL Server (Read/Write) and Jet (Read-only)
Data definition (DDL)	Not supported	Through ADOX
Direct access to SQL Server	Through ODBC	Through OLE DB
Multidimensional recordsets	Not supported	Through Microsoft Data Shape provider
Recordset events	Not supported	Yes
Updateable multi-join recordsets	Not supported	Supported if joins do not preclude it

As you can see in Table 11-1, ADO supports much more functionality than ODBCDirect does. This means that it is really the best choice when working with SQL Server data. One of the other advantages to using ADO is that it can be referenced in all 32-bit versions of Access. If you use Access 2000, it is the default data library. If you want to use it in Access 95 or 97, you can add a reference to it in your code, and you are free to use it with any data source you like. You should also consider the fact that ADO is a newer technology and is constantly evolving. New features are being added often, and support for virtually all functionality in SQL Server and Access is getting closer and closer. You can use ADO to retrieve data, run commands, and create entire databases from scratch. ODBCDirect, on the other hand, is gradually being phased out of Access. True, it was only added in Access 97, but it is very unlikely that, if the feature survives the next version of Access, there will be any improvements in functionality added to it. When compared with ODBCDirect, ADO is a much better choice.

And the Winner Is…

As you can probably guess, my suggestion for data access when connecting to SQL Server using code is to use ADO. ODBCDirect simply cannot handle a lot of the features that you will likely want to implement when using SQL Server. Also, support for ODBCDirect will probably be dropped in the version of Access after 2000 (no one has told me, I'm just guessing). So, if you are using Access at this time, you will probably find that all of your ODBCDirect code will be outdated in the very near future. Using ADO now ensures that your application will upgrade smoothly with a minimal amount of rework in the future. This will make you and your successors happier when the time comes to upgrade.

Despite ADO's capabilities, we cannot completely ignore DAO. The fact remains that any manipulation of tables and queries that are linked into a standard (non-ADP) database must be done through DAO. Creating and deleting linked tables, modifying pass-through queries, and accessing data in forms bound to ODBC data can still be done using DAO. Because it has already been made clear that DAO will continue to be supported (at least for one more version), we should take a look at this technology.

Using DAO to Manage Local Objects

If you are using ODBC linked tables and ODBC pass-through queries, chances are that you will occasionally want to make changes to these objects from code. You may want to change connection properties, modify SQL strings, or perform some other action on the linked objects. In a standard Access database, these actions cannot be done using ADO or ODBCDirect—you must use DAO to manipulate your objects. There is a myriad of documentation available on how to use Access VBA and DAO to manipulate standard access objects, such as Jet tables, queries, forms, reports, macros, and modules. For this reason, I won't attempt to rehash these topics in this chapter. What I will concentrate on is managing SQL Server linked tables and pass-through queries only. If you are using database projects and you won't be connecting ODBC tables in standard Access databases, feel free to skip to the section entitled "Working with Data." It has some nice juicy bits about ADO and database projects that you will probably find more helpful. For those interested in managing ODBC-linked tables, please read on.

Managing ODBC-Linked Tables

Apart from the regular management of tables in an Access database, you will probably want the ability to manage certain characteristics of ODBC-linked tables. The two main items you will want to handle with ODBC attached tables are the ability to attach new tables and the ability to change existing connection information. Both of these items can be handled in a standard Access database using DAO.

The most important of these items is attaching new tables and views from your SQL Server database. There are two methods that can be used to do this. You can attach the table using a DAO TableDef object, or you can use the TransferDatabase function provided as part of Access VBA. However, in order to use either of these functions, you need to know how to configure connections for SQL Server data sources.

In order to view the base information that you will need, attach a table from a SQL Server database using the methods described in Chapter 10. Open the table in design view, ignore any warnings, and choose Viewà Properties when the table is open. Look at the Description property. This property includes the information that Access uses to connect to the SQL Server table. The following code is an example of the connection information:

```
ODBC;
DSN=Access2SQL;
SERVER=SQL7;
WSID=MyComputer;
DATABASE=Access2SQL;
Address=127.0.0.1,1433;
TABLE=dbo.tblWorkOrderTask
```

Normally, all of this information would appear as a single, unbroken string, but I have separated it for you, so that it is easier to understand. ODBC connection information is always configured as a string containing multiple values separated by semicolons. Each value is set using the syntax `settingname=settingvalue`. The only exception to this is the first value, ODBC, which tells Access that this is an ODBC connection. Before we look at this string in detail, I should tell you that this string is for a table that was attached with the Save password option turned off. We will discuss the implications of this in the "Preventing Password Caching" section.

Each setting defines a particular piece of information that Access needs in order to connect to the ODBC data source. In this particular example, the main piece of information to look at is the setting for the DSN item. As you might guess, this tells Access what ODBC DSN should be used to connect to the SQL Server database. The name that follows the equal sign is an existing DSN defined on the source computer. The rest of the settings are retrieved by Access from this DSN, but are stored in the connection string to enable Access to get to the data source faster. Each of the items in the connection string are discussed later in this section.

If you attach a table or view using the Link Tables command, they always appear as shown in the previous example, based on a DSN. However, there is one detail that you might not find in the Access documentation—you do not need a DSN to connect a table or view. With the right knowledge, you can actually connect a table using what is called a "DSN-less connection." With this type of connection, you must supply more information than is required with a DSN connection. There is not much documentation available that can tell you what properties are required because this is not common practice. Fortunately, you can cheat to find out what information you need. In order to do this, create a File DSN on your computer, and then examine the file using a text editor. Or create a System or User DSN, and then examine the Registry settings that it creates. The text in a File DSN follows the Access convention of connection strings of using the `property=value` syntax. The following example is from a File DSN:

```
[ODBC]
DRIVER=SQL Server
UID=sa
Address=127.0.0.1,1433
DATABASE=Access2SQL
WSID=Access2SQL
SERVER=SQL7
```

As you can see, some of the information is identical to the information in a DSN connection. The main difference is that there is a DRIVER setting in this connection. When using SQL Server, this is always "SQL Server". When you create a DSN-less connection, you must include the base information necessary to connect to the database. The minimum settings you require are the driver, server, database, and the address (just in case it cannot be resolved). You can use the names for these parameters provided in a file DSN, or you can use the names created in the Registry when you create a User or System DSN. The names for each item might differ somewhat between the DSN types, but the resulting connection remains the same.

Each of these settings has a special meaning when connecting to SQL Server. Some of them are created by Access without your input, and some of them are information that you must provide. Table 11-2 details some of the more common settings that you might see or use. It also indicates when you must provide them and with what type of connection.

Table 11-2. ODBC Connection Settings

SETTING	VALUE TO PROVIDE	USE WITH DSN	USE WITH DSN-LESS	COMMENTS
Address	IP Address and port for connecting to SQL Server ()	Never; configured in DSN	Always	172.0.0.1,1433, for example.
AnsiNPW	Yes or No	Never; configured in DSN	When not using default.	This tells ODBC to use ANSI standard nulls, paddings, and warnings. Yes is default.
DATABASE	Name of the database	When not using DSN-configured default	Always	You can override the default database set in a DSN when using this setting.
Description	Description of DSN	Never; configured in DSN	Never	Retrieved from DSN if one is used.
DRIVER	Use "SQL Server" (without quotes)	Never	Always	Use the "friendly name" of the driver listed in DSN drivers tab.
DSN	Name of the DSN	Always	Never	--
Language	Language of connection (for example, us_english)	Only when not using system default	Only when not using system default	Allows you to have different users on the same database but using different languages.
PWD	Password for login	When necessary	When necessary	User may be prompted if not set.
QuotedId	Yes or No	Never; configured in DSN	When not using default	DSN-less connections if you want to set it to No (use quoted identifiers). Yes is default.
SERVER	SQL Server to which you want to connect	When not using DSN-configured default	Always	--
StatsLog_On	Yes or No	When necessary	When necessary	This will cause the ODBC driver to log statistics to the default ODBC log file. No is default, so not required.
TABLE	Name of the table	Never	Never	Added by Access
Trusted_ Connection	Yes or No	Never - configured in DSN	When connecting using NT authentication	Specifies that SQL Server uses NT authentication
UID	Login user name for SQL Server	When necessary	When necessary	User will be prompted if not set
WSID	Name of the workstation connecting	When not using default	When not using default	Local computer name is always default

With the information in Table 11-2, you can create a DSN-less connection. A simple connection string using this type of connection could be

```
ODBC;DRIVER=SQL Server;Server=SQL7;DATABASE=Access2SQL;
```

That's all the base information you need. If do not provide login information, you are prompted to login to the system. If you want to include the login information in your connection string, simply add the parameters:

```
UID=username;PWD=password;
```

to the end of the connection string, substituting your user name and password in the appropriate settings. If you are using integrated security, you can leave these settings out of the connection string and use the following string:

```
Trusted_Connection=Yes;
```

Let's take a look at how this is actually implemented.

There are two methods that you can use to attach a table into Access. The first method is to use the Access VBA TransferDatabase method. This is a method of the DoCmd object, and it uses the following syntax:

```
DoCmd.TransferDatabase [transfertype], databasetype, databasename _
  [, objecttype], source, destination[, structureonly][, saveloginid]
```

When you are attaching a SQL Server table, the first parameter, transfertype, must be the VBA constant acLink. The next parameter must specify that you are connecting to an ODBC data source; this is done by using the string: ODBC Database (enclosed in quotes). Next, provide your ODBC connection string as the value for the databasename parameter. Select the acTable constant as the value for the objecttype argument, enter your source table name as the source, and the name you want it to have in Access as the destination. The structureonly parameter does not apply in the case of linking tables, so you can ignore it. Finally, set the saveloginid to True or False, depending on whether you want to save the login information with the table. With the DSN-less connection we have been building, you could attach a table called Orders using the following code:

```
Dim strConn as String
strConn = "ODBC;DRIVER=SQL Server;Server=SQL7;DATABASE=Access2SQL;"
strConn = strConn & "UID=sa;PWD=;"
DoCmd.TransferDatabase acLink, "ODBC Database", strConn, acTable, _
  "Orders", "Orders", , False
```

When this code runs, the table will be attached into your database. If there is any problem with the connection string, you will be prompted to enter the connection information using the SQL Server login screen shown in Figure 11-1.

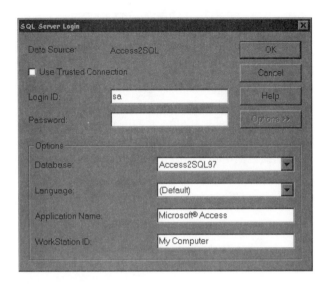

Figure 11-1. SQL Server Login

Figure 11-1 shows this dialog with the Options section expanded. If you are attaching a SQL Server view or a table for which Access cannot determine a unique index, you will also see the Select Unique Record Identifier dialog shown in Figure 11-2.

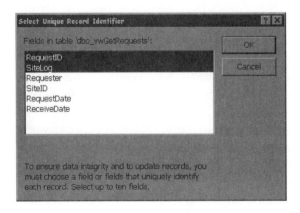

Figure 11-2. Select Unique Record Identifier

This command has one major problem. If the name you want to use for the table in Access is already in use in the local Access database, you do not receive any error messages. Instead, the table is added with a number after the name. In the case of this example, if there is already a table named Orders in the Access database, the SQL Server table is linked in as Orders1 (or Orders2, or Orders3, etcetera). This can be a major problem if you want to ensure that you are working with the correct table when you use it at a later time. You can fix this by checking to make sure that there isn't a table by that name already using code, or you can use the other method of attaching tables, adding a new TableDef to the DAO TableDefs collection.

As you are probably aware, each database object in DAO contains a collection of TableDefs. This is a collection of all of the tables defined in the database, whether they are local or attached tables. In order to add a linked SQL Server table or view into Access using DAO, you must create a new TableDef object, set the properties necessary to define the connection, and then append it to the TableDefs collection. This is accomplished using the following code:

```
Dim tdf As TableDef, db As Database
Set db = CurrentDb                      'Set the current database
Set tdf = db.CreateTableDef("Orders") 'Create a new TableDef
                                        'Set the connection string
tdf.Connect = "ODBC;DSN=Access2SQL;UID=sa;PWD=;"
tdf.SourceTableName = "Orders"          'Specify the SQL table
db.TableDefs.Append tdf                 'Append the table
```

This code shows you all that you need to know to connect a table from SQL Server when using DAO. The first step is to use the CreateTableDef method to create a new TableDef object in the code. Next, you must set the Connect property, specifying the ODBC connection string needed to connect to the database. This is built using the syntax just discussed. Next, set the SourceTableName to the name of the table as it exists in SQL Server. Finally, append the new TableDef to the TableDefs collection using the Append method. That's really all there is to it.

But what happens if your connection information changes and you don't want to reattach all of your tables all over again using the new connection information? Well, you can use DAO to manage this change for you. You can change the connection string for a table at any time by assigning the table to a TableDef object, changing the Connect property, and refreshing the link using the RefreshLink method of the TableDef object; for example:

```
Dim tdf As TableDef, db As Database
Set db = CurrentDb                          'Set the current database
Set tdf = db.TableDefs("Orders")            'Assign the TableDef object
                                            'Set the connection string
tdf.Connect = "ODBC;DSN=Access2SQL;UID=sa;PWD=;"
tdf.RefreshLink                             'Refresh the table link
```

As discussed earlier, when you make changes to a table or view definition on SQL Server, those changes will not necessarily be propagated to the Access interface. If you want to update Access with any changes on SQL Server, you can use the RefreshLink method on a TableDef object that is linked to the SQL Server object and the definition will be automatically be updated. You may have noticed that this method was used in the previous chapter in the RebuildODBCAttachments function. You cannot, however, change the SQL Server table to which the table is attached. This can only be accomplished by deleting the old link table and creating a new one that connects to a different table or view.

When using a standard Access database with SQL Server linked tables, it is still possible to create local Access tables or link Jet tables into the database. When working in the database, you may want to loop through all of the tables and make changes only to those tables that are ODBC attached tables. This means that you will probably want to test to see if the table is a linked ODBC table before you make any changes to it. This is one place where DAO can definitely help out. Each table has a property that defines what type of table it is and some of its characteristics. This information is stored in the Attributes property of a TableDef object. Any table that is attached using ODBC will have a bit set in the Attributes property that corresponds to the DAO constant dbAttachedODBC. To test a table to see if it is an ODBC attached table, simply compare the bits in the Attributes with this constant using the And operator to see if the value is greater than zero, as in

```
boolIsODBCTable = ((tdf.Attributes And dbAttachedODBC) > 0)
```

Preventing Password Caching

One factor that may not have been covered sufficiently is that when you connect to a table using code and you are using SQL Server standard authentication, if you do not provide the full login information including the user name and password, you will be prompted to enter this information. This happens for each connection that you add or change, so it can be quite inconvenient. Also, it provides your users with access to the standard ODBC login screen, where they might change the database or other connection information. To work around this problem, it is best to provide a user name and password in the connection string (if you are not using integrated security). However, when you provide the user name and password in the connection string, Access automatically caches the security information with the table, so users are not forced to login the next time they open the database. There is no way to prevent this from happening from within Access itself. However, you can change your SQL Server database so that Access will know not to store this information.

In order to do this, you must add a new table to your SQL Server database. This table must be named "MSysConf". It allows you to set some basic configuration values for Access connections to SQL Server when ODBC is used, and it must be configured to the specifications in Table 11-3

Table 11-3. MSysConf Table Configuration

FIELD NAME	DATA TYPE	ALLOW NULLS	PURPOSE
Config	SMALLINT	No	Number of the configuration option to set.
chValue	VARCHAR(255)	Yes	Not used; always Null.
nValue	INTEGER	Yes	Configuration option setting.
Comment	VARCHAR(255)	Yes	Description of the configuration option.

Once you create this table, you must add a record to it to disable password caching in Access. Enter a record with the field values of Config = 101, chValue = NULL, nValue = 0, Comment = Null (or your own comment if you like). In order for this change to take effect in your database, you must reset the Connect property for each attached table and refresh the links. Otherwise, the setting will only affect new tables. Once this is done, you can be sure that users will not be able to cache their login information. In fact, the Save Password option in the Link Tables dialog will be disabled. If you want to enable password caching again, change the field nValue = 1 and reconnect your tables as before.

Using DAO to Manage Pass-Through Queries

Now that you know how to manage ODBC connected tables, you may be wondering how to handle pass-through queries. Although they have some limitations, they can be quite useful tools if you need read-only data for items such as reports, combo boxes, or list boxes. As with all other types of queries in a standard Access database, you can use DAO to manage this type of query.

As you are probably aware, queries in an Access database are managed in DAO using the QueryDefs collection of a Database object. Each query is represented as a single QueryDef object within the collection. When you want to manipulate a pass-through query, you simply open the query as a QueryDef object, set the properties you need to modify, and, if it is a new query, append it to the QueryDefs collection.

When working with pass-through queries in Access, there are four properties of the QueryDef object that will be of interest to you. These properties, listed in Table 11-4, allow you to define the configuration and behavior of your query.

Table 11-4. Select QueryDef Properties

PROPERTY	TYPE	PURPOSE
Connect	String	Specifies the ODBC connection string to use to access the SQL database.
MaxRecords	Long	Sets a maximum number of records that can be returned to the client when the query is run (zero means no limit).
ReturnsRecords	Boolean	Specifies whether the command will return data to Access or not.
SQL	String	SQL or Transact-SQL command to execute on the server.

The Connect property is probably the most important of all the properties. This setting is identical to the Connect property of a linked table, and you should use the string format to set it. If it is not set, your query will attempt to run locally and errors will occur. This string, just like a TableDef's Connect property, must start with "ODBC;", which must be followed by the necessary connection information.

The MaxRecords and ReturnsRecords properties of a QueryDef allow you to set the query properties Max Records and Returns Records described in Chapter 10. They allow you to define how the query will work with data from SQL Server.

Finally, the SQL property defines the actual command that you are sending to SQL Server through ODBC. If you want to create a pass-through query, simply provide the SQL Server command string that will do the job for you.

Let's take a look at an example. Suppose you want your pass-through query to run a stored procedure on SQL Server and return the results of that procedure to Access. This stored procedure should return a list of companies that you can use as the source for a combo box. The following code could be used to create a new pass-through query called "qsptCompanies":

```
Dim db As Database
Dim qdf As New QueryDef      'Creating a new QueryDef
Set db = CurrentDb
'Set the QueryDef name
qdf.Name = "qsptCompanies"
'Assign the connection string
qdf.Connect = "ODBC;DSN=Access2SQL;UID=sa;PWD=;"
```

```
'Set the SQL command to execute on SQL Server
qdf.SQL = "EXEC uspGetCompanies"
'If we want to see the data we must set ReturnsRecords
qdf.ReturnsRecords = True
'Limit to 1000 companies to save resources
qdf.MaxRecords = 1000
'Finally, append the new qdf to the database
db.QueryDefs.Append qdf
```

This code creates a new QueryDef object, sets all of the necessary properties to make it a pass-through query, and then appends it to the QueryDefs collection of the database object. You can also do this using the CreateQueryDef method of the Database object. When you use the CreateQueryDef method, however, you do not need to declare the QueryDef as New, and it will automatically be appended to the collection for you. In order to add the same query as the previous query using the CreateQueryDef method, you could use the following code:

```
Dim db As Database
Dim qdf As New QueryDef        'Creating a new QueryDef
Set db = CurrentDb
'Create the QueryDef and set the SQL string
Set qdf = db.CreateQueryDef("qsptCompanies")
'Assign the connection string
qdf.Connect = "ODBC;DSN=Access2SQL;UID=sa;PWD=;"
'Set the SQL command after setting the connection
qdf.SQL = "EXEC uspGetCompanies"
'If we want to see the data we must set ReturnsRecords
qdf.ReturnsRecords = True
'Limit to 1000 companies to save resources
qdf.MaxRecords = 1000
```

This code also adds a new QueryDef to the Access database. There is one item to watch for when using the CreateQueryDef method. This method has two optional arguments: Name and SQLText. Although you can provide values for both of these parameters, you should not set the SQLText parameter when using a pass-through query. This is because Access assumes that you are trying to create a standard Jet query, and it parses the SQL statement you use. If the statement is not valid for Access or for the database you are using, Access raises error 3129—Invalid SQL statement. In order to avoid this issue, set the query's Connect property before assigning a SQL statement.

As with tables, you can change the properties of a query at any time using code by simply opening it as a QueryDef object and setting the necessary properties. For example, you could change the connection information for a query using almost identical code to changing the connection for a table.

```
Dim qdf As QueryDef, db As Database
Set db = CurrentDb                          'Set the current database
Set qdf = db.QueryDefs("Orders")            'Assign the QueryDef object
                                            'Set the connection string
qdf.Connect = "ODBC;DSN=Access2SQL;UID=sa;PWD=;"
```

The only difference is that QueryDefs do not have to be refreshed when you change them.

Just as you may want to check tables to see if they are ODBC attached tables, you may want to test queries to see what type of query they are. This information is stored in a QueryDef's Type property. This property is a value of type QueryDefTypeEnum defined in the DAO library. Depending on whether or not the pass-through has its ReturnsRecords property set to Yes or No, this will be one of two values. If the pass-through returns records, this value will be equal to the enumerated constant dbQSQLPassThrough. If it does not, the value will be dbQSPTBulk. If you are checking a QueryDef to see if it is a pass-through query, you must account for both of these possibilities, as in:

```
boolIsPassThrough = (qdf.Type = dbQSQLPassThrough) Or _
  (qdf.Type = dbQSPTBulk)
```

Working with Data

As our earlier comparison made evident, the best data technology to use when working with SQL Server data in code is ADO. ADO provides extended functionality that allows you to connect to SQL Server and use the SQL Server engine to its full potential. ADO is the default data library in Access 2000. One of the real advantages to using it in earlier versions of Access is that it allows you to create code now that upgrades flawlessly when you decide to make the change to Access 2000 or other future versions of Access. This means that all of your code will be useable without having to be changed to handle a new data library.

Before you start using ADO, you need to add the necessary libraries to the references collection in your code. If you do not already have a copy of the Microsoft Data Access Components library on your computer, you should download it from the Microsoft Web site at *http://www.microsoft.com/data* and install the necessary files. The program you need to download is called mdac_typ.exe and installing it will install all of the DLLs you need to work with ADO in Access 95 or 97. If you are working with Access 2000 or you are running your application on Windows 2000, these DLLs will have been installed on your machine, but you should check the site to see if you have the latest version. To find out what version is installed on your machine, check the value of the FullInstallVer value under the Registry key HKEY_LOCAL_MACHINE\SOFTWARE\Microsoft\DataAccess.

In order to add a reference to ADO in your database, open any module and select Tools à References. Scroll down the list to the item called Microsoft ActiveX Data Objects 2.5 Library and select the checkbox beside it to add the reference.

The ADO library on your computer may have a different version than 2.5. The version number listed could range from 1.5 and higher. Choose the highest version number or download the most recent version from Microsoft and install it. When you highlight the library in the References dialog, a Path or Location for the file should be displayed in the bottom of the dialog. The most recent DLL is currently called msado15.dll to prevent compatibility issues with changing versions. If multiple versions are listed, check the DLL for each version, and select the one that lists msado15.dll as the library file. You should also ensure that you have the latest version by downloading mdac_typ.exe from the URL listed previously. This will guarantee that you have the most recent version with all of the latest fixes.

Once you have added a reference to ADO to your database, you are ready to go ahead and work with SQL Server data.

> **NOTE** *For a comprehensive introduction to using ADO with Microsoft Access, see the ADO articles available in the downloads for this book on the Apress Web site at www.apress.com. For more complete information on using ADO, including best practices and advanced programming examples, see ADO Examples and Best Practices by William R. Vaughn (Apress, 2000) and Serious ADO: Universal Data Access with Visual Basic by Rob Macdonald (Apress, 2000).*

ADO Connections

The base object in the ADO object model is the Connection object. This object is used to connect to a database and contains all of the information necessary to do so. Any other objects used in ADO require a valid connection object to define what data source they are connecting to. In order to use an ADO Connection, you must configure it to connect to your data source. This can be done using one of two methods. You can use a single connection string similar to an ODBC connection string that is defined as a number of settings using the syntax setting=value followed by a semicolon. Or you can build the connection string by setting each property of the connection individually, using the Properties collection of the Connection object. Each of these methods is demonstrated later in this section. However, as with ODBC connection strings, you should understand the connection properties that you must set in order to connect to SQL Server. In order to make ADO Connections as generic as possible, Microsoft decided that any provider specific properties should be set through the Properties collection of the Connection object. The values in this collection will change depending on the type of data source you use, so you must first tell the Connection what type of data source you will be using. This is done using the Provider property. In the case of SQL Server, this property should always be set to "SQLOLEDB", as in the following code:

```
Dim cnn As New ADODB.Connection
cnn.Provider = "SQLOLEDB"
```

Once this property is set, you can then define all of the rest of your connection information using the various settings in the Properties collection. Table 11-5 contains a list of some of the more important properties that you may want to set when connecting to SQL Server.

Table 11-5. SQLOLEDB Properties

PROPERTY	DATA TYPE	PURPOSE
Connect Timeout	Long	Amount of time to wait in seconds before connection fails if not established.
Data Source	String	Network name or alias of the SQL Server you want to use.
Initial Catalog	String	Name of the SQL Server database you want to use.
Initial File Name	String	Initial SQL Server or MSDE file to use when connecting to the database by file name.
Integrated Security	Boolean	Use integrated security (do not set any value for this property unless you set it to True).
Network Address	String	Server IP Address and port to use when connecting to SQL Server (such as "172.0.0.1,1433").
Password	String	Password to use when connecting (if using SQL Server security).
User ID	String	User ID to use when connecting (if using SQL Server security).

In order to set each property listed in Table 11-5, you must assign a value to the corresponding item in the Properties collection of a Connection object, as in the following code:

```
Dim cnn As ADODB.Connection
Set cnn = New ADODB.Connection
cnn.Provider = "SQLOLEDB"
cnn.Properties("Data Source") = "SQL7"
cnn.Properties("Initial Catalog") = "Access2SQL"
cnn.Properties("User ID") = "sa"
cnn.Properties("Password") = ""
```

This code specifies the most basic information necessary to connect to a SQL Server database. You can set any of the other properties as necessary using exactly the same syntax.

The other way to enter this information is to specify the ConnectionString property of the Connection. As with ODBC connection strings, this can be done by using the `setting=value;` syntax, as shown next:

```
Dim cnn As ADODB.Connection
Set cnn = New ADODB.Connection
cnn.ConnectionString="Provider=SQLOLEDB;Data Source=SQL7;" & _
  "Initial Catalog=Access2SQL;User ID=sa;Password=;"
```

This code creates a connection with the same settings as the previous example.

Although you can use the latter method to create a connection string, it is recommended that you set each property individually. This makes your code more readable and allows you to quickly find and change settings when the need arises.

Connections in ADPs

The discussion on Connections has so far left out the concept of working with an ADP, and for very good reason. If you are using an ADP, your connections are handled for you. Rather than creating a new connection and having to set the properties for it each time you need to connect to SQL Server, you can use a the connection information already established in your project. This connection can be accessed using the code:

```
Set cnnMySQLConnection = CurrentProject.Connection
```

This code copies the connection information in your ADP directly into the Connection object cnnMySQLConnection, so you don't have to worry about configuring each connection you want to use. In fact, you can totally bypass the use of Connection objects if you will always use the same settings as defined for your project. You can simply assign the CurrentProject.Connection value to a Recordset or Command object as necessary.

One difference between ADP connections and those that you may create on your own is that ADP connections do not use the standard SQL Server OLE DB provider (SQLOLEDB). Instead, they use the Microsoft Data Shaping Service provider. This provider is really a provider on top of a provider. It allows you to create and use multidimensional data sets from specific data providers. For this reason, you can create shaped recordsets if you desire. (Consult the ADO documentation for a complete description of how data shaping works and how you can use it.) However, if you want to access the base information outside of the data shape provider to connect to SQL Server (and reduce your overhead a bit), you can use the BaseConnectionString property of the CurrentProject object. This property returns a string that you can use as the connection information for any ADO objects you want to use with the SQLOLEDB provider.

Running Commands with SQL Server

In ADO, Command objects are used to execute textual commands and call stored procedures on a data source. When using Commands with SQL Server, there are a few details you should know about how their behavior differs from Commands used against Jet data.

When using Command objects with SQL Server, you have the ability to pass parameters to the stored procedure through the Command object. This functionality is also available with the Access provider, but there is one major difference. Parameters in Commands against SQL Server can be input or output Parameters, or both. What this means is that if you call a stored procedure that has parameters that have the OUTPUT keyword in the declaration, you can use ADO to retrieve the values from these parameters after the stored procedure has completed. In order for ADO to know that you will need the value back from SQL Server, you need to specify the *direction* of the parameter as appropriate. Suppose you have a stored procedure that inserts a new record into a table and one of the output parameters is the identity value for the newly created record. The stored procedure definition might look like this:

```
CREATE PROCEDURE uspAddCustomer
    (@vchCustomerName varchar(50),
      @vchContactName varchar(50),
      @intCustomerID int OUTPUT )
AS
INSERT INTO Customers (CompanyName, ContactName)
VALUES (@vchCustomerName, @vchContactName)

SELECT @intCustomerID = @@IDENTITY

RETURN @@ERROR
```

This may be a very simple procedure, but it does illustrate the point at hand. In order to call this procedure using ADO, you would need to create a new Command object, connect it to SQL Server, create parameters for each parameter in the stored procedure and append them to the Command's Parameters collection, and then execute the command. The main difference in each parameter's direction information is that you must specify the Direction property of the Parameter object you create. To call this stored procedure, you could use the following code:

```
Dim cmd As New ADODB.Command
Dim prm As ADODB.Parameter
'Configure the Command object
cmd.ActiveConnection = strMyConnectionString    'Supply a string
cmd.CommandText = "uspAddCustomer"
cmd.CommandType = adCmdStoredProc
'Setup the first input parameter
Set prm = cmd.CreateParameter("@vchCustomerName", adVarChar, _
  adParamInput, 50, "Millenium Inc.")
cmd.Parameters.Append prm
'Setup the second input parameter
Set prm = cmd.CreateParameter("@vchContactName", adVarChar, _
  adParamInput, 50, "Frank Black")
cmd.Parameters.Append prm
'Setup the output parameter
Set prm = cmd.CreateParameter("@intCustomerID", adInteger, _
  adParamOutput)
cmd.Parameters.Append prm
cmd.Execute
```

This code uses the CreateParameter method of the Command object to create each parameter. The various properties of the Parameter object, including the Direction, are set in this method. The syntax for this method is

```
Set parameter = command.CreateParameter (Name, Type, Direction, _
  [Size], [Value])
```

Once the Parameter is created using this method, the Parameter should be appended to the Command's Parameters collection. Setting the Direction property of the Parameter to adParamInput or adParamOutput allows you to instruct the Command as to whether you want data back from the call.

If you want to retrieve the return value from a stored procedure, you must create another parameter on the Command specifying that it is a return parameter. This is also done using the Direction argument. The actual parameter name is not important, but ADO uses the default name "RETURN_VALUE", so you should stick to that convention. You could add the return value to the previous command using the following code:

```
Set prm = cmd.CreateParameter("RETURN_VALUE", adInteger, _
  adParamReturnValue)
cmd.Parameters.Append prm
```

Note that when you create Parameters for a Command, they must be created in the order in which they appear in the stored procedure. ADO always evaluates the parameters by ordinal position, not by name. If you make errors in the order of the parameters, you may get unexpected results. When you explicitly define return parameters, you should configure these as the first parameters in the list. Failure to do so will generate errors.

Now, what do you do if you don't know what parameters exist in the stored procedure? When your code is executing and it needs information on the parameters of a stored procedure, you cannot necessarily go back to SQL Server and check the procedure definition. Fortunately, the answer is quite simple. You can create your Command object, set the ActiveConnection, CommandType, and Command-Text properties, and then call the Refresh method of the Parameters collection, as in:

```
cmd.Parameters.Refresh
```

You can then use your code to interrogate Parameters collection and the properties of each parameter to determine what information needs to be supplied. Use this functionality judiciously, though, as it requires an extra network round trip between your application and SQL Server.

One final note about parameters used with ADO Commands. If your Command calls a stored procedure that returns data as well as returning parameters and you are using that data in your code, you must set the Recordset object to Nothing before you can access the output parameters. The following code illustrates this issue:

```
Set rst = cmd.Execute
'Do something with the recordset here
Set rst = Nothing
'Now you can access the output parameters
Debug.Print cmd.Parameters("@intOutputValue")
```

Basically this means that the values in your output parameters will be uninitialized until the recordset that was returned has been dealt with. As Microsoft says, "This behavior is by design." Be aware of it, so that you do not run into issues with your application when you begin your coding.

Recordsets and SQL Server

Generally, there is not too much difference between using a SQL Server-based ADO recordset and an Access-based ADO recordset. In fact, ADO was designed so that this type of provider transparency would aid developers. Regardless, SQL Server does have many capabilities that Access does not have, so those are the areas where you need to know how to work with recordsets in ADO.

One of the major differences between SQL Server stored procedures and Access queries is that stored procedures have the capability to return multiple recordsets from a single procedure. The problem with this in ADO is how to use each recordset that is returned. The answer is the NextRecordset method of the Recordset object. This command can be used on any statement that returns compound recordsets, such as a stored procedure or a command that includes multiple SELECT strings (you can do this with SQL Server by delineating the SELECT statements with semicolons). However, you must do all of the necessary processing with each recordset in the order retrieved before you can move on to the next. The NextRecordset method automatically clears the current Recordset object and returns a new Recordset object, so you must assign the return value to another Recordset object. This can be the original Recordset variable you used or another one. The syntax for the method is

```
Set recordset2 = recordset1.NextRecordset
```

The following example calls a stored procedure that returns two recordsets and simply prints the number of records in each Recordset to the debug window.

```
Dim rst As New ADODB.Recordset
Dim cmd As New ADODB.Command
Dim lngI As Long
cmd.CommandText = "uspMultiRecordset" 'SP that returns two rsts
cmd.ActiveConnection = CurrentProject.BaseConnectionString
cmd.CommandType = adCmdStoredProc
rst.Open cmd                          'Open the cmd with the rst
Debug.Print rst.RecordCount           'Print the recordcount
Set rst = rst.NextRecordset           'Open the next recordset
Debug.Print rst.RecordCount           'Print the recordcount
```

If you require access to multiple recordsets at a time, you should always use separate commands or queries to return them. This ensures that you do not lose one recordset when you need to access another.

SQL Server-based ADO Recordsets have another major difference from Access-based ADO recordsets—they can be dynamically assigned (in code) to an Access 2000 form as the data source for the form and still be updateable. Access 2000 introduced a new property on Access forms, the Recordset property. This property can be set to an ADO or DAO Recordset object that has been created in code. This means that you can create a recordset in code, do whatever needs to be done with it, and then directly display the data in a form without having to have the form requery the database. This allows you to use a client-side recordset and not have to send it back to the server or database file before the user can see it. However, if you assign an ADO recordset to the form, it can only be updated if it is based on a SQL Server connection. ADO Jet data can be displayed, but it will be read-only. To use this functionality, open any Recordset object based on SQL Server data and assign it to a form using the form's Recordset property. You will have to create the form in advance (using the interface or using code) and bind the objects you create to fields in the recordset (or a dummy used for this purpose). The easiest way to do this is to create a control for each field in the Recordset (text box is the best), and just bind it to the field you want to use with it. Then, open the form in datasheet view to save yourself from having to format the form itself.

Asynchronous Commands and ADO Events

One of the advantages of working with ADO over working with ODBCDirect is the fact that not only does ADO support asynchronous commands, it also supports events. If you don't quite understand what this means, the following information provides a little primer.

Normally, when you open an object in your code or call a function to do some work, the code where the call originated stops. This pause in execution lasts as long as the other process is running. When the other function is done, the calling procedure regains control and continues working away. This is called synchronous execution. Only one action can take place at a time, and if any item takes a long time, all execution must stop until the long running item has completed its work. Asynchronous processing is exactly the opposite of synchronous processing. When you call an asynchronous command, you actually spawn a separate process that does not interfere with the running command. If you call a long running command asynchronously from within your code, the command starts, but your own code does not wait for it to complete before moving on to the next line of code.

All of the ADO objects support asynchronous operations. Connections and Recordsets can be opened asynchronously, and Commands can be executed asynchronously against a Connection. This is a bonus to any program that has long running data calls that you don't want your users to get held up by. But it does introduce another problem—how do you tell when an asynchronous command completes? The answer is, you use *events*.

Just as the forms, reports, and controls you use support events, so do ADO objects. In order to use the events in the ADO objects, you must first declare an ADO Connection or Recordset object in the declarations section of a class module (you cannot use standard modules). When you do this, you must use the VBA WithEvents keyword. To declare a Recordset object in your code and capture the events it raises, you would use the code:

```
Private WithEvents mrst As ADODB.Recordset
```

Once this is done, you can then select the object you just created in the class module from the Object Box (the drop-down list at the top of your module on the left side). With the object selected, you can select one of the events from the Procedures/Events Box (the drop-down list at the top of your module on the right side). The procedure for each event is created when you select it using the Visual Basic ObjectName_EventName naming convention used for the event procedure name, as illustrated in Figure 11-3.

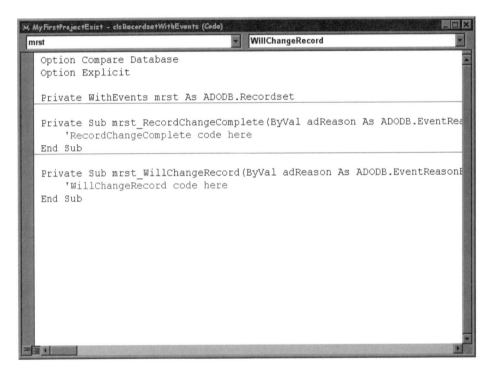

Figure 11-3. Recordset WithEvents

The necessary parameters are supplied for you automatically when you create these procedures.

Each object has its own set of events that correspond to the actions you may want to track against each item. A full description of the events can be found in the ADO documentation supplied with Microsoft Data Access Components (MDAC), or you can consult any of the resources mentioned earlier for a faster, more Access related explanation.

The main areas where you may want to use events are in processing of record-sets and execution of commands. You open a recordset that contains a large amount of data asynchronously, and then program the Recordset's FetchComplete event to notify your application when all of the data is available. Or you can execute a long running Command asynchronously and have the Command's Connection object notify the application that the processing is done by adding code to the Connection's ExecuteComplete event. Either way, you or your users can continue to work without being held up by the long running code.

Using ADO to code your data access can add some really incredible functionality to your application and ensure that you are ready for the next version of Access.

The Choice Is Yours

Choosing the right data access method in your code can make a big difference in your application's performance and future upgrade path. ODBCDirect was added to DAO in Access 97, but chances are that it will not survive in the next version of Jet. Because all 32-bit versions of Access are capable of using ADO to access SQL Server data, ADO is your best choice for coding against SQL Server data. ADO provides more capabilities than ODBCDirect, and this functionality is likely to improve even more in the future.

CHAPTER 12

Optimizing Access for SQL Server

BY NOW, YOU KNOW MOST of what you need in order to move an Access application to SQL Server. I've covered how to create a SQL database, how to move your data, and how to use SQL Server data from within Microsoft Access. You are ready to begin or are well into your conversion from Access to SQL Server. But there is one more detail you need to know before you can complete your project, which is how to optimize your Access application for SQL Server databases.

Throughout this book, I have provided you with the information necessary to make your application as efficient as possible. I would like to take you one step further by discussing how to optimize your application. This chapter is entirely devoted to optimizing Access applications that use SQL Server as their backend database system. This information can take you to a new level of development; a level where you have the understanding that can make you a truly great client/server developer.

Although there are many differences in development when working with Access database projects and when using ODBC linked tables in a standard Access database, many of the concepts that make for a good Access client/server application apply to both types of database applications. These concepts can help any application perform better and ensure that your users are going to be happy with the result of your work.

Reducing Data Transfers

When developing Access applications that interface with SQL Server, probably the most important improvement you can make is to reduce the amount of data that is sent across the network at any one time. This does not necessarily mean that you must take away from the user experience. Rather, it means that you should reduce the data that the user requests from the server to a manageable amount. There are a number of techniques to do this, and a few of the major ones will be discussed in this section. I can't tell you what to do specifically in your database. I can, however, provide you with some guidelines, techniques, and specific advice. These techniques will show you what to watch for in your own development, so that you can apply the concepts to the unique characteristics of your project.

Filtering Data on the Server

One of the easiest techniques that you can use to reduce the amount of data that goes to the client is to filter data on the server. You should attempt to reduce the data being sent to the client before it ever leaves SQL Server. You can do this in a number of ways.

If you are using an ADP or do not need to update the data, you should use stored procedures to return the data to Access. Use parameters in your stored procedures to filter data returned to the client application. This ensures that only the necessary data travels over the network, and Access has less data to handle internally. Also, don't forget that you can limit data using views. Any view you want to create can contain a WHERE clause that limits the data that is returned. If you can filter data using preselected criteria, do so.

Another design choice that comes into play in this area is filter-by-form. The filter-by-form feature is one of the worst features ever added to Access. Not only does it generate large amounts of unnecessary overhead, it also seems counterintuitive to many users. In a situation where an Access database uses SQL Server data, employing the filter-by-form feature takes away your control of what work the database should do. Users do not usually have the knowledge of the database necessary to understand what kinds of filters work well against the data. Filtering fields that are not indexed and leaving out indexed columns results in an unoptimized query being sent to the server. You are almost always better off supplying a user with criteria selections and using stored procedures or views to handle the filtering. It makes a big difference in the amount of traffic running to and from your server and improves the performance of data searches on the server itself.

Bound Controls

One of the reasons Access is such a popular development environment is because binding controls to data in a database is so easy. Most development environments require that you handle retrieving data and binding it to controls yourself, or they do not provide all of the functionality that Access does in bound controls. However, this leads to one major problem with Access/SQL Server development—overusing bound controls.

Each control that you bind to data requires Access to retrieve the contents of a field from the database. The more controls that you bind to a field, the more data must be returned from the database. Because binding controls to data is so easy in Access, Access developers tend to think of this as the least important factor in the development of an application. As a result, developers are inclined to use bound controls almost anywhere they can. When developing an application against SQL Server, you should sit back for a moment and consider whether the data you are binding in your forms really needs to be included. Do you really need *all* of the information from parent tables when entering data on a subform? Will your users use all of the fields that you are returning to your form? If it is possible to eliminate some of these fields, you should do so.

You should also be very careful about the number of list and combo boxes that you use on your forms. I stated earlier that you should use stored procedures to populate these items. However, you should also use them judiciously. Each combo or list box on a form requires a separate query to be sent to SQL Server and a separate set of data to be returned. Each time you reopen a form or requery the combo or list box's contents, this information is requeried from the database. This means that you are increasing the load on the server and adding traffic on the network. If these controls are used only to display information and not for editing an underlying record, do not automatically assume that a list or combo is required. Often the information can be adequately retrieved into a text box or left out of the form altogether. This technique could dramatically improve the application's performance.

Combo and list boxes can also be improved by reducing the data that they present to users. If you have a large list of items that your users might want to select from, you may want to limit this list to a manageable amount of data. For example, if you want to give users a list of Orders in a combo box, you could use two different stored procedures to return the values for this list. The first stored procedure would only return the last 100 (or other appropriate quantity) of the Orders placed. This allows users to select from a limited set of records, assuming that it is likely that they will want to look at a recent order. You could then include a checkbox on your form that users could select to have all orders listed. This checkbox would change the source of the combo box, so that it uses another stored procedure to retrieve all of the necessary values. By making the short list the default, you reduce much of the data transfer that must occur in the regular use of your application.

Access Settings

One of the common ways to limit the data returned by any query is to set the Max Records property of the query. When you reduce the number of records users can return at any one time, you reduce the amount of data being transmitted across the network. You could again provide users with an option to retrieve all of the records if necessary. However, most users will use the default settings you provide and will end up using less data.

If you are using ODBC in a standard Access database, you can also prevent a few of the possible trips that Access takes to the server. Normally, when connecting to SQL Server via ODBC, Access tries to log in to the database using the current Jet login information. If you have not configured Jet security, the default login user "Admin" with a blank password is passed to the server when Access attempts to retrieve some data. If Jet security is configured, the login and password that the user opens the database with is passed to SQL Server. This adds a few extra trips to

the server that are not really necessary if you are using SQL Server security to handle the connections. To prevent Access from doing this, set the TryJetAuth setting
in the Registry for Microsoft Access under the key HKEY_LOCAL_MACHINE\
Software\Microsoft\Office\8.0\Access\Jet\3.5\Engines\ODBC for Access 97 or
HKEY_LOCAL_MACHINE\Software\Microsoft\Office\9.0\Access\Jet\4.0\Engines\
ODBC for Access 2000. If the key or value does not exist, create them. TryJetAuth
should be a string value (REG_SZ) with a value of 0 if you want to prevent Access
from attempting to connect to SQL Server using the current Jet security login
information, as shown in Figure 12-1 (more settings that you can use in this location in the Registry are listed in Table A-2 in Appendix A).

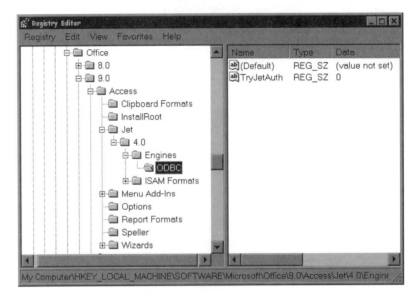

Figure 12-1. TryJetAuth setting

Client-Side Processing

One of the best ways to reduce network traffic is to use client-side recordsets when
dealing with SQL Server data. This happens automatically in an ADP, and you can
do this manually in your code. Client-side recordsets essentially disconnect the
recordset from the server and allow you to work with a local copy of the data. You
can work with the data on your machine, adding records, making modifications,
or deleting records as necessary without the server being contacted again. When
you have completed the tasks you need to run against the data, you can submit all
of the changes in a batch. In ADO, you can do this by setting the CursorLocation
property of a Recordset or Connection object to adUseClient. When you have done
all of your work with a recordset, you can then update the data on the server by

calling the UpdateBatch method of the Recordset object. This sends all of your changes to the server in a single action, rather than as each record is modified.

You can further improve client-side recordsets by only submitting the changed records, rather than the whole recordset. To do this in ADO, set the MarshalOptions property of the Recordset object to the enumerated constant adMarshalModified-Only before you call the UpdateBatch method. This causes ADO to send only those records that have been modified or added to the recordset, rather than sending the entire contents of the recordset back across the network and leaving SQL Server to determine what needs to be updated.

Increasing Throughput

Your application can also be optimized to increase the throughput of Access and SQL Server. This means making the jobs faster that Access and SQL Server must perform by providing them with hints or better methods to work with your data. You can also design your SQL Server database so that Access can better understand how to deal with the data, and you can use data in such a way that Access passes the processing back to the server in the most efficient manner.

SQL Database Design

There can never be enough said about the benefits of good database design. A good design can completely change the behavior of a database and how its clients interact with it. For this reason, there are many books available that are devoted to this subject. I would urge you to pick up one of these books if you want to make your application as fast, reliable, and inexpensive as possible. When it comes to using Access as a client, however, there are a few factors that you should watch out for when creating your SQL Server database.

As discussed in Chapter 8, timestamps can be extremely useful when working with SQL Server data. Although you may not see it when it happens, timestamps reduce the load on the server when data is updated. Fewer fields must be compared on a single data modification statement and the server performs the updates faster. You also have more control over concurrency—the problem you run into when two users attempt to update the same record at the same time. Timestamps reduce the amount of time it takes to update data and increase the reliability of updates to the data. Using timestamps allows the ODBC or OLE DB driver to update data more efficiently.

You can also improve the methods that Access uses to update tables by designing SQL Server indexes appropriately. The principal rule in this case is to always cluster the primary key or the most frequently used *unique* index on a table. You should then include the field(s) in this index in any SELECT statements that access the table, regardless of whether you need the data or not. This allows Access to determine the best unique index to use when data must be updated. If you also use this clustered index as the main criteria for any data selection, your application will perform better.

You can also improve the performance of SQL Server databases by limiting your use of large data types, like text and image types. Retrieving, setting, and updating data in these types of columns can be very slow (and, in SQL 6.5, prone to errors). SQL Server must do extra work to handle large data types, so performance on the server suffers. You also cause your Access application to have to work harder when these data types are manipulated locally. If it is possible to avoid using this data types, do so. If you do require them for a particular application, ensure that you request the column that includes this data only when you need it.

Access Database Design

There are a few changes that you can make to your Access application that will increase the throughput on the server. The general goal when using Access with external data is to ensure that as much processing is done on the server as possible.

One of the ways in which you can improve throughput from Access is to ensure that whenever you request data from SQL Server that must be filtered, you should limit the filtering to only those columns that are indexed. Basically, this means that you should only use WHERE clauses in your requests that filter fields already indexed in the base table. This is called *index covering,* and it provides the SQL Server query optimizer with a better restriction for planning how the data is retrieved. If you find that a particular field is constantly being used as a criteria for some filter, index that column so that SQL Server can return the data to the client as quickly as possible.

When using ODBC-linked views and tables, you should be careful how you create local queries that use that data. With standard queries on this data, Access evaluates the query to see how much of the processing can take place on the server. If all of the processing can be done on the server, Access sends the request directly to SQL Server. If Access is unsure about some portions of the query, all of the base data necessary to run the query is retrieved from SQL Server and processed locally.

In order to prevent this from happening, there are a few design issues to watch for in your standard queries. Do not use multiple-table joins in a query. Access often cannot determine if SQL Server is able to understand a complex join that contains multiple tables, so the contents of all of the tables are brought to the client and the join is performed locally. This can lead to bottlenecks in your application. You should also avoid using VBA functions in any portion of your queries other than in the SELECT statement itself. Avoid functions like Nz, DLookup, IIf, and any custom functions you have created. Access immediately takes over the processing and again requests all of the data from the server before the function is run locally. You can avoid this by using the functions only in controls on forms and reports.

You can also use nested queries—one to retrieve filtered data from SQL Server and the other to execute the VBA function on the results of the first query.

Finally, when using recordsets based on SQL Server data in your code, you should optimize the locking of the data on SQL Server. If the data does not need to be updated, set the LockType property of the Recordset object to the constant adLockReadOnly. This tells SQL Server that it does not need to maintain any tracking on the data once it is sent to the client. The read-only setting frees the server to work on other tasks, rather than tracking data that you will never commit back to the database. You should also use forward-only recordsets wherever you can. Although these recordsets can only be browsed in one direction, they do reduce the amount of overhead involved in handling the data. If you need to scan a read-only recordset and you aren't going to use it more than once, you can create a forward-only recordset by setting the CursorType property of an ADO Recordset to the constant adOpenForwardOnly or the Option argument of the OpenRecordset DAO method to the constant dbOpenForwardOnly before you open the recordset

Using ADO, you can also completely disconnect recordsets from the server by setting the ActiveConnection property to Nothing, using the code

```
Set rst.ActiveConnnection = Nothing
```

This removes any reference to the connection on which the recordset is based. This also reduces the memory requirements in your code by reducing the objects that ADO must manage. You can set this property back to a valid connection later on, and then submit your changes. The update is managed in exactly the same way as if you had never removed the connection reference. Setting the ActiveConnection to Nothing releases the connection to SQL Server that is used in your code, so that the server can release the resources used by the connection. This technique should be used wherever possible to reduce the possibility of overloading the connections on the server.

A Plan for the Future

Now that you understand the work that is involved in migrating a database, you may be interested to learn how you can avoid some of this work in the future. Chances are that once you migrate one system to SQL Server, you will start to see the potential to migrate others. This does not necessarily mean that you will migrate them. It just means that you can see a possibility that they may need to be upsized at some point in the near or distant future. For this reason, you may want to design your Access applications in such a way that migrating it to SQL Server requires as little effort as possible.

As I have tried to stress throughout this book, planning is one of the best tools you can use in any application design. Planning can make or break a project.

When you are designing your next Access application, take into account the potential that the application may be migrated to SQL Server. One of the keys to success is to plan the design of your application so that it works with Access data in much the same way that it will have to work with SQL Server data. This can save you from having to do a lot of extra work when the time comes to migrate. Furthermore, you can do this without adversely affecting the performance of your Access application. In some cases, this can even improve your application's performance. The following sections contain some tips that can help you to ensure the success of a future migration.

Tip #1: Use Queries to Enhance Security

One of the challenges in developing any database application is to design adequate security. This is intended to prevent users from taking unplanned actions on your database objects. When working with SQL Server, it is best to use views and stored procedures as the only means of users accessing data. This allows you to limit the data that users can access and ensures that they can only access that data using the methods that you choose. With direct access to the tables, users might be able to view sensitive data or modify data in a way that conflicts with your database design.

Access databases can be designed with this concept in mind. You can create queries that access or modify data in your tables as you need them. You can then restrict users from being able to directly edit the tables in the database and only give them access through queries that use the data in the tables. By using the WITH OWNER ACCESS option in a SQL statement, you can give users full rights to edit the data that is returned (you can set this option in a query by adding the option after the query SQL statement or by selecting the Owner's option in the query's Run Permissions property). When it comes to bulk data modification, you can use action queries to perform the necessary function. This allows you to restrict users' abilities to update tables in ways that can be hazardous to the performance of your application.

Using queries more often in your Access database allows you to become accustomed to securing your database in this manner. It also allows you to better determine what security settings are necessary if you decide to move the database to SQL Server.

Tip #2: Perform Bulk Updates Using Stored Queries

One of the major concerns I run into when I look at some of the code I wrote when I first started using Access is the number functions that open recordsets in code and loop through the records in order to update each one. This type of data manipulation uses a great deal more resources than it should. I should have been using UPDATE, INSERT, and DELETE queries as necessary. When you make the move to SQL Server, this type of code is incredibly hard on system resources. If your dataset is connected to the server, modifications to each record require at least one round-trip to and from the server. This adds overhead to your network and your application.

I have found that there is almost always a better solution to be found using action queries. True, sometimes you need to run customized VBA functions on the data, but you should check these functions to ensure that there is no way that they can be done using queries. Quite often you will find that at least some, if not all, of the functionality can be ported into SQL statements.

When you make the move to SQL Server, you will not have any access to VBA functions. Bulk updates should *always* take place through stored procedures or SQL action statements. Doing otherwise adversely affects the operation of your database. Fortunately, SQL Server includes the Transact-SQL programming language, so you can do more in SQL Server stored procedures that you can in an Access query. However, you should attempt to use queries in Access wherever you can, so that you become accustomed to developing databases in this manner. You will also find that your Access SQL skills will improve over time. These skills can easily be applied to a SQL Server database in the future, with only a few changes to accommodate the differences between the two systems.

Tip #3: Use Parameters Now

Using parameters in Access queries is a practice that most Access developers avoid. There is a very good reason for this. Apart from parameters that reference controls on forms, there is no way to provide values for arbitrary parameters when opening forms and reports. This means that if you create a real parameter in your code called something like lngCustomerID, you cannot provide the value for this parameter if you want to bind the query to a form. If you do, your users receive a dialog asking them to enter the parameter value each time the form or report is opened. So where can you use them?

Not all of the places where you use queries need to be bound to forms and reports. Quite often, you use recordsets in code to accomplish some task. Or you update data using an Execute call on a command or QueryDef object from code. This type of data is often filtered using a dynamically created WHERE clause. If this is the case, you should create a parameter query that takes the values you would normally build in code. For example, let's suppose that you often change the shipping rates for customers depending on the state in which they live. You might be tempted to write a function such as the following:

```
Public Sub UpdateShipRate(ByVal curNewRate As Currency, _
                          ByVal strState As String)
    Dim db As Database
    Dim strExecute As String
    strExecute = "UPDATE tblRate SET tblRate.ShipCost = " & _
      Format$(curNewRate, "Currency") & _
      " WHERE tblRate.State = '" & strState & "'"
    Set db = CurrentDb()
    db.Execute strExecute
End Sub
```

This does the job very well. You can update ShipCost in any State as needed. However, you should use a parameterized query with this code instead of dynamically building the SQL string. The SQL statement for your new query would be

```
PARAMETERS curNewRate Currency, txtState Text;
UPDATE tblRate SET tblRate.ShipCost = [curNewRate]
WHERE tblRate.State = [txtState]
```

This query provides Access with the up-front knowledge about the data types of the parameters that are to be used. If you don't want to create the parameters using SQL statements, you can access the parameters list from the query design grid by selecting Query➡Parameters. This query requires two parameters, just like your code did. You can then call this query in your code by using a DAO QueryDef object or an ADO Command object and simply supplying the necessary parameters. The same function, rewritten to use DAO and the new query (called qupdShipRate), could be written as follows:

```
Public Sub UpdateShipRate(ByVal curNewRate As Currency, _
                          ByVal strState As String)
    Dim db As Database, qdf As QueryDef
    Set db = CurrentDb()
    Set qdf = db.QueryDefs("qupdShipRate")
    qdf.Parameters("curNewRate") = curNewRate
    qdf.Parameters("txtState") = strState
    qdf.Execute
End Sub
```

If you want to write this function to use ADO, you could use the following code:

```
Public Sub UpdateShipRate(ByVal curNewRate As Currency, _
                          ByVal strState As String)
    Dim cmd As New ADODB.Command, lngRecordsAffected As Long
    Set cmd.ActiveConnection = CurrentProject.Connection
    cmd.CommandText = "qupdShipRate"
    cmd.CommandType = adCmdStoredProc
    cmd.Execute lngRecordsAffected, Array(curNewRate, strState)
End Sub
```

Each of these functions would do the same job as the first example. The main advantage is that the query is compiled in Access and executes faster. This type of updating is also more "SQL Server–friendly" and is easier to use after a migration.

Tip #4: Increase Maintainability with Stored Queries

The previous example brings up one very important benefit to using queries instead of dynamically calling SQL text in your code: Your code and your queries will be much easier to maintain. How many times have you made a change to a field or table name and found that there are many forms, reports, and modules that you must then search through in order to update the references to this change? When you move your SQL statements out of code and out of form, report, combo, and list box sources, you will find that these objects instantly become easier to maintain. In fact, you should aim to move all SQL statements out of these objects and into queries.

Although this action dramatically increases the number of queries in your database, you will find that your application becomes much easier to maintain. Instead of having to remember all of the places you need to look to find the references to your objects, you can simply check the SQL statement on each query and easily determine where changes need to be made. In Access 2000, you can even enable Name AutoCorrect, and your changes will be self-maintaining. If you embed your SQL strings in code, this cannot happen.

Finally, the best advantage to using this type of design is that your move to SQL Server will be as painless as possible. Because all of your data access functionality is handled in one area, you can easily upsize your database to SQL Server without fear of missing some items. If you use the Upsizing Wizard in Access 2000, these objects are automatically migrated for you, and you can simply make modifications to improve the design and performance of the application without having to worry about the need to search for any items that you may have missed.

Tip #5: Use ADO for Coding against Data

Another technique that you can use to ensure that your database will scale to SQL Server with as little work as possible is to use ADO as your data access technology in your code. If you use ADO as your data access technology, you may not need to make more than a few changes to your code to make it work with SQL Server data. The syntax for working with data in ADO is identical between SQL Server and Access. You may have to change the names of the objects that you call in your code as well as the names of the parameters you set, but if you upgrade from a standard Access database to a database project, you won't have to change much else.

The best way to ensure that you don't have to change too much is to use the CurrentProject.Connection property in Access 2000 to set any connection you use to your database. This property holds the current ADO connection information to the application database. In a standard database, this is the connection information to the local database. When you switch to an ADP, this connection information is automatically set to the appropriate value for your SQL Server database.

If you are using Access 95 or 97, this connection information is not available. However, you can simulate this feature with a small amount of code. Create a new module called CurrentProject in your database, and add a single function—the Connection function—that returns an ADO Connection to the current database. A very simple version of this function might look like this:

```
Public Function Connection() As ADODB.Connection
    Dim cnn As New ADODB.Connection
    cnn.Provider = "Microsoft.Jet.OLEDB.3.51"
    cnn.Properties("Data Source") = CurrentDb.Name
    cnn.Open
    Set Connection = cnn
End Function
```

In order to make your function callable using the same syntax as Access 2000, you must name the module "CurrentProject". You can then retrieve a connection to the current database with code that is identical to Access 2000:

```
Set cnn = CurrentProject.Connection
```

If you decide to upgrade your database to an ADP in the future, just delete this module and your upgrade should work as if it was never in Access 97.

A Final Word

Making the move to SQL Server from Access is a big decision, and contrary to some of the documentation available, there is a lot of work involved. It is essential that you take the time to plan the move before you jump in. Start the plan early, and your migration will go smoothly. You should also design your new applications with the idea that they might eventually be moved to SQL Server. This will lead you to become a better developer and improve the way that you work.

Although I have discussed particular versions of Access and SQL Server, many of the techniques I have stressed apply equally to any version of Access or SQL Server. Keep them in mind no matter which version of Access or SQL Server you are using. I look forward to providing you with even more information when SQL Server 2000 is available.

APPENDIX A
Selected Tables

SQL Server Data Types

The data types available to you differ a great deal between Access and SQL Server. The following table lists all of the data types that can be used in SQL Server and their sizes and accuracies. For a description of what data type to choose in which situation, see "Choosing the Appropriate Data Type" in Chapter 8.

Table A-1. SQL Server Data Types

DATA TYPE	DESCRIPTION
binary	Fixed-length binary (e.g., Word file) to a maximum size of 8,000 bytes in SQL 7 and 255 bytes in SQL 6.5.
bit	Integer (whole number) that is either a 1 or a 0.
char	Fixed-length non-Unicode text data to a maximum length of 8,000 characters in SQL 7 and 255 characters in SQL 6.5.
datetime	Date/time data between January 1, 1753 and December 31, 9999. Accurate to 3.33 milliseconds.
decimal	Fixed precision (maximum total number of digits that can be stored left and right of the decimal) and scale (maximum total number of digits that can be stored right of the decimal) between -10^{38} and $10^{38}-1$.
float	Floating point precision number between $-1.79E308$ and $1.79E308$.
image	Variable-length binary (such as a file) to a maximum size of $2^{31}-1$ (2,147,483,647) bytes.
int	Integer between -2^{31} ($-2,147,433,648$) and $2^{31}-1$ (2,147,483,647).
money	Monetary data accurate to 4 decimal places between -2^{63} ($-922,337,203,685,477.5808$) and 2^{63} (922,337,203,685,477.5807).
nchar	(SQL 7 only) Fixed-length Unicode text data to a maximum length of 4,000 characters.
ntext	(SQL 7 only) Variable-length Unicode text data to a maximum length of $2^{30}-1$ (1,073,741,823) characters.

Table A-1. SQL Server Data Types (Continued)

DATA TYPE	DESCRIPTION
numeric	Same as decimal.
nvarchar	(SQL 7 only) Variable-length Unicode text data to a maximum length of 4,000 characters.
real	Floating point precision number between –3.4E38 and 3.4E38.
smalldatetime	Date/time data between January 1, 1900 and June 6, 2079. Accurate to one minute.
smallint	Integer between -2^{15} (–32,768) and $2^{15}-1$ (32,767).
smallmoney	Monetary data accurate to 4 decimal places between –214,748.3648 and 214,748.3647.
text	Variable–length non–Unicode text data to a maximum length of $2^{31}-1$ (2,147,483,647) characters.
timestamp	Unique identifier based on time and date of record modification. Cannot be modified directly.
tinyint	Integer between 0 and 255.
uniqueidentifier	(SQL 7 Only) A globally unique identifier (GUID), such as the ones that Access creates for replication information.
varbinary	Variable-length binary to a maximum size of 8,000 bytes in SQL 7 and 255 bytes in SQL 6.5.
varchar	Variable-length non-Unicode text data to a maximum length of 8,000 characters in SQL 7 and 255 characters in SQL 6.5.

Microsoft Access ODBC Registry Settings

When using ODBC with Microsoft Access, there are a number of Registry settings you can use to affect how Access deals with ODBC data. See Table A-2. These Registry settings must be entered under the key

HKEY_LOCAL_MACHINE\SOFTWARE\Microsoft\Office\8.0\Access\ Jet\3.5\Engines\ODBC

for Access 97, or under the key

HKEY_LOCAL_MACHINE\SOFTWARE\Microsoft\Office\9.0\Access\ Jet\4.0\Engines\ODBC

for Access 2000. If the key does not exist, create it in order to add the Registry values that you need to use.

Table A-2. ODBC Jet Registry Settings

NAME	TYPE	DEFAULT	DESCRIPTION
LoginTimeout	REG_DWORD (DWORD)	20	Number of seconds to wait for the server to respond before a login attempt times out and is considered failed.
QueryTimeout	REG_DWORD	60	Number of seconds to wait for a synchronous query to complete before it is cancelled and considered failed.
ConnectionTimeout	REG_DWORD	600	Number of seconds to wait before an idle connection is closed.
AsyncRetryInterval	REG_DWORD	500	Number of milliseconds to wait between polling server to determine status of an asynchronous request.
AttachCaseSensitive	REG_DWORD	0	Determines whether to match table names exactly or to find the first table name matching the request, regardless of letter case. 0 means match first, 1 means match exact name.
AttachableObjects	REG_SZ (String)	'TABLE', 'VIEW', 'SYSTEM TABLE', 'ALIAS', 'SYNONYM'	Server object types that can be attached as linked tables. Separate each item by a comma and enclose each item in single quotes (as default is).

Table A-2. ODBC Jet Registry Settings (Continued)

NAME	TYPE	DEFAULT	DESCRIPTION
SnapshotOnly	REG_DWORD	0	Determines whether to include or ignore indexes on linked tables, forcing recordset cursor type. If 0, indexes are used if possible and dynaset-type recordsets can be used. If 1, indexes are ignored and all recordsets are snapshot only.
TraceSQLMode	REG_DWORD	0	Specifies whether SQL statements sent to a data source by the ODBC driver should be logged to the file sqlout.txt. 0 for no, 1 for yes.
TraceODBCAPI	REG_DWORD	0	Species whether ODBC API calls generated by requests should be logged to the file odbcapi.txt. 0 for no, 1 for yes.
DisableAsync	REG_DWORD	1	Indicates whether to use synchronous queries at all times or to use asynchronous calls if possible. 0 to use asynchronous calls if possible, 1 for never to use them.
TryJetAuth	REG_DWORD	1	Indicates whether to try connecting to the ODBC data source using the current Jet user and password before prompting for other login. 0 for no, 1 for yes.
PreparedInsert	REG_DWORD	0	Indicates whether to use an INSERT statement that includes all fields in the table for the updated record or only those fields that were updated. 0 for only affected columns, 1 for all.
PreparedUpdate	REG_DWORD	0	Same as PreparedInsert, but for UPDATE instead.
FastRequery	REG_DWORD	0	Specifies whether to use prepared SELECT statements for parameterized queries and allow the statement to be reused without having to be reprepared each time. 0 for no, 1 for yes.

INDEX

Symbols

\ (backslash) operator, 61

\# (pound) sign in identifiers in SQL Server 6.5 and 7, 66–67

\#\# (double hash) sign, using with temporary tables in T-SQL, 235–236

\#\# (double pound) sign in identifiers in SQL Server 6.5 and 7, 67

\$ (dollar) sign in identifiers in SQL Server 6.5 and 7, 66–67

& (bitwise AND) operator in T-SQL, 232

+ (string concatenation character) operator in T-SQL, 233

< (less than) operator in T-SQL, 232

!< (not less than) operator in T-SQL, 232

<= (less than or equal to) operator in T-SQL, 232

<> (not equal to) operator in T-SQL, 232

= (equal) sign, using with stored procedures in SQL Server, 224

= (equal to) operator in T-SQL, 232

!= (not equal to) operator in T-SQL, 232

> (greater than) operator in T-SQL, 232

!> (not greater than) operator in T-SQL, 232

>= (greater than or equal to) operator in T-SQL, 232

? (question marks) in tables, 215

@ (at) sign
   in identifiers in SQL Server 6.5 and 7, 66–67
   using with T-SQL, 224
   using with variable names in T-SQL, 227

@@ (double at) sign
   before SQL Server variable names, 236
   caution against using with identifiers in SQL version 6.5, 66

@@ERROR system variable in SQL Server, 236

@@TRANCOUNT system variable in SQL Server, 239

^ (bitwise exclusive OR) operator in T-SQL, 232

_ (underscore) in identifiers in SQL Server 6.5 and 7, 66–67

| (bitwise OR) operator in T-SQL, 232

A

aaaaa characters
   before primary keys in Access 2000 wizard, 91
   before primary keys in Access 97 wizard, 79

Access, 2
   Admin user ID, 29
   analyzing tables when migrating to SQL Server, 41–47
   Autonumber fields, 43
   benefits of prototyping applications, 25
   clustered indexes, 44
   compacting databases, 30
   connecting SQL Server database to, 249, 258–263
   connecting to SQL Server database from, 38–40
   contrasting client/server architecture to, 2
   creating tables with fields related to other fields, 191
   cross-tab queries, 48
   Double data type, 44
   hardware requirements, 31
   lengths of Text fields and Memo fields, 43
   Long Integer data type, 43
   managing list and combo boxes on, 308–309
   managing tables, 8
   Memo data type, 209
   primary keys, 44
   query process, 28
   read-only forms, 49
   record locking feature, 29
   repairing databases, 30
   role of unique indexes, 38
   setting rules with Validation Rule property, 45
   Single data type, 44
   software requirements, 31
   system.mdw file, 29
   testing stored procedures, 247–248
   using cascading deletes with forms, 52
   using ODBC tables, 263–266
   using steps to migrate to SQL Server, 131–132

Access 2000, CurrentProject.Connection property, 318

Access 2000 wizard. *See also* Access 97 wizard, migration, upsizing wizards entries
   versus Access 97 wizard, 79
   caution about upsizing data with, 96
   creating new databases with, 80–83
   guidelines for use of, 95–97
   managing application changes with, 87–89
   migrating defaults with, 85
   migrating indexes with, 85
   migrating table relationships with, 85–86
   naming databases with, 81
   upsizing options for, 84–86

Access 97 wizard. *See also* Access 2000 wizard, migration, upsizing wizards entries
   creating new databases with, 69–71
   downloading, 60
   guidelines for use of, 95–97
   migrating defaults with, 73